The Autodesk
Architectural Desktop 3
Book

The Autodesk Architectural Desktop 3 Book

Book

A Comprehensive Guide

H. Edward Goldberg, AIA
Registered Architect

Prentice
Hall

Upper Saddle River, New Jersey
Columbus, Ohio

Library of Congress Cataloging in Publication Data

Goldberg, H. Edward,
    The Autodesk Architectural desktop 3 book / H. Edward Goldberg.
        p. cm.
      includes index.
      ISBN 0-13-040644-9
      1. Architectural drawing--Computer aided design--Handbooks, manuals, etc. 2.
Autodesk Architectural desktop--Handbooks, manuals, etc. 3. AutoCAD. I. Title.

NA2728 .G65 2002
720'.28'40285--dc21   2001043672

Editor in Chief: Stephen Helba
Executive Editor: Debbie Yarnell
Media Development Editor: Michelle Churma
Production Editor: Louise N. Sette
Production Supervision: Lisa Garboski, bookworks
Design Coordinator: Diane Ernsberger
Text Designer: STELLARViSIONs
Cover Designer: Jeff Vanik
Cover art/photo: Jeff Vanik
Production Manager: Brian Fox
Marketing Manager: Jimmy Stephens

This book was set in Janson by STELLARViSIONs. It was printed and bound by Courier
Kendallville, Inc. The cover was printed by Phoenix Color Corp.

Pearson Education Ltd., *London*
Pearson Education Australia Pty. Limited, *Sydney*
Pearson Education Singapore Pte. Ltd.
Pearson Education North Asia Ltd., *Hong Kong*
Pearson Education Canada, Ltd., *Toronto*
Pearson Educación de Mexico, S. A. de C.V.
Pearson Education—Japan, *Tokyo*
Pearson Education Malaysia Pte. Ltd.
Pearson Education, *Upper Saddle River, New Jersey*

10 9 8 7 6 5 4 3 2
ISBN: 0-13-040644-9

I dedicate this first book to the women I love,
my mother, Lillian,
my wife, Judy,
and my daughter, Allison.

Acknowledgments

I would like to thank Art Liddle, co-editor of *CADALYST*, for first introducing me to Autodesk Architectural Desktop 1, and for giving me a chance to hone my communication skills by writing about ADT in his magazine. I also want to thank Sara Ferris, Art's co-editor, for being a pleasure to work with and for always having a bright smile.

I would like to thank all the wonderful and dedicated people at the AEC division of Autodesk in New Hampshire for their professional assistance and for their friendship. Of that group, special thanks go to Clay Freeman, Julian Gonzalez, and Paul Gold.

I would also like to acknowledge the reviewers of this text: Douglas C. Acheson, IUPUI (IN); and David Braun, Spokane Community College, (WA).

Contents

PART I

Concept   27

PART II

Design   61

PART III

Documentation   213

PART IV

Desktop   281

The Autodesk
Architectural Desktop 3
Book

Autodesk Architectural Desktop Release 3

For the last few years CAD has been undergoing a revolution; in fact, many people are now calling CAD for architecture CAAD (computer-aided architectural design). Rather than using CAD as just an electronic extension of normal drafting, software companies are now beginning to take advantage of the power of the computer to help the designer during the design phase of the project as well as during the documentation phase.

Many CAD developers make claims about the ease of use of their programs, but it has been my experience that the new generation of software for the AEC industry must contain a large amount of empirical information in order for it to increase efficiency. Because buildings vary widely and building designers work in many different ways, these programs must be customized to the particular user. In my opinion, all these new programs have a large setup and learning curve. Once these programs have been set up and mastered, they definitely increase productivity.

Autodesk Architectural Desktop Release 3 is really AutoCAD specialized for architectural design and documentation. Its underlying graphics engine is AutoCAD. The better you understand AutoCAD, the better you will do with Architectural Desktop. If you are new to AutoCAD, I highly recommend that you first become familiar with that program before moving on to the Architectural Desktop specifics. AutoCAD itself is a very capable program, but it does have a large learning curve. Of most importance is the ability to work in Paper Space and understand how the Dimension Styles work, how to use XREFs, and how to work and view in three-dimensional space.

The Concepts

The developers of Architectural Desktop Release 3 have a long-term goal of total object-oriented drag-and-drop forward and rearward integration. This means they are heading for CAAD software in which objects such as doors and walls are no

Tip Architectural Desktop 3 cannot be purchased separately from AutoCAD 2000. If you already own a stand-alone copy of AutoCAD 2000, remove it from your computer before loading Architectural Desktop Release 3.

longer "drawn" by draftspersons but are intelligent objects that act like the real object and can contain information such as cost. The program will eventually be able to interpret these objects that the designer will place in a three-dimensional virtual world, make suggestions and corrections, and automatically create the 2D plans, sections, and details. Although the program has not reached this point yet in its third iteration, it has become quite sophisticated.

Architectural Desktop Release 3 uses three different concepts for eventually creating documentation.

1. The Mass Model Concept

The mass model concept is unique to Architectural Desktop Release 3. It is based on a modeling tradition called mass modeling used by many architects. In this system, the architect or designer makes a cardboard, wood, or clay "study model" of the building and then creates the documentation from it. In Architectural Desktop Release 3, one can make virtual massing models. These massing models can then be sliced into floorplates, or horizontal sections from which walls can be automatically generated.

2. The Space-Planning Concept

The space-planning concept is one that has been used by architects and designers for years. In this concept, rectangles and circles represent building program areas. The designer then places these forms in relationship to each other to create *flow diagrams*. After the relationships have been established, they are then used to help create the form of the structure. In Architectural Desktop, the developers have taken this one step farther by combining a 3D component to the relationships. Every space-planning object also contains information about floor-to-ceiling heights and floor-to-floor heights. After the space planning has been completed, the space plan can automatically be converted into three-dimensional walls, into which doors, windows, etc., can be added.

3. The Virtual Building Concept

The virtual building concept places components of the building much as one would place the objects in the real world. Instead of drawing lines and circles, one places doors, windows, walls, roofs, etc.; to this end Architectural Desktop has a myriad of parametric tools. The virtual building is the system most used by architects and designers in Architectural Desktop. This system is the easiest for new users to learn.

Installing Autodesk Architectural Desktop Release 3

Installing Autodesk Architectural Desktop 3 has become very simple. Insert the single CD into your CD reader, and follow the directions. In about 10 minutes the program will be installed on your computer, and you will be asked for an authorization number. You do not have to have this number to immediately run the program, but you will get a warning that the program will only run for 30 days before you must supply the number. It is easy to get the number either by phone, fax, or Internet, but many people are so eager to get started that they wait a couple of days before authorizing.

Starting Autodesk Architectural Desktop

1. From the start menu (Microsoft Windows), choose programs>AutoCAD Architectural Desktop 3> AutoCAD Architectural Desktop.

   or

2. At the desktop (Microsoft Windows), click on the Architectural Desktop Release 3 icon (depending on the way Windows has been configured, this is either a single-or double-click with the left mouse button).

After you have saved an Autodesk Architectural Desktop drawing, you can also start the program by dragging and dropping that drawing onto the Architectural Desktop icon. This will automatically start Architectural Desktop 3 and bring up that drawing.

At this point a simple toolbar will appear with five icons, only three of which are active (not grayed out). The three active icons are File New, File Open, and question mark (help).

If you choose the **File New** icon, the **AutoCAD Today** dialog box appears. It is broken into two parts; the top part is labeled My Drawings, and it gives you direct access to your program. The bottom part gives you access to the Web. Autodesk, because it is connected to the Web, keeps the bottom part current.

If you choose the **File Open** icon, the standard AutoCAD Select File dialog box appears. Here you can select a previously edited drawing through the file tree.

As is typical of AutoCAD, upon which Architectural Desktop is built, there are many redundancies built into the command structure. This is true of the **AutoCAD Today** dialog box.

The **My Drawings** section also gives you access to your drawing files and consists of three tabs.

1. Open Drawings
2. Create Drawings
3. Symbol Libraries

Open Drawings

Open Drawings allows you to select the last edited drawings or use the browser (Browse button) to explore for other drawings, on the system, on the Internet, or on diskettes and CDs. You can search the drawings by Most Recently Used, History (by Date), History (by Filename), and History (by Location).

Create Drawings

Create Drawings allows you to create new drawings from drawing templates, from scratch, or from a Wizard.

Symbol Libraries

Symbol Libraries allows you to access or edit the **Design Center** symbol libraries.

Creating New Drawings

You can create new drawings in several ways. You can start from scratch and set the basic settings yourself, you can use a Wizard to help you step through the setup process, or you can start from a Template file that you have preset or has been preset by someone else. These methods are explained in detail in the AutoCAD 2000i user guide that accompanies the Architectural Desktop Release 3 manual.

The developers who made Architectural Desktop Release 3 have created several templates for you. They have been created in both imperial and metric measurement systems. If you are new to the program, it's probably in your best interest to use these templates until you are familiar enough with the program to create your own templates.

Hands On

After starting Architectural Desktop, choose **File New > Create Drawings** tab > Templates dropdown >**(A)** >Aec arch [imperial-intl].dwt. The program will cycle for approximately 1 second and then the screen will appear with the grid showing, along with 11 tabs at the bottom of the drawing area. The first tab is the **Model** tab, which is used for general drawing in full scale. The other tabs have been preset to help you work in different modes. With the display system (which we discuss later), certain viewports will display your drawing in different ways. A good example of this is the reflected viewport. In this viewport, which is used for reflected ceiling plans, the display system has been set so that the door headers don't display in the plan. This is the typical way in which an Architectural Desktop–reflected ceiling plan is drawn. If you change this viewport to a 3D display, the viewport will show the door headers. This is a very important part of the way that Architectural Desktop works.

The Options Dialog Box

The Options dialog box is used to customize the program for your needs. Try the following exercise to get an idea of how the dialog box works.

1. Start Architectural Desktop.
2. RMB in any viewport to bring up a cascade menu.
3. Select Options; the Options dialog box will appear.
4. Select the Display tab.
5. Make sure the Display Scroll Bars in the Drawing Window checkbox is <u>unchecked</u>.

This will eliminate the scroll bars at the right of your screen and give you more space in which to work.

6. Select the System tab.
7. Under General Options, change the startup to Show Traditional Startup Dialog.
8. Select the User Preferences tab.
9. Under Windows standard behavior, select the right-click customization button and make sure all the shortcut menus are activated.
10. Select the AEC Dwg. Defaults tab.
11. Under walls settings, set the wall-cleanup radius to 8 in.

Main Toolbar Dropdown, Toolbars, and Command Line Entry

Although there are several ways for interacting with Autodesk Architectural Desktop Release 3, the methods that I prefer are either the use of the cascading menus from the main toolbar dropdown or the specialized toolbars. I do use the command line, but only for simple one- or two-letter commands, such as L for line or E for erase.

Specialized Toolbars

Besides the standard toolbars in AutoCAD 2000i, there are 38 additional toolbars available for Architectural Desktop. Only a limited number of these toolbars are necessary on the screen at any one time, depending on the operations you need to perform. The dialog box necessary to make operative selected toolbars can be accessed in three ways. Try the following three methods for turning on the toolbars.

Method 1

1. Start Architectural Desktop.
2. Select View | Toolbars.
3. At the Customize dialog box, select AECARCHX in the menu group.
4. Scroll down, select the Walls checkbox, and close the dialog box.

The Walls toolbar will now appear in your drawing space; move it or dock it in a convenient spot.

Method 2

1. Start Architectural Desktop.
2. Move your cursor over any toolbar icon, and RMB.
3. At the Customize dialog box, select AECARCHX in the menu group.
4. Scroll down, select the Walls checkbox, and close the dialog box.

Method 3

1. Start Architectural Desktop.
2. Move your cursor over any empty area in the top toolbar area, and RMB.
3. For Architectural Desktop toolbars, select AECARCHX.
4. Select the Walls toolbar.

The toolbar will now appear in your drawing space. Move it or dock it in a convenient spot. Repeat one of these methods and open up all 38 of the Architectural Desktop Release 3 toolbars. It will never be necessary to have all the toolbars open at one time; just select the toolbars that are necessary for the particular operation that you are about to perform. By using profiles, you can automate which toolbars will be available at a given time.

Profiles

The profiles are set in the Options dialog box.

1. Start Architectural Desktop.
2. Open the AEC Layout Tools, Doors-Windows-Openings, and Walls toolbars.
3. RMB in any viewport to bring up the Cascade menu.
4. Select the Profiles tab, and click on the Add to List button.
5. At the Add Profile dialog box, under profile name type **Wall Drawing Tools**; apply and close.

You now have created a profile that will bring up the previously mentioned toolbars whenever you select the wall drawing tools profile. Go ahead and try it; but first close all the toolbars. Remember, Architectural Desktop Release 3 remembers the last setup that you used.

6.   With all the toolbars closed, RMB and select options. Choose the Profiles tab, select Wall Drawing tools, and choose the Set Current button.

Customize your profiles to speed up the selection of toolbars for any given operation.

How to Use This Book

The exercises in this book have been designed to illustrate most of the major commands used in running this program. Rather than require the student to study a lot of verbiage, I prefer the "hands-on method," with each exercise walking you through the typical use of the commands for that subject. As with AutoCAD itself, there are many ways to achieve the same result in Autodesk Architectural Desktop Release 3, so feel free to use the method you like best. I have also taken the attitude that the student has a general knowledge of basic AutoCAD, so I include few basic AutoCAD exercises. Because I believe that using the least number of keystrokes is the sign of a good operator, I do not use the full typed name of the commands unless that is the only way to start an operation.

The program comes with a very comprehensive index and online help. This book is intended to augment that help and to show you methods and tricks to improve your productivity.

LMB and RMB

For ease of explanation in this book, I use the notation RMB. Because Autodesk Architectural Desktop Release 3 uses the Windows operating system, there are many controls that can be selected by clicking the left mouse button (LMB) or the right mouse button. RMB indicates you should make a right-mouse-button click. As with most Windows programs, RMB, or right-mouse-button-clicking, will usually bring up context-sensitive menus (menus that change in relationship to the particular operation being made).

AEC Objects

In Autodesk Architectural Desktop 3, AEC Objects are specific architectural objects such as walls, doors, and windows that can be programmed to act and appear in a specific manner. It is these AEC Objects that give Autoesk Architectural Desktop most of its power and productivity.

Radio Buttons and Checkboxes

Although not specific to Architectural Desktop, the concepts of radio buttons and checkboxes are very important.

Radio Buttons

When available, radio buttons are found in groups, but only one can be input at a time. If one of the radio buttons in a group is chosen, the others turn off.

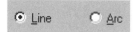

Checkboxes

When available, checkboxes indicate on or off. If they are in a group, several checkboxes can be selected at a time.

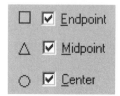

Context-Sensitive Menus

In Autodesk Architectural Desktop 3, selecting an AEC Object and clicking the right mouse button brings up menus that, among standard commands such as copy, paste, and move, pertain to the AEC Object selected. For example, RM3 on a window

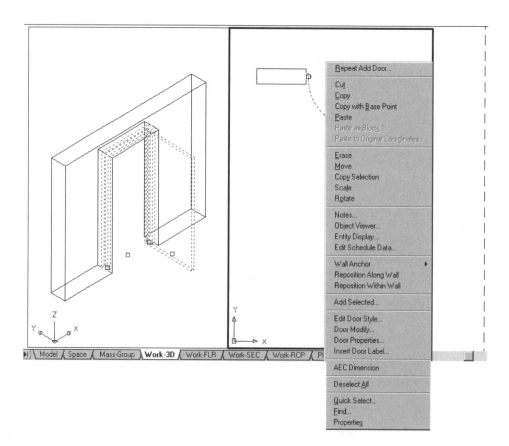

brings up the Edit Window Style, Window Modify, Window Properties, and Insert Window Label menus.

New Add Dialog Box Rollup Feature

There has been an important change to the typical Add and Modify dialog boxes. At the upper-right corner of the dialog box to the left of the Close Dialog Box icon is a *pushpin* icon. Placing the pushpin in the horizontal position selects Enable Rollup. Selecting the upper-left corner of the dialog box and checking Enable Rollup can also activate this function. Enable Rollup causes the dialog boxes to minimize whenever your cursor is not on the box. Moving your cursor near the box activates the full box. Activating this feature creates much more usable "real estate" within which to work.

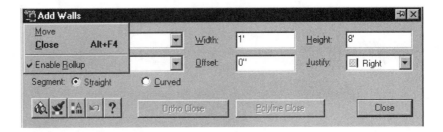

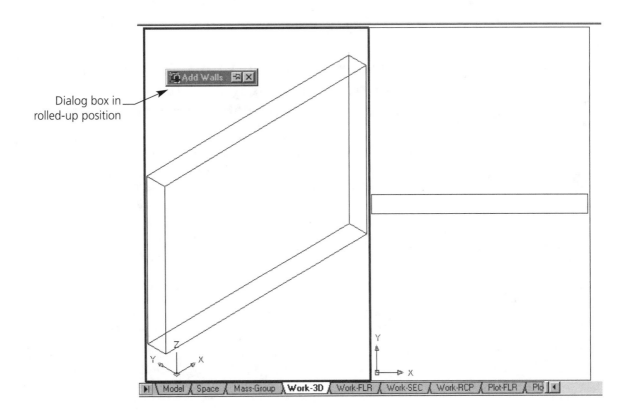

Dialog box in rolled-up position

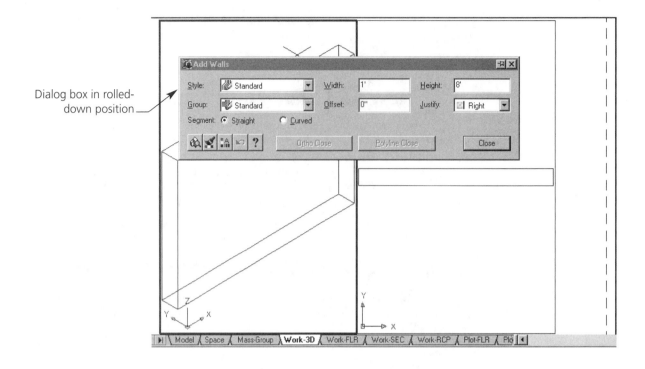

Dialog box in rolled-
down position

New Insert Door, Window, Opening, Window Assembly and Add Selected Options on the RMB Contextual Menu

By RMB on AEC Wall Objects, you can insert doors, windows, openings, and window assemblies without going to the icons or toolbar menus.

By RMB on AEC Objects and selecting Add Selected from the Contextual menu, you can add the identical AEC Object and style without going to the icons or toolbar menus.

Typical Architectural Desktop
Add and Modify Dialog Boxes

AEC Objects are input by Add dialog boxes. These contain settings for the Style of the AEC Object and other important settings such as size and alignment, depending on the object.

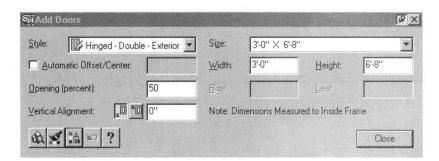

The AEC Object's properties can be reached from the Add dialog box as well as from context-sensitive menus associated with the AEC Objects.

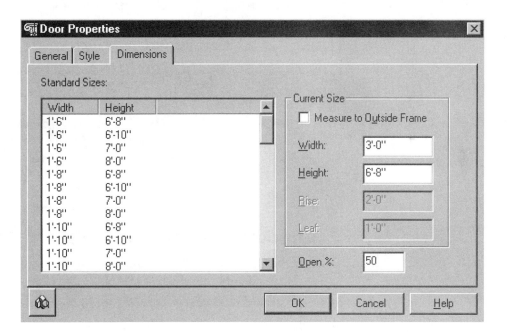

A Viewer is always available to view the AEC object being added or modified.

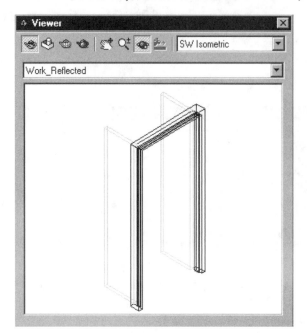

AEC Objects can be modified while in place by using the Modify dialog boxes. These are similar to the Add dialog boxes but have subtle differences in options.

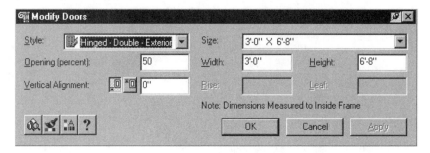

Autodesk Architectural Desktop 3 Definitions

AEC   Acronym for Architecture, Engineering, and Construction–related information.

AEC Arch (Imperial)   Using the English measuring system (inches, feet, etc.).

AEC Arch (Metric)   Using the metric system.

Massing Model   Block model system used by many architects during the initial design stage.

Layout Tab   Modifiable tabs at the bottom of the Architectural Desktop 3 drawing screen. Each tab represents one drawing page.

View Ports   Model Space divisions within the Layout tabs.

Plan View   Top view looking down, typically shown 3 ft 6 in. above the finished floor level.

Elevation   Orthographic view looking at a building at eye level.

Section   Slice through a building or part of a building showing its component parts.

RCP   Reflected ceiling plan; architectural drafting convention showing the ceiling plan as if one were lying on one's back and looking up. Typically used for lighting plans.

Edit Style of an AEC Object

Editing a style of an AEC Object sets all the parameters for an object under that name. For example, when you edit a Windows style, you create a window of a particular width, depth, sash width, sash depth, glass thickness, etc. You also set design rules such as the type of window (double-hung) or whether it has a particular shape. Most styles have a display props tab, which allows for setting of things such as line types, hatches, and line type scale. Often under the Edit Display Props tab, an AEC Object will have other properties that can be controlled. A typical example of this is a stair object that would have a cut plane. The cut plane controls the elevation through which the stair is displayed in plan.

Modifying an AEC Object

Once an AEC Object has been placed in a drawing, it can be modified in several ways. To request modification, select the object and RMB. A Contextual menu will appear, allowing modification for that particular AEC Object. Another method is to go to the Main toolbar and select Design, select the AEC Object type, and then select Modify for that type of object. An example of this is the modification of a wall. Either RMB on the wall and select Modify Wall, or go to the Main toolbar and select Design | Walls | Modify Wall.

Properties of an AEC Object

Properties of an AEC Object show not only their style and dimension, but also control interaction with similar objects and other AEC Objects. Often properties will display more controls for that particular AEC Object. Properties for AEC Wall Objects, for example, also control Wall Cleanups, Wall Modifiers, and 3D Modifiers.

General Definitions

CAD   Computer-aided design. The use of the computer as an electronic pencil.

CAAD   Computer-aided architectural design. Specialized software for the architectural profession; most recently developed to aid in the design process and the documentation process.

Object-Oriented CAD Programs   The latest direction in which CAAD and MCAD developers are proceeding. Structures are not input by lines, but as real-world objects containing information and reacting with other objects in a real-world manner; the beginnings of artificial intelligence.

Parametric Software   Software that usually works hand in hand with object-oriented programs. The object parameters, such as height, width, and material, are controlled through dialog boxes.

Portal Site   Organized entranceway to associated sites; i.e., an AEC portal may belong to a company that has AEC venture partners and contains links to them.

Visualization Streamer   The latest Internet technique, which allows a real-time or premade walkthrough visualization to be sent over the Web without long delays for download.

ASP   Applications Service Provider; refers to a software manufacturer whose application software resides on its server, and which rents its use. The entire program is never downloaded to the end user. This system requires a fast Internet connection.

Intranet   An internal business network set up with an Internet interface.

Extranet   A private dedicated Internet-like system that can be accessed from the outside or through the Internet.

E-business   Referring to business transactions done over the Internet.

Styles, Properties, and Display Props

Many of Architectural Desktop Release 3's AEC Objects are style-based. This means that AEC Objects such as doors, windows, walls, etc., are basically the same object modified by their style. Although each AEC Object has its own parameters to be set, the Wall Style Properties dialog box shown here is typical of the type of dialog box one can expect when editing any object's style.

All default settings can be changed at the command line when inserting wall.

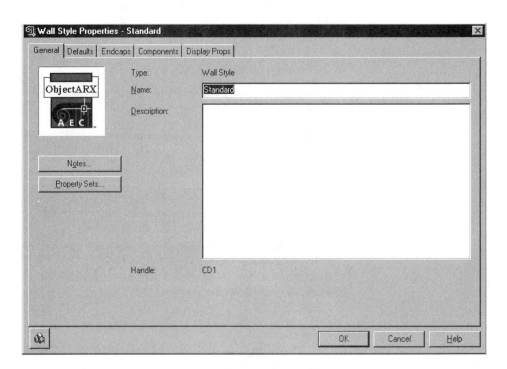

Default wall dimension settings for this style

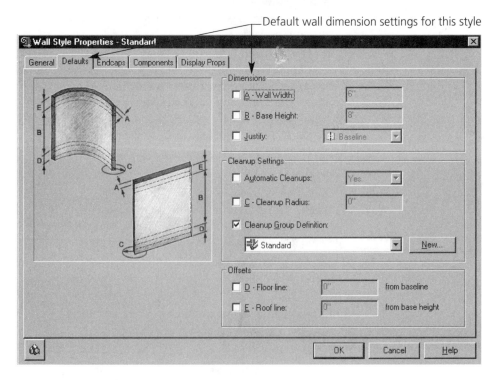

The Display System

The display system in Autodesk Architectural Desktop 3 controls how AEC Objects are displayed in a designated viewport. By using the display system, it is possible to have one viewport display a building in 3D (model) while having another viewport display that same building as a reflected ceiling plan.

The display system is made up of three components: **Display Representations, Display Representation sets,** and **Display Configurations**.

Display Representations

A Display Representation is responsible for drawing a graphical representation for a physical object such as a door, wall, window, etc. The Display Representation does not contain physical information about the object, such as type or size; on the other hand, the objects don't know how to represent themselves graphically, but they do contain physical information and react as they would in real life. To generate an image of an object in a viewport, a Display Representation uses the physical data stored in the object (door, window, etc.), such as width and height, and graphical data stored in the Display Props, such as linetype, color, and lineweight. For example, when a plan view is required, the appropriate Display Representation puts the object information together with the appropriate entities (such as lines, arcs, and hatch), linetype, and lineweight to display a graphic representation of the object in plan view. If the object changes size, the Display Representation will place the new graphics on the screen.

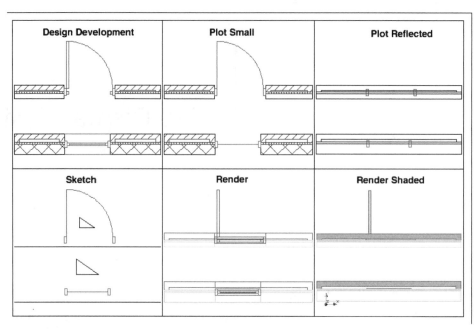

Different Display Representations of the Same Walls in Different Viewports

Display Representation Sets

A Representation Set is a collection of Display Representations. A good example would be a Representation Set called Work_Plan. When you create the Representation Set Work_Plan, you will place in it all the Display Representations you specified for each type of object Door, Window, Wall, etc., in that view.

The Display Manager icon on the AEC Setup toolbar brings up the Display Manager screen.

Display Representation Set Work_Plan is highlighted because the Work-FLR Layout tab was selected when the Display Manager was opened. Note that the Work_Plan Representation Set shows most of the AEC Objects using the Plan View checkbox.

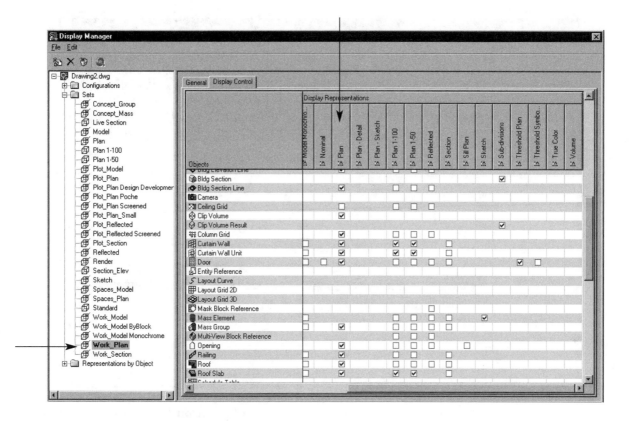

Display Configuration

Display Configurations does the final display control. A Display Configuration references one or more Display Representation sets and controls the display of objects in your drawing when viewed from different directions. Assigned to the Model tab or to a Layout viewport, the purpose of the Display Configuration is to control the display of objects in the viewport when viewed from different directions (top, bottom, front, back, right, left, or 3D (model)). You can create two types of display configurations: fixed-display configurations and view-direction-dependent display configurations. Fixed-display configurations use a single display representation set regardless of the view direction. There is also a choice of using either the view direction in the current viewport or one of the six orthogonal views (top, bottom, left, right, front, and back) to display multiview blocks. For example, if you want to create a "stacked" set of floor plans, which you could view in isometric, you would use the plan display rep set and select Top as the view direction. If you used the current viewport view direction, all multiview blocks would display their model representation. View-direction-dependent display configurations match display representation sets to the six orthogonal views (top, bottom, left, right, front, and back), so the display of objects in a viewport changes, depending on the current view in the viewport. If you do not specify a display representation set for one of the view directions, or if you apply a view to the viewport that is not orthogonal, then a default display representation set controls the display in that viewport.

The following is a Display Configurations screen. Notice that the Work display configuration contains Work_Model, Work_Plan, and Work_Section Display Representation Sets.

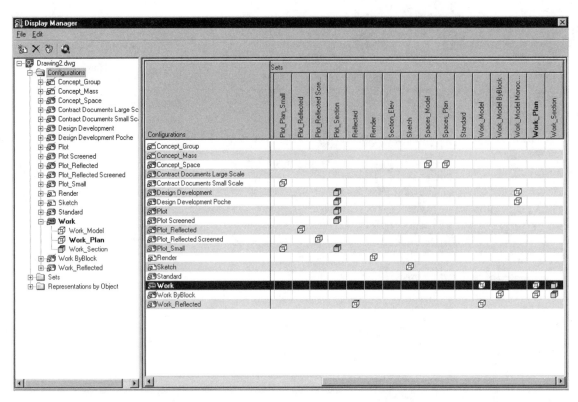

Double-clicking on a Display Configuration brings up another screen showing which view each Display Representation uses.

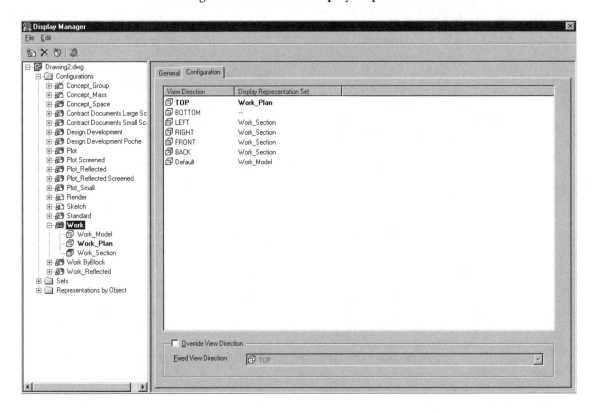

Hands On

Using the Display Manager.

1. Go to the work 3D Layout tab.

2. Erase all existing viewports and create three new viewports, one vertical and two horizontal.

3. Go to Model Space. Set the left viewport to TopView, the top-right viewport to TopView, and the lower-right viewport to SW Isometric View.

4. In the left viewport, draw a 16-ft square building using the Stud-4 Rigid-1.5 Air-1 Brick-4 wall style and add three windows and a door, as shown in Figure 1.

5. Activate the upper-right viewport; then click on the Set Current Display Configuration icon in the AEC Setup toolbar.

6. Set the upper-right viewport to Plot_Reflected; then activate the lower-right viewport, click on the Set Current Display Configuration icon again, and set the viewport to Sketch (Figure 2).

7. Repeat this process, trying out all the different Display Configurations.

   Display Configurations allow you to see your buildings in different representations at the same time.

Figure 1

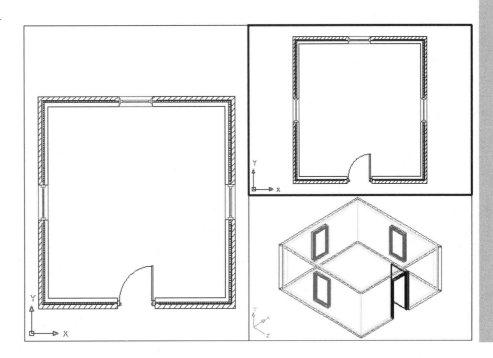

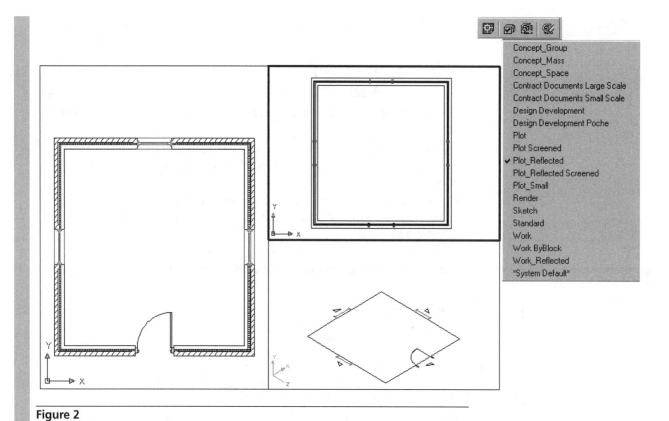

Figure 2

Templates

Autodesk Architectural Desktop Release 3 comes with **19 standard templates**. They can be accessed from the new My Drawings dialog box. If you wish to use the traditional start-up dialog, it can be accessed by going to Options | System | General Options and selecting the traditional start-out dialog box. The programming staff created each of the templates to satisfy a specific design need. Within each of the templates the layout has been labeled, viewports have been created, and displayed configurations have been assigned to the viewports. The following lesson is designed to help familiarize you get with the templates.

Hands On

1. Select File | New from the Standard toolbar or choose the new icon from the top Icon toolbar.
2. At the Select How to Begin dropdown, choose Template.
3. Select the Aec arch (imperial-intl).dwt template.
4. Using the lower-left screen cursors, move the Layout tabs until you see the Template-Overview tab. Select that tab.
5. Zoom in full screen on the Work-Sec representation.

The Template-Overview tab shows all the tabs in the template plus the Display Configuration, Display Representation set, View Orientation, and Zoom Scale of each viewport.
Every AEC Template has a Template-Overview tab.

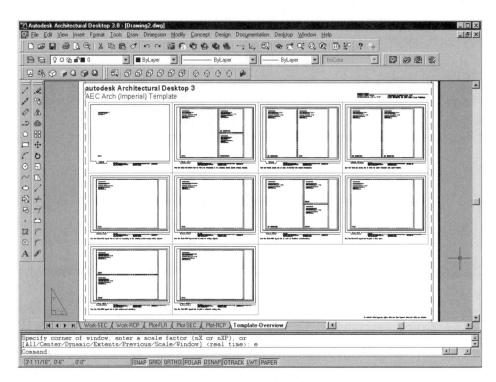

The following is a closeup of Template-Overview showing viewport settings.

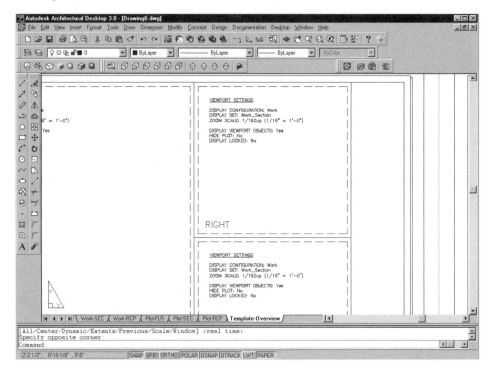

Using the Layout Tabs

The 19 template drawings that come with Autodesk Architectural Desktop Release 3 contain preset layout tabs, depending on the particular template. Following is a sampling of typical layout tabs and their use. It is highly advised that you open up all the sample templates that come with the program and make yourself aware of the different layouts.

Because the layout tabs make use of AutoCAD's Paper Space capability, it is also advisable for you to become familiar with this capability by reading me AutoCAD 2000i user's guide.

MODEL Tab

The Model Layout tab does not contain viewports. It is highly recommended that unless you are an advanced AutoCAD user, you should not use this layout tab.

MASS GROUP Tab

The Mass Group Layout tab contains the viewports used to work on massing studies. Massing studies make use of Mass Elements and Mass Groups.

SPACE Tab

The Space Layout tab contains the viewports used to work with spaces and space boundaries.

Work-3D Tab

The work 3D Layout tab contains the viewports used for working on everything in your building except for things in the ceiling, which are reserved for the reflected ceiling plans.

WORK-FLR Tab

The Work-FLR Layout tab is exactly the same as the Work 3D Layout tab except that it contains only one viewport.

WORK-SEC Tab

The Work-Section Layout tab contains viewports for working on sections elevations.

WORK-RCP Tab

The Work-RCP Layout tab contains a viewport for working on reflected ceiling plans.

PLOT-FLR Tab

The Plot-FLR Layout tab contains viewports for arranging floor plans in plan view for plotting.

PLOT-SEC Tab

The Plot Section Layout tab contains viewports for arranging elevation and section drawings for plotting.

PLOT-RCP Tab

The Plot-RCP Layout tab contains viewports for arranging reflected ceiling plans for plotting.

Customizing Templates

Templates are really specialized AutoCAD drawings. You can customize them to contain your company logos, title sheets, etc. The easiest way to create a customized template is to open an existing template, make changes to it, and save it as a template under a new name.

Hands On

1. Activate the <u>Viewports</u> and AEC Setup toolbars, and place them in a convenient spot.

2. Using the Aec arch [imperial-intl].dwt template, select the Work-3D Layout tab.

3. Press the <u>PAPER</u> button to place the layout in Paper Space, and delete the viewport borders (Figure 3).

4. Select the <u>Display Viewports Dialog</u> icon from the <u>View toolbar</u> to bring up the <u>Viewports</u> dialog box.

5. At the Viewports dialog box, select the <u>New Viewports</u> tab.

6. Select <u>Three: Left</u>, change the Setup to <u>3D</u>, set the Change view to <u>Top</u> for the left viewport, <u>Front</u> for the top right viewport, and <u>SW Isometric</u> for the bottom-right viewport, and then press the <u>OK</u> button (Figure 4).

7. Press the <u>Enter</u> key at the command line to accept <Fit>.

8. Select each Viewport and press the <u>Set Current Display Configuration</u> icon from the AEC Setup toolbar.

9. When the <u>Set Current Display Configuration</u> menu appears, select <u>Work</u>.

You have now set the typical <u>Work-3D</u> Layout used in the exercises in this book.

10. <u>Select File | Save As</u> from the <u>Main</u> toolbar to bring up the <u>Save Drawing As</u> dialog box.

Figure 3

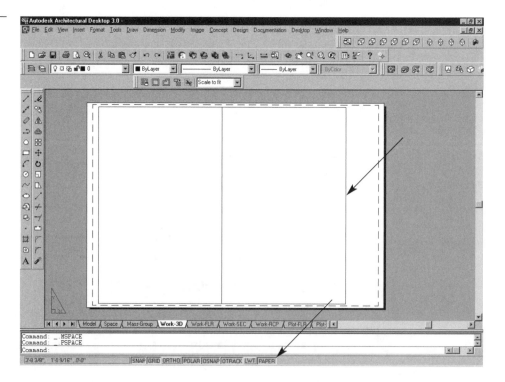

Figure 4

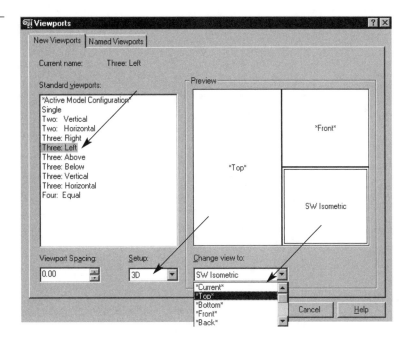

11. At the Save Drawing As dialog box, select **AutoCAD Drawing Template File [*.dwt]** from the <u>Files of Type</u> dropdown list.
12. Save the file name as Aec arch [imperial-intl] again (Figure 5).

Figure 5

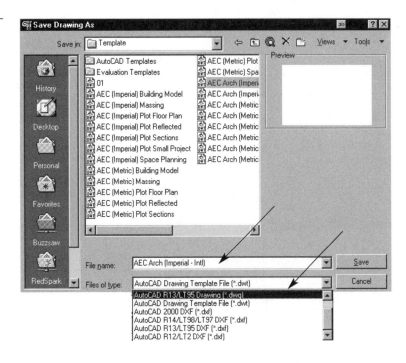

Concept

Design

Documentation

Desktop

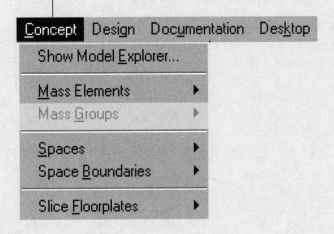

Concept	Design	Documentation	Desktop
Show Model Explorer...			
Mass Elements	▶		
Mass Groups	▶		
Spaces	▶		
Space Boundaries	▶		
Slice Floorplates	▶		

Section 1

Mass Elements and Mass Groups

When you finish this section, you should be able to do the following:

✔ Understand the purpose of Mass Elements and Mass Groups.
✔ Design with Mass Elements and Mass Groups.

Designers often use massing models to get a sense of the scale and placements of structures in a building. Real massing models are made of wood, plastic, cardboard, etc., and are usually quick conceptual objects. Autodesk Architectural Desktop Release 3 also contains tools to help you in the conceptual design process. Among these tools are Mass Elements and Mass Groups for creating virtual massing models. The system starts with Mass Elements (primitives similar to wooden building blocks) of many different solid shapes. It then allows you to add and subtract these volumes by creating Mass Groups. You can then section the final results into floors and eventually convert them into construction documents if you want to.

Mass Elements

Mass Elements can be input into a drawing by selecting them from the Mass Elements toolbar.

Mass Elements are specialized solid primitives that you can either control parametrically or modify on the screen by pulling grips.

 Tip To save space, we use RMB and LMB to represent "click the right mouse button" and "click the left mouse button," respectively.

You can also input Mass Elements into a drawing by selecting Mass Elements | Add Mass Element from the Concept drop-down menu in the main toolbar.

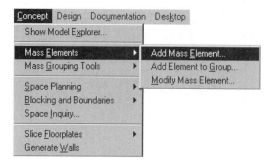

Hands On

The following exercise walks you through the basics of adding and modifying Mass Elements.

1. Start Architectural Desktop Release 3 with the Aec arch [imperial-intl].dwt template.
2. Select the Mass-Group Layout tab, and activate the left 3-D viewport.
3. RMB on any icon, select Customize, select the Toolbars tab, select AECARCHX from the menu group, and check the Mass Elements checkbox. Place the Mass Elements toolbar in a convenient location.
4. Select the <u>Box</u> icon from the <u>Mass Elements</u> toolbar to bring up the <u>Add Mass Element</u> dialog box.
5. At the Add Mass Element dialog box, change the width to 30 ft and the depth to 20 ft, and lean the height at 10 ft (Figure 1–1).
6. Activate the left 3-D viewport and press the Enter key twice.

You have now placed a Mass Element in the viewport; notice that the Mass Element does not appear in the right viewport. This is because the right viewport has been configured to show Mass Groups, not Mass Elements.

7. Select the Mass Element, RMB, and choose <u>Element Modify</u> from the Contextual menu.
8. Change the width to 50 ft, and change the depth to 30 ft. Then select the apply button and close the dialog box.

Figure 1–1

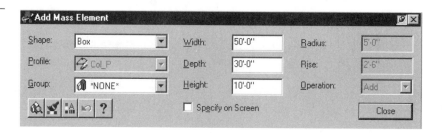

You have now modified a Mass Element using the Modify Element dialog box.

9. Select the Mass Element again, stretch the right corner grip 25 ft in the 0° direction, and LMB to complete.

10. Again select the Mass Element, RMB, and choose <u>Element Modify</u> from the Contextual menu.

Notice that the width in the Modify Mass Element dialog box has changed. You have just changed the Mass Element by stretching it on the screen (Figure 1–2).

11. Select the Mass Element again, RMB, and choose Element Modify from the Contextual menu.

12. From the shape dropdown in the Modify Mass Element dialog box, choose Cylinder and press OK to close the dialog box.

You have now changed the Mass Element primitive. Repeat this process several times until you can modify all the Mass Element primitives (Figure 1–3). You can place Mass Element primitives either by specifying their width, depth, and height in the <u>Add Mass Element</u> dialog box or by checking the <u>Specify on Screen</u> checkbox, also located on this dialog box. By checking this checkbox, you will be able to set the Mass Element's size in all directions as you are placing it.

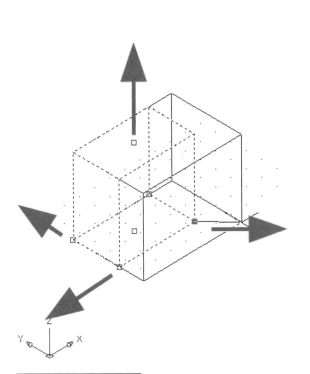

Figure 1–2
Stretching Mass Elements on screen.

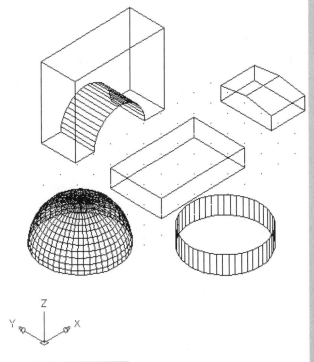

Figure 1–3
Mass Element Primitives.

Creating a Concept Building Using Mass Elements and Mass Groups

Hands On

1. Start Architectural Desktop Release 3 with the Aec arch [imperial-intl].dwt template.
2. Select the Mass-Group Layout tab and activate the left 3-D viewport.
3. Select the Box icon from the Mass Elements toolbar to bring up the Add Mass Elements toolbar.
4. At the Add Mass Element dialog box, change the width to 60 ft, the depth to 40 ft, and the height to 10 ft.
5. Activate the Front View and select the Array icon from the Modify toolbar.
6. In the Array dialog box set Rows to 4 and Columns to 1, and set the Row offset to 10 ft.
7. Select the Rectangular Array radio button, press the Selected objects button, and select your 60′ × 40′ × 10′ Mass Element. Press the Enter key, and when you return to the Array dialog box, press the OK button to end the command.

You have now made Mass Element into a four-story structure that is 40 ft high (Figure 1–4).

8. Change the view to Top view.
9. Place a 6-ft radius by 10-ft-high cylinder at upper left corner of the structure. (Center the cylinder at the corner of the structure.) **This will become the stairway.**
10. Go to Desktop | Utilities | Reference AEC Objects.
11. At the Command line, type AD (for Add), and press the space bar or Enter key.
12. Select your Cylinder, and at the Command line direction Insertion point:, pick the center of your cylinder and take a copy to the upper right corner of your arrayed 60-ft × 40-ft × 10-ft Mass Element.

Figure 1–4

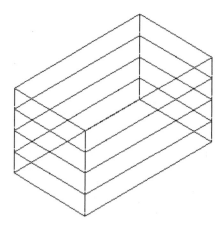

Figure 1–5

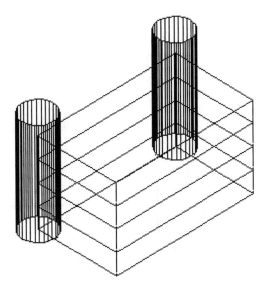

13. Select the left cylinder again and RMB. Choose <u>Element Modify</u> from the Contextual menu, and at the <u>Modify Mass Element</u> dialog box, change the height of the Cylinder to 50 ft (Figure 1–5).

   Notice that the right Cylinder also changes. Reference AEC Objects change when their parent object changes. You will see this command again in the Desktop section of this book.

14. Select the second box to activate its grips. With object snap <off>, stretch the box rearward 10 ft. This is best done in top view (Figure 1–6).

Figure 1–6

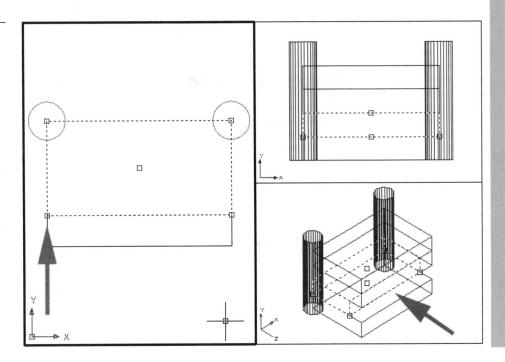

Figure 1–7

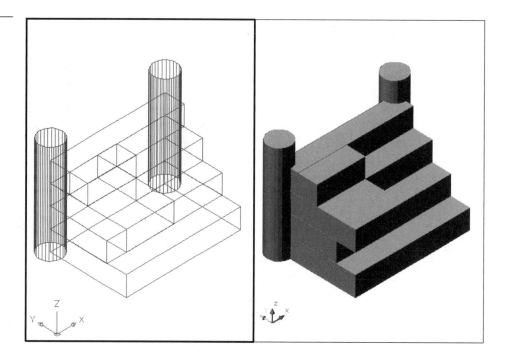

15. Repeat this process, adding, stretching, and modifying Mass Elements until you create mass elements similar to Figure 1–7. **Save this exercise.**

Mass Groups

You can input Mass Groups into a drawing by selecting them from the Mass Groups toolbar.

You can also input Mass Groups into a drawing by selecting Mass Groups | Add Mass Group from the Concept dropdown menu in the Main toolbar.

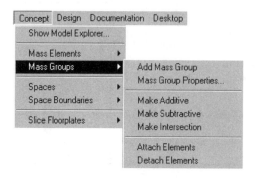

Hands On

1. Use the previous exercise.
2. Activate the <u>Mass Groups</u> toolbar, and place it in a convenient spot.
3. Activate the left viewport.
4. Select the <u>Set Current Display Configuration</u> icon from the <u>AEC Setup</u> toolbar, and check <u>Concept Mass</u> from the Contextual menu.
5. Activate the right viewport.
6. Select the <u>Set Current Display Configuration</u> icon from the <u>AEC Setup</u> toolbar, and check <u>Concept Group</u> from the Contextual menu.

Your Mass Elements will disappear in the right viewport because the Concept_Group Display Configuration shows only Mass Groups.

7. Select the <u>Add Mass Group</u> icon from the Mass Groups toolbar.
8. Place a <u>Mass Group icon marker</u> in the right viewport, and press the Enter key (location does not matter).
9. Select the <u>Mass Group icon marker</u>, RMB, and select Attach Elements from the Contextual menu.
10. Select all the Mass Elements in the left viewport.

You now have Mass Elements in the left viewport and a Mass Group in the right viewport (Figure 1–8).

11. Activate the right viewport.
12. Select the Mass Group composition, RMB, and select <u>Show Model explorer</u> from the Contextual menu to bring up the Model Explorer dialog box.

Figure 1–8

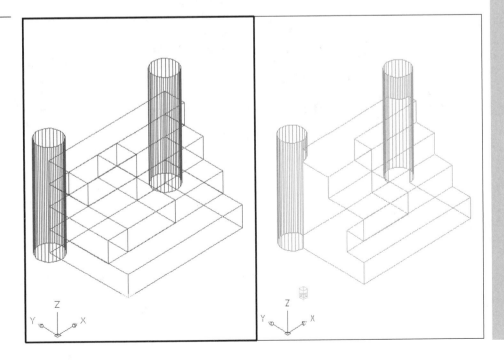

Figure 1–9

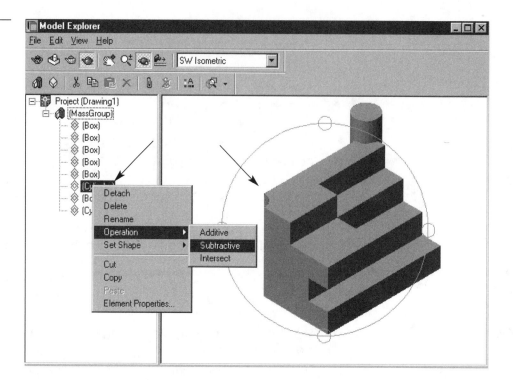

13. At the Model Explorer dialog box, expand the Mass Group in the Tree View.

14. RMB on the icon next to the cylinder to bring up the Contextual menu.

15. Select <u>Subtractive</u> and the cylinder will subtract from the composition (Figure 1–9).

You can modify the composition by modifying the Mass Elements in the left viewport and/or by making the Mass Group elements additive, subtractive, or intersecting.

The creation of a Mass Group is the last step in the creation of a massing design. From this design, you will be able to create spaces and walls. Save this exercise.

Section 2

Spaces

When you finish this section, you should be able to do the following:

- ✔ Add, Modify, Convert, and Generate Spaces.
- ✔ Set Space Styles.
- ✔ Inquire, Generate, Divide, and Join Spaces.
- ✔ Use Interference Conditions.

Buildings are often designed by first compiling their needed spaces. The relationship between these spaces as well as their size and volume often dictate the shape of a building. Autodesk Architectural Desktop Release 3 uses space objects to aid the architect and designer when using this design concept.

Space objects are AEC objects that represent the three-dimensional space, including floors, ceilings, room height from the top of the floor to the bottom of the ceiling, and floor thickness and distance above the ceiling. There are several ways you can make space objects. You can add them from styles, convert them from linework, convert them from wall enclosures, or make them automatically from space boundaries.

You can input spaces into a drawing by selecting them from the Spaces toolbar.

You can also input spaces into a drawing by selecting Spaces | Add Space from the Concept drop-down menu in the main toolbar.

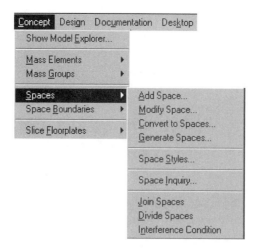

Space objects are AEC objects that represent three-dimensional space, including floors, ceilings, room height from the top of the floor to the bottom of the ceiling, and floor thickness and distance above the ceiling (Figure 2–1).

Until you add Space Boundaries (see the next section for Space Boundaries), it is hard to visualize the entire volume, including the space above the ceiling (Figure 2–2).

Creating Space Styles

To help understand how space styles are created, try the following tutorial.

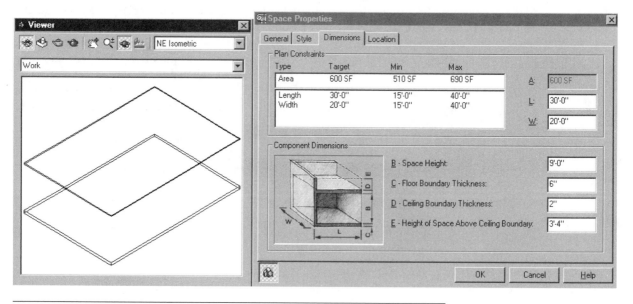

Figure 2–1

Figure 2–2

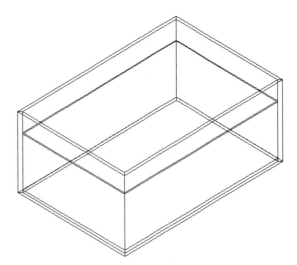

Hands On

1. Using the Aec arch [imperial-intl].dwt template, select the Space Layout tab.
2. Select the <u>Space Style</u> icon from the Spaces toolbar.
3. Create a new style and call it "Bath Room."
4. Double-click on the Bath Room style and bring up the <u>Space Style Properties</u> dialog box.
5. Set the settings as shown below.

You would like your bathroom to be 5 ft x 10 ft and 50 ft². Knowing that your design might vary somewhat, you allow for some variance. Accept that the bathroom might get as big as 80 ft², but the length and width can never be less than 10 ft x 5 ft, respectively. The settings restrict the space object maximum and minimum settings on input.

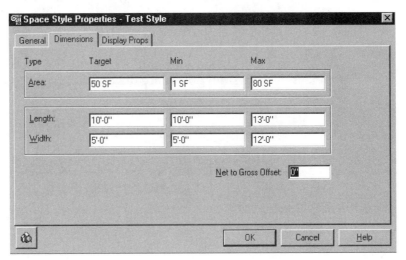

6. Go to the Space Layout tab and activate the Top View viewport.

7. Select the Add Space icon from the Spaces toolbar. **Make sure Enable Rollup is turned off.**

In this exercise you want to watch the dimensions change, so turn Enable Rollup off to cause the Dialog box to stay open at all times.

8. At the Add Space dialog box, select the Bath Room Style.

9. Make sure the Specify on Screen checkbox is unchecked.

10. Click the Lock icon next to the Width input window; then check the Specify on Screen checkbox.

Checking the Specify on Screen checkbox locks the width dimension but allows the other dimensions to vary on screen.

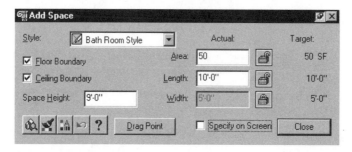

11. Click in the Top viewport to set a corner of the space object.

12. Drag the mouse around and notice that the width doesn't change.

13. Complete the command and exit.

The Add Space dialog box shows a maximum of 65 ft² because the length maximum was set at 13 ft.

14. Select the Bath Room space object in the Top viewport.

15. RMB and select Modify Space from the Contextual menu.

16. In the Modify Space dialog box, change the 5-ft width to 8 ft and press the Apply button.

Locking dimensions are only for input. The Modify Space dialog box always overrides the Add Space dialog box.

Generating Spaces

Space objects can also be created from walls, polylines, lines, circles, etc. The following tutorial illustrates the use of the Generate Spaces command.

Hands On

1. Using the Aec arch [imperial-intl].dwt template, select the Space Lay-out tab.
2. Activate the Top View and draw the sample floor plan (Figure 2–3).
3. Select the <u>Generate Spaces</u> icon from the Spaces toolbar.
4. In the Generate Spaces dialog box, set the selection filter to **<u>All Linework</u>**.
5. Select the floor plan you have just drawn.
6. At the <u>Generate Spaces</u> dialog box, choose the Standard Style and select an internal point in the floor plan (Figure 2–4).

Figure 2–3

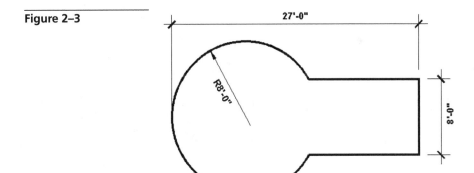

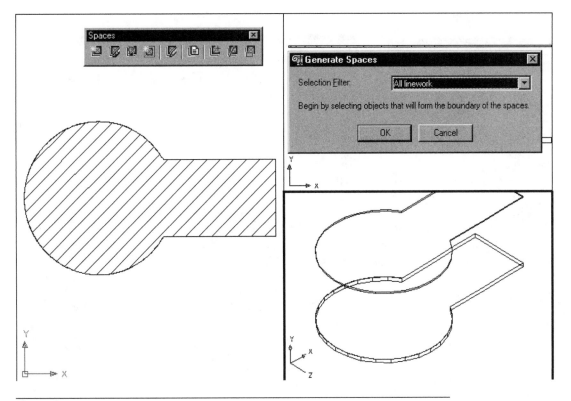

Figure 2–4

Dividing Spaces

Hands On

1. Using the preceding tutorial, select the <u>Divide Spaces</u> icon from the Spaces toolbar.
2. Select the Space Object in the Top View viewport, and Draw a division, as shown in Figure 2–5.
3. Select the <u>Space Inquiry</u> icon, and you will see the areas of the two spaces you have created (Figure 2–6).

Figure 2–5

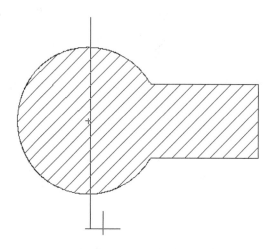

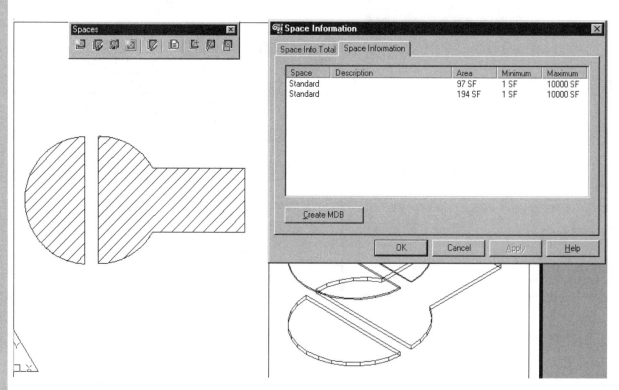

Figure 2–6

Interference Condition

Hands On

1. Using the previous tutorial, change to the Work-3D Layout tab.
2. Select the Top viewport.
3. Add 8 1-ft-square columns (use <u>Design | Structural Members | Add Column</u>). They must pass through both the ceiling and the floor.
4. Select the Interference Condition icon from the Spaces toolbar.
5. At the command line, choose the Add option.
6. Select the Space Object, and then select the Columns. Exit the command (Figure 2–7).

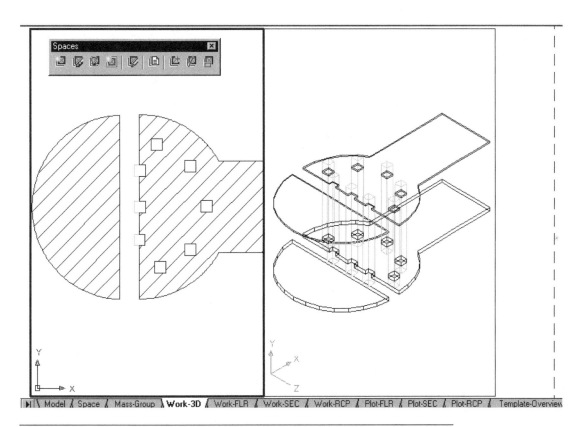

Figure 2–7
Using Interference Conditions, you can easily subtract areas from a Space Object.

Section 3

Space Boundaries

When you finish this section, you should be able to do the following:

- ✔ Add, Modify, and Convert to Boundaries.
- ✔ Understand the relationship between Spaces and Space Boundaries.
- ✔ Add and Edit Boundary Edges.
- ✔ Understand the "Manage Contained Spaces" concept.

Solid Form and Area Separation

You can combine Spaces and Space Boundaries to create a complete representation of the space, the interior space, and the surrounding boundaries. Space Boundaries can represent either a solid boundary (Solid Form) or the indication of the separation between areas (Area Separation). Solid-Form Boundaries are equal to and act just like walls; they are the only type that you can convert into walls. Area-separation boundaries have a thickness of zero and cannot be converted to walls.

Use Space Boundaries and Spaces to make subtle changes in elevation, room height, interstitial space, etc., during the conceptual design process.

You can input **Space Boundaries** into a drawing by selecting them from the Space Boundaries toolbar.

You can also input **Space Boundaries** into a drawing by selecting Space Boundaries | Add Boundary from the Concept dropdown menu in the Main toolbar.

Concept   Design   Documentation   Desktop

Show Model Explorer...

Mass Elements   ▶
Mass Groups   ▶

Spaces   ▶
Space Boundaries   ▶   Add Boundary...
                         Modify Boundary...
Slice Floorplates   ▶   Convert to Boundaries...

                         Attach Spaces to Boundary
                         Merge Boundaries
                         Split Boundary

                         Add Boundary Edges
                         Edit Boundary Edges
                         Remove Boundary Edges

                         Anchor to Boundary

                         Generate Walls

Creating and Modifying Space Boundaries

Hands On

1. Activate the Space Boundaries toolbar and place it in a convenient place on your screen.
2. Using the Aec arch [imperial-intl].dwt template, select the Space Layout tab.
3. Activate the Top View viewport.
4. Select the <u>Add Boundary</u> icon from the <u>Space Boundaries</u> toolbar.
5. At the Add Space Boundary dialog box, set the <u>Segment Type</u> to Solid Form, Height to 12 ft, and Width to 6 ft, select Line, and <u>uncheck</u> the Manage Contained Spaces checkbox (Figure 3–1).
6. Create a 10-ft × 10-ft Space Boundary enclosure.
7. Change the Manage Contained Spaces checkbox to <u>checked</u>, and create a second 10-ft × 10-ft Space Boundary enclosure (Figure 3–2).

   The second Space Boundary contains a space object because the Manage Contained Spaces checkbox is <u>checked</u>.

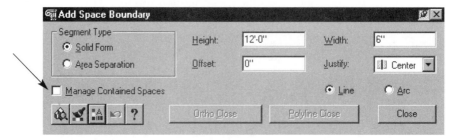

Figure 3–1

Figure 3–2

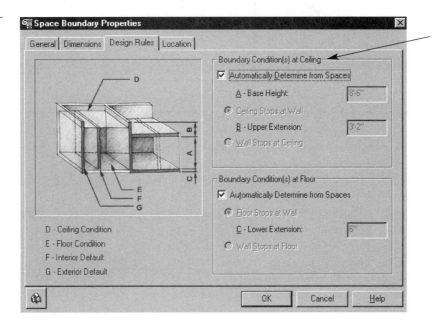

Boundary Conditions Determined from Spaces

Hands On

1. Using the previous exercise, RMB on Space Boundary no. 2, and select Space Boundary Properties from the Contextual menu.

2. At the <u>Space Boundary Properties</u> dialog box, select the <u>Design Rules</u> tab.

3. Check the <u>Automatically Determine from Spaces</u> checkboxes for <u>Boundary Condition(s) at the ceiling</u> and <u>the floor</u> (Figure 3–3). Press OK.

Figure 3–3

Figure 3–4

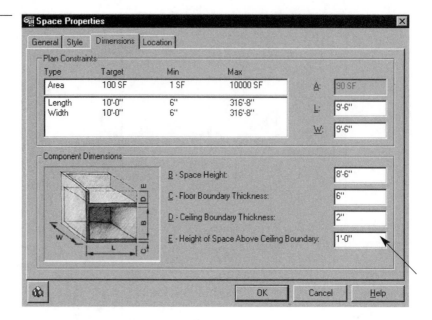

4. Select the space object in Space Boundary no. 2, RMB, and select Space Properties from the Contextual menu.

5. In the <u>Space Properties</u> dialog box, select the <u>Dimensions</u> tab.

6. Change <u>E</u> - Height of Space Above Ceiling Boundary to 1′-0″ (Figure 3–4).

Space Boundary no. 2 changes because the space properties changed. In this case the Space controls the Space Boundary. Figure 3–5 shows the situation before and Figure 3–6 shows the situation after the change.

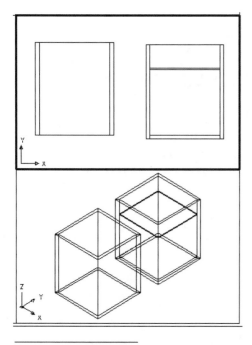

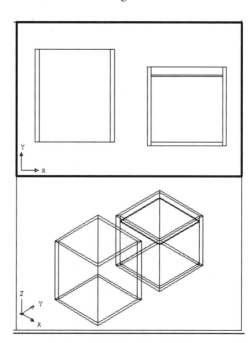

Figure 3–5   **Figure 3–6**

Figure 3–7

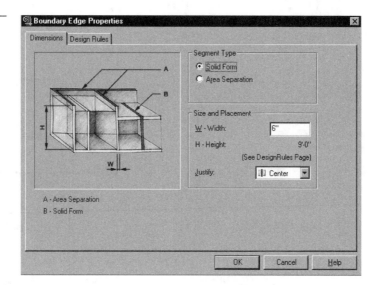

 If you create a Space Boundary and it doesn't seem to have any height on the screen, make sure it is set for Solid Form, not Area Separation (Figure 3–7).

Vary the settings in the **Space Properties** dialog box, and observe all the changes in the Space Boundary.

Convert to Boundaries

Convert to Boundaries is similar to Convert to Spaces or Generate Spaces (see the exercise in Section 2). The difference is in terminology. After you select this routine, you are presented with three Command Line options: Edges / Space / Slice. Edges converts arcs, circles, or polylines. Space converts Spaces, and Slices converts Floor Slices created from Massing models. Use the floorplan shown in the "Generating Spaces" exercise in Section 2 to practice using this routine.

Attach Spaces to Boundary and Merge Boundaries

Attach Spaces to Boundary and Merge Boundaries are similar. Both are used to connect Space Boundaries together. Attach Spaces to Boundary allows you to attach an existing Space Object to a Space Boundary. When this is done, the two Space Boundaries act as one. Merging Boundaries joins two Space Boundaries together to act as one.

Try the following exercise to understand these concepts.

Hands On

1. Activate the Space Boundaries and Spaces toolbars and place them in a convenient place on your screen.
2. Using the Aec arch [imperial-intl].dwt template, select the Space Layout tab.

Figure 3–8

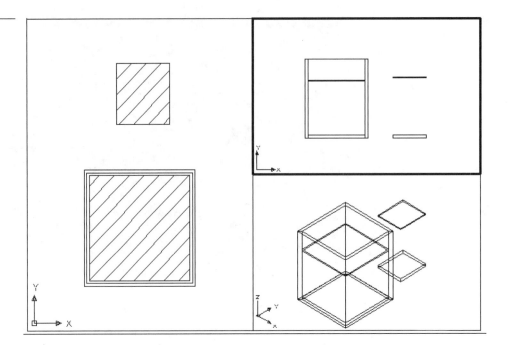

3. Activate the Top View viewport.

4. Select the <u>Add Space Boundary</u> icon from the Space Boundaries toolbar.

5. At the Add Space Boundary dialog box, <u>check</u> the <u>Manage Contained Spaces</u> checkbox. Make sure the <u>Solid Form</u> radio button is also selected.

6. Create a 10-ft × 10-ft Space Boundary enclosure.

7. Select the <u>Add Space</u> icon on the Spaces toolbar.

8. Add a Space object approximately half the size of the Space Boundary you previously made (Figure 3–8).

9. Select the <u>Attach Spaces to Boundary</u> icon from the Space Boundaries toolbar.

10. At the command line request, select the Space Boundary you created in Step 6, and then select the Space Object created in Step 8.

Although the command line will say that one space was merged, nothing will seem to have happened. That is because the new boundary created around the Space Object is an Area Separation, not a Solid Form. To change this do the following:

11. Select the first Space Boundary, RMB, and select <u>Modify Space Boundary</u> from the Contextual menu.

12. Notice that the Varies radio button is selected under Segment Type.

Because you have attached the Boundaries, they act as one, but their Segment type is different (Varies).

13. Select the <u>Solid Form</u> radio button, and click the <u>Apply</u> button.

Both Spaces now have Space Boundaries, and the Space Boundaries act as one.

14.   Turn the object snap <on>.

15.   Select the second Space Boundary, select the center grip, and drag it to the first Space Boundary (Figure 3–9).

The Boundary between the two Space Boundaries becomes one. To test it, insert a door (Figure 3–10).

Figure 3–9

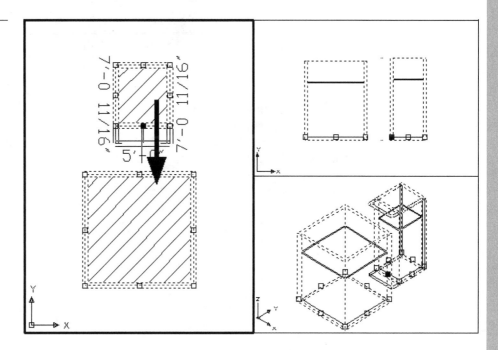

Figure 3–10

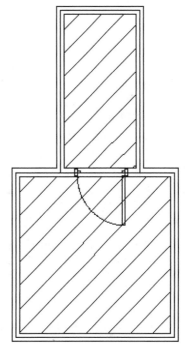

Figure 3–11

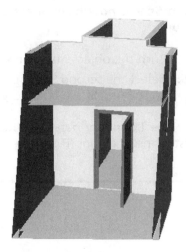

Figure 3–11 shows that the Space Boundaries are truly one. By using the 3D Orbit tool and selecting the Front Clipping Plane to cut away the front of the Space and Space Boundary, you can see the door really passes through the Space Boundary.

16.   **Save the exercise** for later use.

Add, Edit, and Remove Boundary Edges—Insert Joint

Hands On

1.   Using the previous exercise, select the Space Boundary, RMB, and pick Edit Edges from the Contextual menu (Figure 3–12).
2.   Select segment **a**, and at the <u>Boundary Edge Properties</u> dialog box uncheck <u>Automatically Determine from Spaces</u> for the Boundary Condition(s) at Ceiling.
3.   Select the Space Boundary, RMB, and pick <u>Edit Edges</u> from the Contextual menu.
4.   Select segment **c,** and at the <u>Boundary Edge Properties</u> dialog box, uncheck <u>Automatically Determine from Spaces</u> for the Boundary Condition(s) at <u>Floor</u>.
5.   Set **C** - Lower Extention to 6′-0″ and press the OK button.
6.   Select the Space Boundary, RMB, and pick <u>Insert Joint</u> from the Contextual menu.

 Tip   You can set Insert Joint for Space boundaries only from the Contextual menu; it is not available from any toolbars.

Figure 3–12

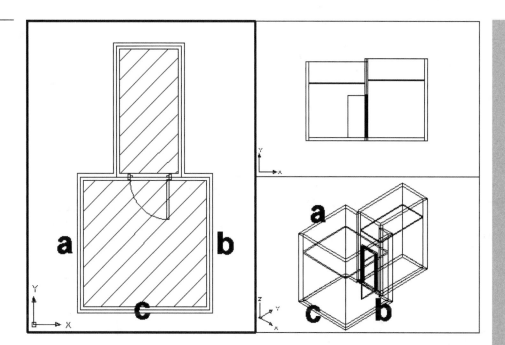

7. Select segment **b,** and insert a joint. <u>Nothing will seem to happen!</u>

8. Select the Space Boundary again, and you will see a new vertex in segment **b**.

9. Select the vertex, hold down the CTRL key on the keyboard, and pull out the segment (Figure 3–13).

10. Select other vertices, again hold down the CTRL key, and pull on segments (Figure 3–14).

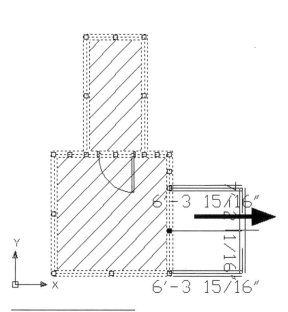

Figure 3–13

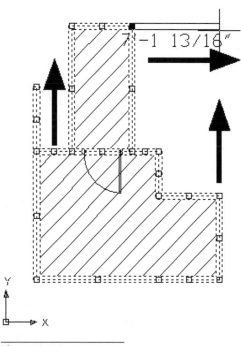

Figure 3–14

Figure 3–15

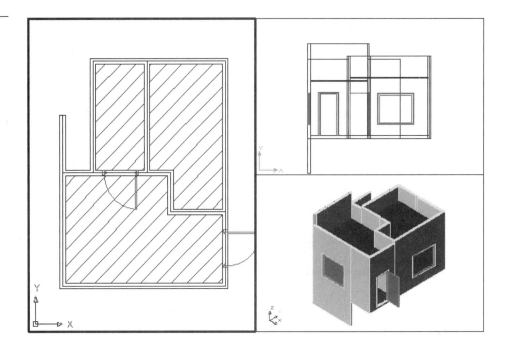

Using all the editing functions for Space Boundaries, you can quickly create a conceptual space plan (Figure 3–15).

11. **Save your exercise.**

Generating Walls

After you have generated a space plan with Space Boundaries and have added doors, windows, etc., it is time to create walls. This is the link in Architectural Desktop from the concept stage to the design stage.

Hands On

1. Using the previous exercise, select the Space Boundary, RMB, and pick Generate Walls from the Contextual menu.
2. If you have added doors and windows, at the Command line respond **Y** to the question Generate New Openings? Again, **nothing will seem to happen!**

    Nothing will seem to have happened because you are in the Space Layout tab, and it is not configured to show Walls.

3. Switch to the Work-FLR Layout tab.

Figure 3–16

4. Turn off the A-Area-Bdry layer (the Space Boundary is on that layer, and you don't want it to show).

If you understand the Display system, you can configure the Work-FLR Layout tab to <u>not</u> display Space Boundaries.

5. Select the SW Isometric View, and select Flat Shaded, Edges On from the Shade toolbar.

You are now in the Design phase, and you can use any of the tools under the Design toolbar to further refine your building (Figure 3–16).

Section 4

Slice Floorplates

When you finish this section, you should be able to do the following:

✔ Generate and use Slice Floorplates.
✔ Convert Slice Plates into Space Boundaries.

You can generate **Slice Floorplates** in a drawing by selecting them from the Slice Floorplates toolbar.

You can also generate **Slice Floorplates** in a drawing by selecting Slice Floorplates | Generate Slice from the Concept dropdown menu in the main toolbar.

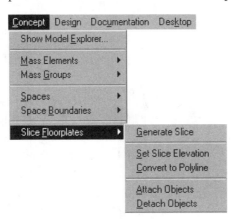

Hands On

1. Using the last exercise from the Mass Groups section, activate the <u>Slice Floorplates</u> and <u>Space Boundaries</u> toolbars, and place them in a convenient spot.
2. Select the <u>Generate Slice</u> icon from the <u>Slice Floorplates</u> toolbar.
3. Type 5 at the command line for the number of slices, and press the space bar or <u>Enter</u> key.
4. In the right viewport, click and drag a rectangle, click, and then press the space bar or <u>Enter</u> key twice, and enter 10′ for the distance between slices. Press the space bar or <u>Enter</u> key to end the command.

The size or rotation of the Slice icon doesn't matter; it is only an indicator icon (Figure 4–1).

5. Select the five Slice icon markers, RMB, and select <u>Attach Objects</u> from the Contextual menu.
6. Select all the objects that make up the Mass Group, and press the space bar or <u>Enter</u> key.
7. Select the <u>Layers</u> icon from the <u>Objects Properties</u> toolbar to bring up the <u>Layer Properties Manager</u> dialog box.
8. At the Layer Properties Manager dialog box, select the <u>A-Mass-Grps</u> layer, and freeze it in the current viewport.

You have now isolated the Slice Floorplates of your design at every 10-ft change in elevation (Figure 4–2).

9. Activate the left viewport (Mass Elements).
10. Select one of the cylinders, RMB, and select <u>Element Modify</u> from the Contextual menu to bring up the <u>Modify Mass Element</u> dialog box.

Figure 4–1

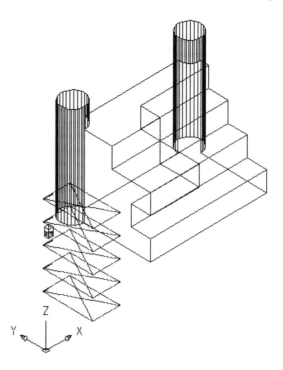

Figure 4–2

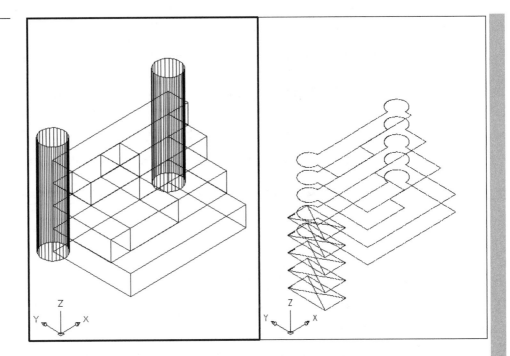

11.   At the Modify Mass Element dialog box, change the Radius to 12'-0"
       and then press the OK button to end the command.

**Notice that as the Mass Element changes radius, the Slice Floorplates
in the right viewport change to reflect the Element's changes. Once you
have created Slice Floorplates, they change in relation to changes in your
model** (Figure 4–3).

12.   Select the Work-3D Layout tab.
13.   Select the Layers icon from the Objects Properties toolbar to bring up
       the Layer Properties Manager dialog box.

Figure 4–3

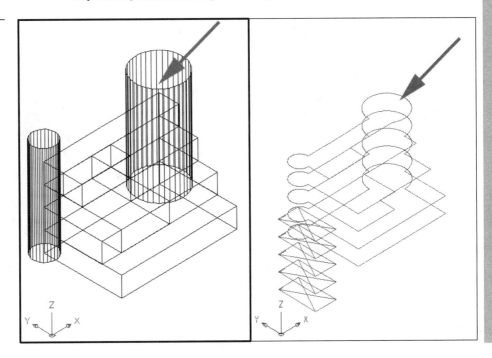

14. At the Layer Properties Manager dialog box, select the <u>A-Mass</u> and <u>A-Mass-Grps</u> layers, and then freeze them in all viewports.
15. Select the <u>Convert to Boundaries</u> icon from the Space Boundaries toolbar.
16. Type **SL** for Slice at the command line, and press the space bar or <u>Enter</u> key.
17. Select all the Slice Floorplates, and press the space bar or <u>Enter</u> key.

The Space Boundary Properties dialog box will now appear.

18. At the <u>Space Boundary Properties</u> dialog box, select the <u>Dimensions</u> tab.
19. At the Dimensions tab, select and activate the <u>A- Solid Form</u> radio button.
20. Change the W-Width to 12″.
21. Change to the Design Rules tab.
22. Uncheck the <u>Automatically Determine from Spaces</u> checkbox.
23. Set the A- Base Height to 10′-0″, and press the Ok button.

You have now created space boundaries from your Slice Floorplates. You will later generate these Space Boundaries into walls (Figure 4–4).

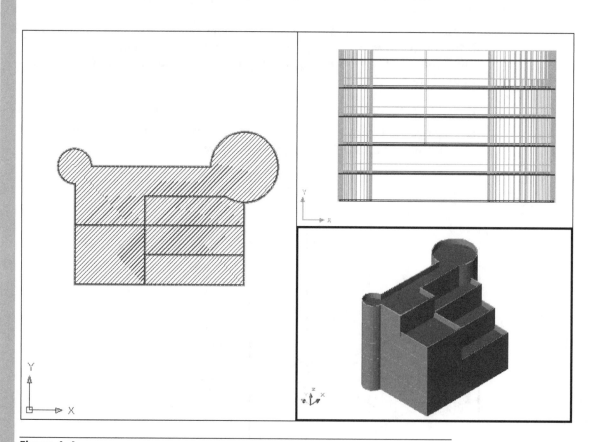

Figure 4–4

Concept

Design

Documentation

Desktop

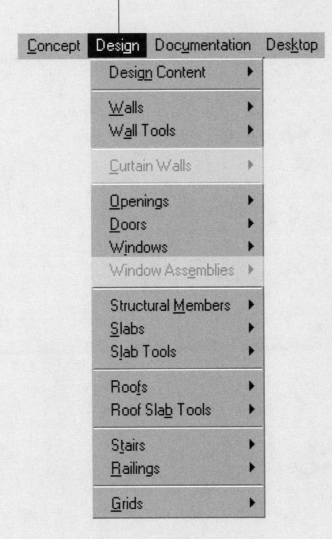

| Concept | Design | Documentation | Desktop |

Design Content	▶
Walls	▶
Wall Tools	▶
Curtain Walls	▶
Openings	▶
Doors	▶
Windows	▶
Window Assemblies	▶
Structural Members	▶
Slabs	▶
Slab Tools	▶
Roofs	▶
Roof Slab Tools	▶
Stairs	▶
Railings	▶
Grids	▶

Section 5

Design Content

When you finish this section, you should be able to do the following:

✔ Understand what Design Content is in Architectural Desktop.
✔ Find Design Content.

In order to create understandable architectural construction documents, designers include symbols of equipment such as bathroom fixtures, beds, chairs, and kitchen cabinets. Autodesk Architectural Desktop 3 includes a very comprehensive set of generic content symbols in both 2D and 3D. You can create much of the content utilizing Architectural Desktop's Multi-View block representation system. (See Sections 28 and 29 in Part 4.) Multi-View Blocks allow the Display System to place the representation of the object in the appropriate view (i.e., 3D in Model view, plan representation in Plan view, etc.).

You can input Design Content into a drawing by selecting the appropriate content icon from the Design Content - Imperial or Design Content - Metric toolbars.

You can also input Design Content into a drawing by selecting the appropriate content from the Design | Design Content menu from the Main Toolbar.

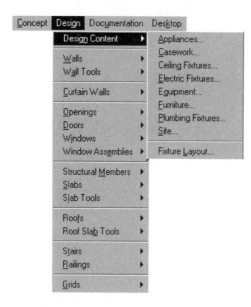

Content

All the symbols and schedules, documentation symbols, and styles are contained in a folder called <u>Content</u> in the main <u>Autodesk Architectural Desktop 3</u> directory. Unless you direct it otherwise, upon installation, Architectural Desktop 3 places the Programs directory on the **C** drive (Figure 5–1).

The program separates content into Imperial, Metric, and Metric DACH subfolders. Depending on your choice of units or the preferences of the country for which you are designing, you will select the appropriate content folder.

Figure 5–1

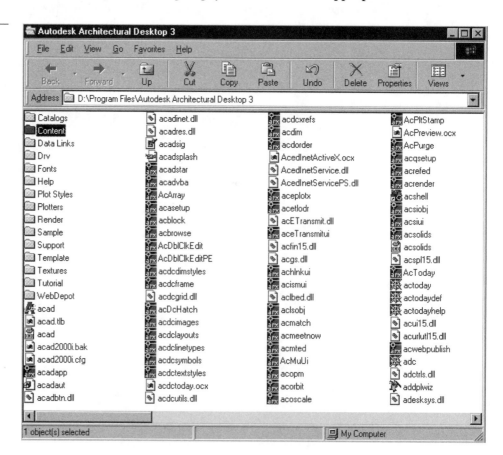

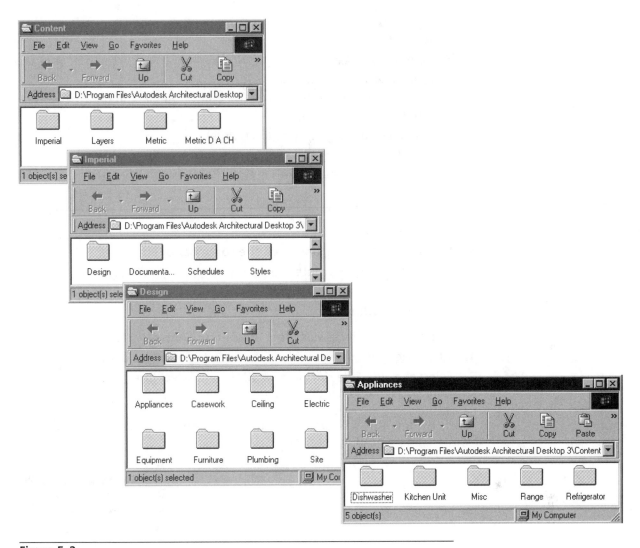

Figure 5–2

Each of these subfolders is then divided into further subfolders containing the actual drawings of the content (Figure 5–2).

The program holds all content in standard AutoCAD drawings (dwg), and it can be modified using standard AutoCAD commands.

Because Autodesk Architectural Desktop 3 uses all AutoCAD 2000i's features, it makes use of the AutoCAD Design Center to access its symbols. You can also drag content from the Internet using Autodesk's iDrop technology.

Using the AutoCAD Design Center to Create a Kitchen

Hands On

Creating the Kitchen

1. Activate the Walls, Design Content - Imperial, Layout Tools, and Anchors toolbars.

2. Using the Aec arch [imperial-intl].dwt template, select the work-3D Viewport tab.

3. Activate the Top View viewport.

4. Place a 15′ × 10′-0″ rectangle.

5. Select <u>Convert to Walls</u> icon from the <u>Walls</u> toolbar, and select the rectangle.

6. Type <u>Y</u> to erase the geometry (rectangle).

7. At the <u>Wall Properties</u> dialog box, select the Standard wall; then change to the Dimensions tab and set the following:
   - Wall Width = 4″
   - Base Height = 8′-0″
   - Justify = Right

8. Select the <u>OK</u> button, and press the space bar or Enter key.

9. Modify the walls to create the enclosure shown in (Figure 5–3).

Adding the Appliances

10. Select the <u>Appliances</u> icon from the Design Content - Imperial toolbar.

11. At the <u>DesignCenter</u>, double-click the <u>Refrigerator</u> folder to open it.

12. Select the Side-Side refrigerator, RMB, and select <u>Insert</u> from the Contextual menu (Figure 5–4).

The refrigerator will come into the drawing in a vertical position with the insertion point at its rear center.

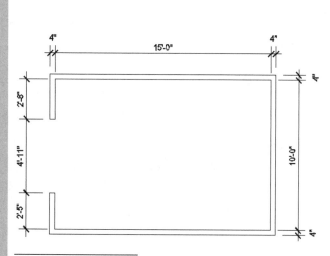

Figure 5–3

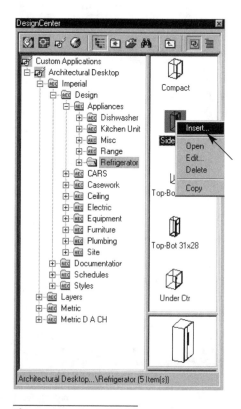

Figure 5–4

13. At the command line, type **B** for Base point, and press the space bar or Enter key.

   This will relocate the insertion point of the refrigerator. Repeating the B will cycle you through the insertion location points.

14. At the command line, type **R** for Rotation, and press the space bar or Enter key.
15. At the command line, type **270**, and press the space bar or Enter key.

This will rotate the refrigerator to the position needed.

16. With the End Point object snap set, place the refrigerator as shown in Figure 5–5.
17. Select the Casework icon from the Design Content - Imperial toolbar.
18. At the DesignCenter, double-click the Base with Drawers folder to open it.
19. Continue to place base cabinets, a stove, and a tall cabinet until you create a kitchen layout similar to Figure 5–6. **Save this drawing as Kitchen.**

The Counter

Autodesk Architectural Desktop 3 provides a wall style called Casework-36 (Counter). There is a problem with this method; you can't cut a hole in the style for a sink. To get around this, you can use the new Slabs object.

Figure 5–5

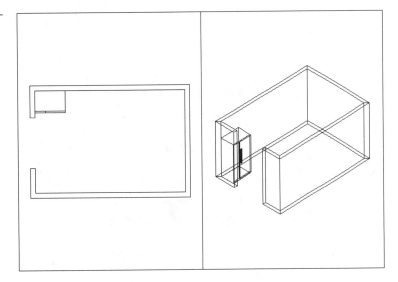

Figure 5–6

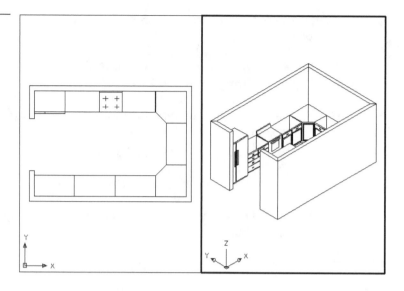

The Splash Edge Style

Hands On

1. Start a new drawing and save it as <u>counter drawing</u>.

2. Select the <u>Rectangle</u> icon from the Draw toolbar, and create a 1-in. ×
   4-in.-high rectangle.

3. Select <u>Desktop | Profiles | Profile Definitions</u> from the main toolbar to
   open the Style Manager dialog box.

4. At the <u>Style Manager</u> dialog box, select the <u>New Style</u> icon, and
   make a new profile style called <u>Splash profile</u>.

5. Select <u>Splash</u>, select the <u>Set From</u> icon from the top of the Style Manager toolbar, and pick the 1-in. × 4-in. rectangle that you created in
   Step 2.

6. Press the Enter key to accept no additional ring, and pick the lower-
   right corner of the rectangle. Press the OK button when the Style
   Manager dialog box reappears.

7. Select <u>Design | Slabs | Slab Edge Styles</u> from the main toolbar to bring
   up the <u>Style Manager</u>.

8. At the Style Manager dialog box, select the <u>New Style</u> icon, and
   make a new slab edge called <u>Splash Edge</u>.

9. Select <u>Splash Edge</u>, RMB, and select Edit from the Contextual menu
   to bring up the <u>Slab Edge Styles-Splash Edge</u> dialog box.

10. At the Slab Edge Styles-Splash Edge dialog box select the <u>Design
    Rules</u> tab.

11. Check the Fascia checkbox, and pick Splash profile from the drop-
    down list (Figure 5–7).

12. Press the <u>OK</u> button, and close all the dialog boxes.

**You have now created the splash edge style. You can keep this style
for any future use.**

Figure 5–7

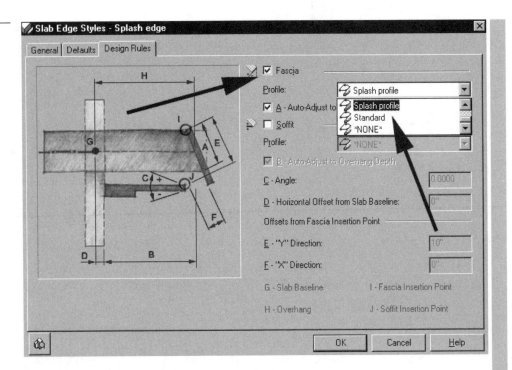

The Kitchen Counter Style

13. Select <u>Design | Slabs | Slab Styles</u> from the main toolbar.
    - At the Style Manager dialog box, select the <u>New Style</u> icon, and make a new slab style called <u>Kitchen Counter Style</u>.
    - Select <u>Kitchen Counter Style</u>, RMB, and select edit from the Contextual menu to bring up the <u>Slab Styles-Kitchen Counter</u> dialog box.
    - At the Slab Styles-Kitchen Counter dialog box, select the <u>Defaults</u> tab.
    - At the Defaults tab, check the <u>Perimeter Edges</u> checkbox and select <u>Splash edge</u> from the dropdown list (Figure 5–8).
    - Change to Design Rules tab in the same dialog box.
    - Check the <u>Has Fixed Thickness</u> checkbox, and set the <u>Thickness</u> to 1.5″, and press the <u>OK</u> button to return to the Style manager.
    - Again, select <u>Kitchen Counter Style</u>, RMB, and select edit from the Contextual menu to bring up the <u>Slab Styles-Kitchen Counter</u> dialog box again.
    - Press the Viewer button at the lower left of the dialog box to check the new Kitchen Counter slab style and make sure that the splash edge is correct (Figure 5–9). **Save this drawing.**

Now its time to place the counter.

1. Open the <u>Kitchen</u> drawing, select the Work-FLR tab, and activate the Top View.
2. Select the Style Manager icon from the AEC Setup toolbar to open up the <u>Style Manager</u>.
3. In the Style Manager dialog box, open the <u>Counter drawing</u> and open its <u>Slab Styles</u> tree.
4. In the Slab Styles tree, select the <u>Kitchen Counter Style</u>, RMB and select <u>Copy</u> from the Contextual menu.

Figure 5–8

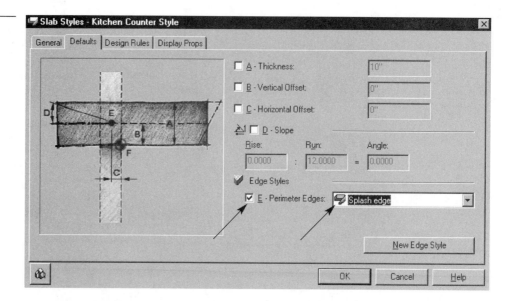

Figure 5–9

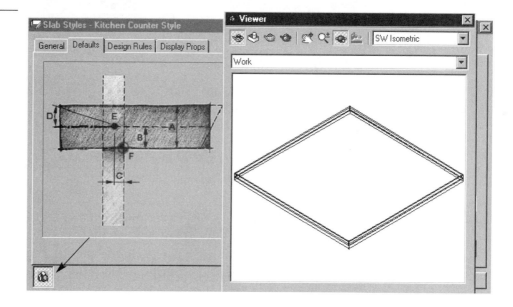

5. Close the <u>Slab Styles</u> tree and the Counter drawing.
6. In the Style Manager dialog box, open the <u>Kitchen</u> drawing and open its <u>Slab Styles</u> tree.
7. In this Slab Style tree, RMB and paste the <u>Kitchen Counter Style</u>.

You now have the Kitchen Counter slab style in your drawing (Figure 5–10).

8. Select the <u>Slab Styles</u> icon from the <u>Slabs</u> toolbar to open the <u>Style Manager</u>.
9. At the Style manager select the <u>Kitchen Counter Style</u>, RMB, and select Edit from the Contextual menu.

Figure 5–10

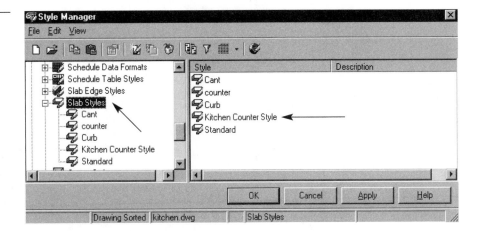

10. At the <u>Slab Styles - Kitchen Counter Style</u> dialog box, check the <u>Vertical Offset</u> checkbox, and enter 2'-10-1/2" for the offset dimension. Press the <u>OK</u> button and close all the dialog boxes.

This will set the counter height for the kitchen counters (Figure 5–11).

11. Select the <u>Add Slab</u> icon from the Slabs toolbar.
12. At the command line, type ST for Style, and press the space bar or Enter key.
13. Enter the full name <u>Kitchen Counter Style</u> exactly as defined in Step 13 of the previous exercise.
14. With object snaps turned on, trace the cabinets needing counters (Figure 5–12).

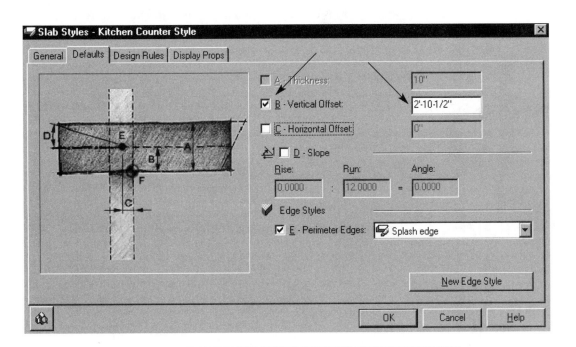

Figure 5–11

Figure 5–12

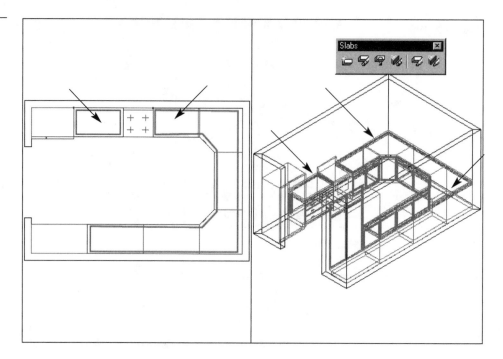

15. Select the counters, activate their grips, and pull the counters out 1 in.

    Counters always overhang base cabinets 1 in. (Figure 5–13).

16. Change the view to SW Isometric.
17. Select the <u>Edit Slab Edges</u> icon from the <u>Slabs</u> toolbar.
18. Select the edges shown in Figure 5–14 and press the space bar or Enter key to bring up the <u>Edit Slab Edges</u> dialog box.
19. At the <u>Edit Slab Edges</u> dialog box, change the <u>Edge Style</u> to <u>None</u> for the three chosen edges, and press the OK button (Figure 5–15).
20. Repeat Step 19 for the other counter.

Figure 5–13

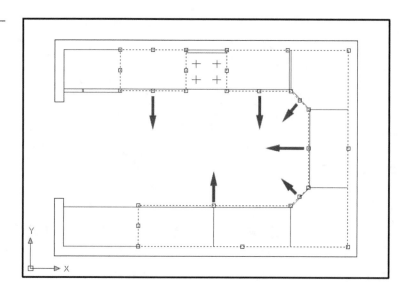

Figure 5–14

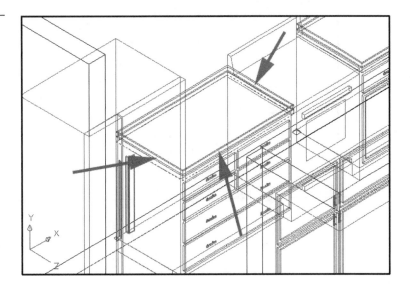

Figure 5–15

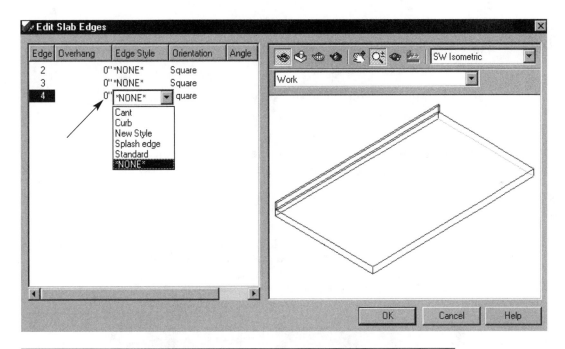

Placing the Sink

21. Change the UCS (User Coordinate System) to a Z height of 2′11-1/2″.

    This allows the sink to be brought in at counter height.

22. Select the Plumbing Fixtures icon from the Design Content - Imperial toolbar to bring up the Design Center.

23. From the Design Center, select and open the Sink folder.

24. Select the Kitchen-Double B sink, RMB, and select Insert from the Contextual menu.

25. Place the sink in the center of the counter (Figure 5–16).

Figure 5–16

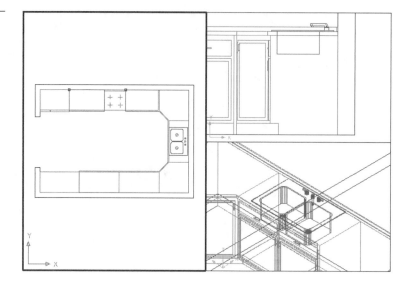

Turning on Gouraud shading shows that the counter cuts through the sink (Figure 5–17).

Real counters need cutouts for sinks.

26. Change to the top view, and activate the Slab Tools toolbar.

27. Select the <u>Rectangle</u> icon and place a rectangle as shown in Figure 5–18.

28. Select the <u>Slab Hole</u> icon from the <u>Slab Tools</u> toolbar.

29. Accept <Add> from the command line, and press the space bar or Enter key.

30. Select the counter when asked to select a slab at the command line, and then select the rectangle you placed in Step 27 of this exercise. Press the space bar, and type <u>Y</u> at the command line to erase the layout geometry. Press the space bar again to finish the command.

The sink and counter shade correctly (Figure 5–19).

Figure 5–17

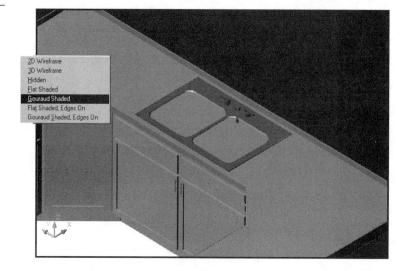

Figure 5–18

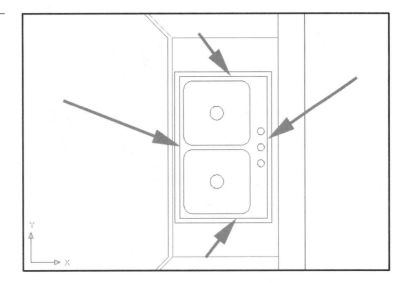

Figure 5–19

31. Place the upper cabinets and a window, and complete the kitchen (Figure 5–20).

Kitchen Section/Elevation

32. Select the <u>Add Elevation Line</u> icon from the <u>Elevations</u> toolbar.
33. Place an Elevation line through the kitchen, as shown in Figure 5–21.
34. Select the elevation line, RMB, select Generate Elevation from the Contextual menu, and generate an elevation of your finished kitchen (Figure 5–22).

As mentioned at the beginning of this section, Autodesk Architectural Desktop 3 contains a great deal of Design Content, and you can make your own. There is also additional content on the Web, and the Autodesk

Figure 5–20

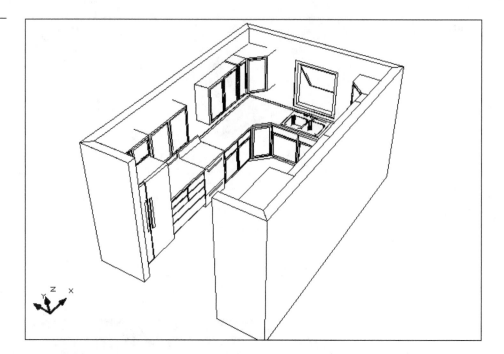

Figure 5–21

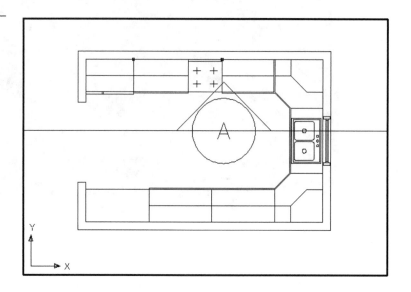

Figure 5–22

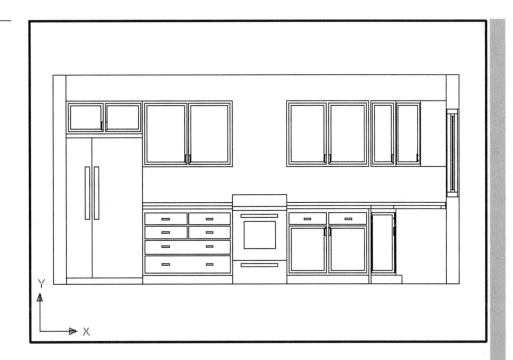

AEC development team is constantly adding content through the built-in AEC web portal -<u>Point a</u>.

Section 6

Walls

When you finish this section, you should be able to do the following:

- ✔ Understand the Add Wall dialog box, including Ortho Close and Justification.
- ✔ Understand the different wall types.
- ✔ Use the Wall and Wall Tools Contextual menus.

You can input walls into a drawing by selecting the Add Wall icon from the Walls toolbar.

You can also input walls into a drawing by selecting the Design | Walls | Add Wall menu from the Main toolbar.

You can also get the Walls menu by RMB in any viewport or by selecting a wall and RMB.

Adding Walls

The Add Walls dialog box is an excellent entry spot for controlling the myriad of wall controls. The following pictures illustrate the various dialog boxes and their pathways to the wall editing system.

Add Walls Icon

The Add Walls icon or Add Walls menu brings up the following dialog box.

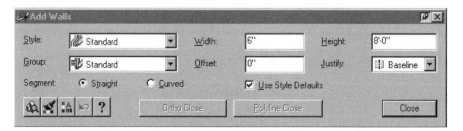

Selecting the style menu on the Add Walls dialog box brings up the Wall Style dropdown menu.

Wall styles dictate the type of wall that you will place in the design.

There are 51 preset wall styles included with the program. By editing the wall styles, you can create any wall.

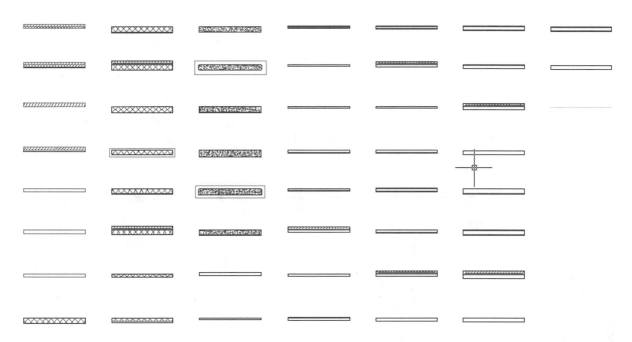

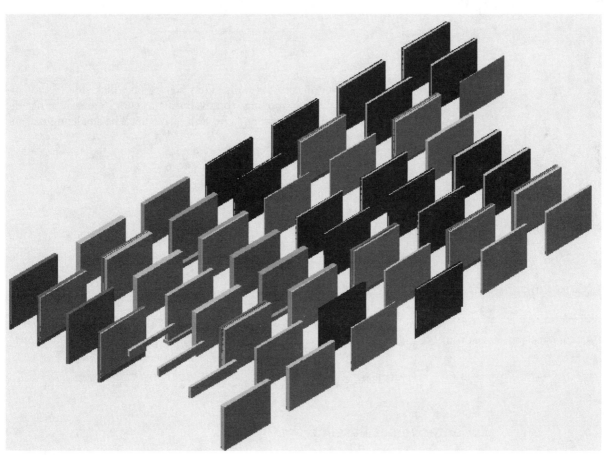

Group

Group refers to cleanup groups. Cleanup groups are very useful when you are trying to create architectural documents that must represent different types of walls located in the same area and you want similar types to interact only with like kind. The most common use is when you have an existing series of walls that will be removed and replaced with new walls. Often the new walls will cross the locations of the existing walls to be removed. Walls of one cleanup group will not interact with walls of another cleanup group. Cleanup groups are set in the Cleanup Groups Definitions menu under the Design | Walls | Cleanup Groups Definitions menu dropdown.

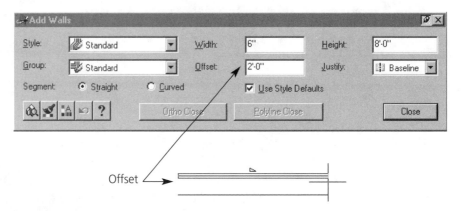

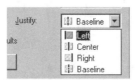

Offset

Justify

There are four justification options for walls. They signify on which side of the cursor line you create the wall when moving from wall start to end. Remember that the triangle that appears indicates the start and end wall direction. The small angle of the triangle points to the wall end.

Left Justified Wall Example

Center versus Baseline

When you insert a wall with **Centerline Justification**, the insertion point will be the center of the wall.

When you enter **Baseline Justification**, the insertion point will be the baseline of the wall. This allows you to line up components such as bricks, etc., as you place walls on top of walls or adjacent to differing materials and wall widths.

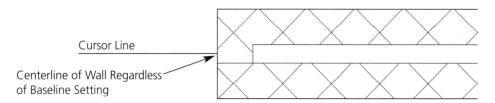

Cursor Line

Centerline of Wall Regardless
of Baseline Setting

Centerline Wall Justification

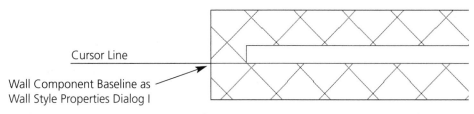

Cursor Line

Wall Component Baseline as
Wall Style Properties Dialog I

Baseline Wall Justification

Ortho Close

Ortho Close is a quick way to close a series of walls at right angles. Try the following simple exercise.

Hands On

1. Using the Aec arch [imperial-intl].dwt template, select the Work-FLR Viewport tab.
2. Selecting the Add Wall icon, place a 10-ft wall 0° to the right.
3. Continue placing a wall 270° to the first wall.
4. Continue placing a 10-ft wall 0° to the right.
5. Continue placing another wall 270° to the last wall.
6. Select the Ortho Close button in the Add Walls dialog box.
7. In response to the directions on the command line, move your cursor to the left and LMB.

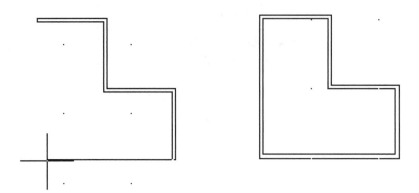

The walls will now close at right angles to the starting point of the first wall.

Modifying Walls

 ### Modify Walls Icon

Modifying Walls allows you to change the Wall style, the cleanup group, the height of the wall, and its justification. Modifying Walls also allows access to the Wall Properties dialog box and all its settings. You can access the Modify Walls dialog box using the Modify Walls icon on the Wall toolbar, by selecting the wall and RMB, and then choosing Wall Modify from the menu or by going to the Design | Walls | Modify Walls dropdown from the main toolbar.

Convert to Walls

 ### Convert to Walls Icon

You use Convert to Walls to convert lines, arcs, circles, or polylines to Walls. The command line tests whether or not the original entities should be retained. Most often the response is YES. You can access Convert to Walls using the Convert to Walls icon on the wall toolbar or by going to the Design | Walls | Modify Walls dropdown from the main toolbar.

Wall Styles

 ### Wall Styles Icon

The Wall Styles icon or the Design | Walls | Wall Styles dropdown from the Main toolbar gives access to the Style Manager for walls. Here you can select, analyze, and edit walls to create new wall styles.

Creating a New Wall Style

New Wall Style

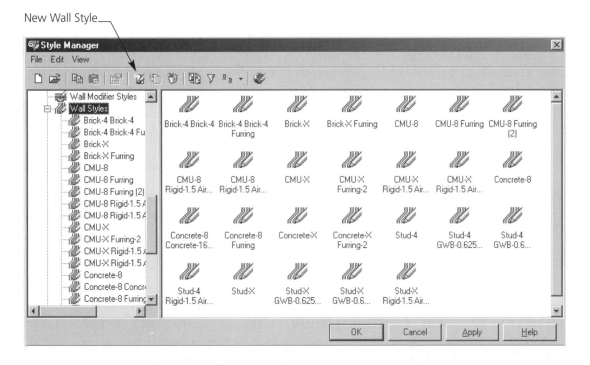

Click Here
to Bring
Up Viewer

Double-
Click to
Bring Up
Wall Style
Properties
Dialog Box
for Editing
Wall Styles

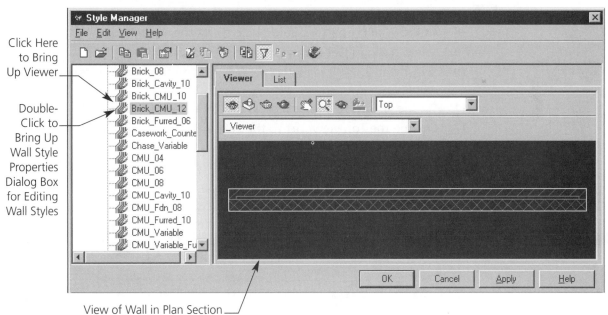

View of Wall in Plan Section

Hands On

1. Start a new drawing using the Aec arch [imperial-intl].dwt template.
2. Select the Work-3D Layout tab, and activate the Top view (left view-port).
3. RMB and select Design | Walls | Add Wall from the Contextual menu.

Figure 6–1

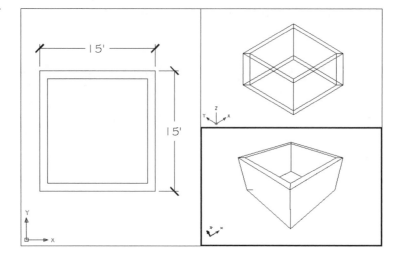

4. Add 4-15' standard straight walls 1-ft wide, 8-ft high, with left justification forming a square building (Figure 6–1).

5. RMB and select <u>Design | Walls | Modify Wall</u>, select all walls, and change the Style to CMU-10 Rigid-1.5 Air 2 Brick 4 (Figure 6–2).

6. Activate the SW Isometetric Viewport (upper right).

7. Select wall A, RMB, and choose <u>Wall Properties</u> from the Contextual menu.

8. At the <u>Wall Properties</u> dialog box, select the <u>Roof/Floor Line</u> tab.

9. Select the <u>Add Gable</u> button, and press OK.

10. Select wall B, RMB, and choose <u>Wall Modify</u> from the Contextual menu.

11. Set the Height to 15', and press the OK button (Figure 6–3).

12. Change the Top viewport to the Left View, and draw a polyline as shown in Figure 6–4.

13. Change the Front View viewport to the Right View, and draw a polyline as shown in Figure 6–4.

Figure 6–2

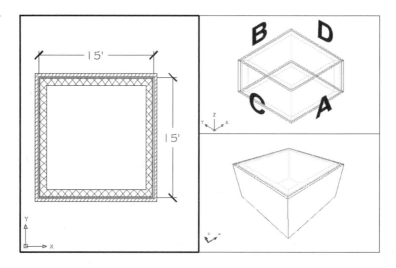

Figure 6–3

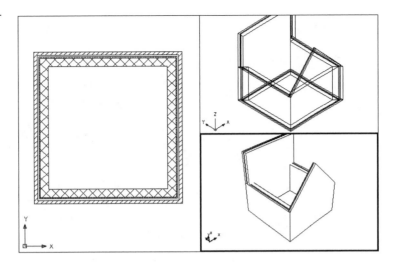

Figure 6–4

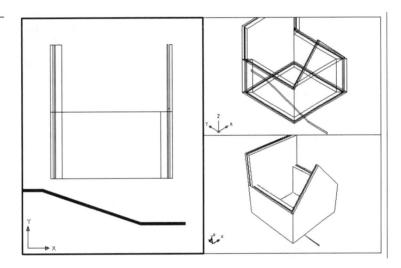

14. Activate the upper-right viewport (SW Isometric View). Select <u>Design | Wall Tools | Floor Line</u>. At the Command Prompt, choose <u>Project</u>.

15. Select walls C and D; then select the polyline below the floor.

Your walls will now project to the polyline (Figure 6–5). Experiment with all the Wall Modifications and Wall Properties tools.

Figure 6–5

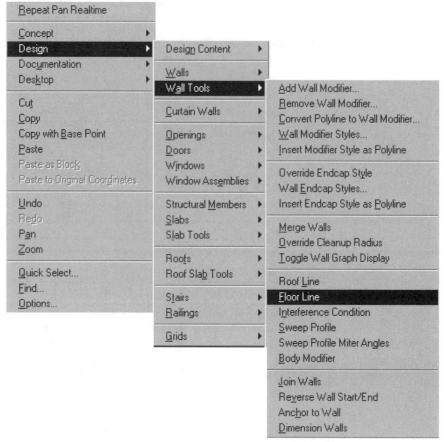

(a)

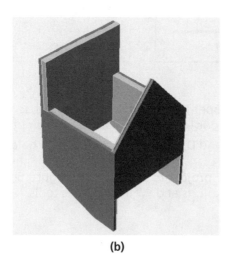

(b)

Section 7

Wall Tools

When you finish this section, you should be able to do the following:

✔ Use Wall Modifiers.
✔ Understand Roof Line and Floor Line wall commands.
✔ Understand Interference Conditions.
✔ Use Sweep Profiles.

You can access **Wall Tools** from the Wall Tools toolbar.

You can also access Wall Tools by selecting the <u>Design | Wall Tools</u> menu from the Main toolbar.

You can also get to the <u>Wall Tools</u> menu by RMB in any viewport.

Wall Modifiers

Not to be confused with Modify Wall, Wall Modifiers change the surface of a wall. If you need a repetitive object, such as an alcove in a wall, use a Wall Modifier.

Add Wall Modifier

Hands On

1. Activate the <u>Wall</u> and <u>Wall Tools</u> toolbars and place them in a convenient place.
2. Using the Aec arch [imperial-intl].dwt template, select the Work-3D Layout tab.
3. Place a 15′ long wall in the Top viewport; make it a 6″ wide Standard Style wall.
4. Select the <u>Add Wall Modifier</u> icon from the <u>Wall Tools</u> toolbar, and select the wall.
5. Click on the wall at a starting point for the pilaster, and then click on the wall again at the point on the wall where you want the pilaster

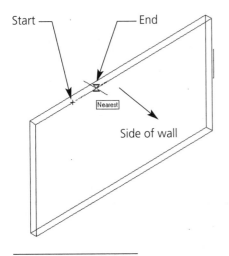

Start — ———— End

Nearest

Side of wall

Figure 7–1

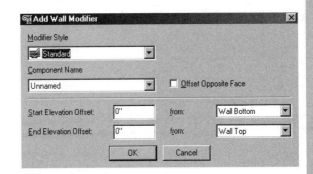

Figure 7–2

Figure 7–3

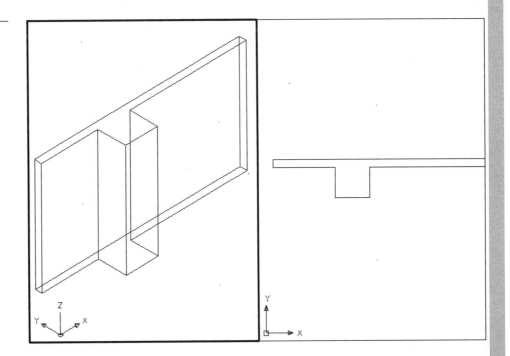

to end. Finally click on the side of the wall for the pilaster to appear (Figure 7–1).

6. Enter the depth of the pilaster (2') in the command line, and press the <u>Enter</u> key to bring up the <u>Add Wall Modifier</u> dialog box (Figure 7–2).

7. At the Add Wall Modifier dialog box press the OK button to create the pilaster (Figure 7–3).

The previous Wall Modifier used the Standard style modifier, but custom wall modifiers can also be created. Custom wall modifiers can be created by converting a polyline to a wall modifier.

Try the following exercise to experience creating a custom <u>Wall Modifier</u>.

Hands On

1. Erase the previous exercise.
2. Place a new 15′ long wall in the Top viewport, and make it a 2′ wide Standard Style.
3. Draw a <u>polyline</u> as shown in Figure 7–4. (Draw it anywhere in the Top view.)
4. Select the <u>Convert Polyline to Wall Modifier</u> icon from the <u>Wall Tools</u> toolbar.
5. At the Command prompt, pick the wall, then select the polyline, select y to erase the polyline and bring up the <u>New Wall Modifier Style Name</u> dialog box.
6. At the New Wall Modifier Style Name dialog box insert the new name <u>alcove,</u> and press the <u>OK</u> button to bring up the Add Wall Modifier box.
7. When the <u>Add Wall Modifier</u> dialog box appears, accept all defaults, and press the <u>OK</u> button to create the <u>alcove</u> wall modifier (Figure 7–5).

Figure 7–4

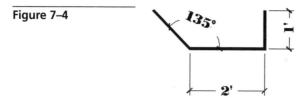

Figure 7–5

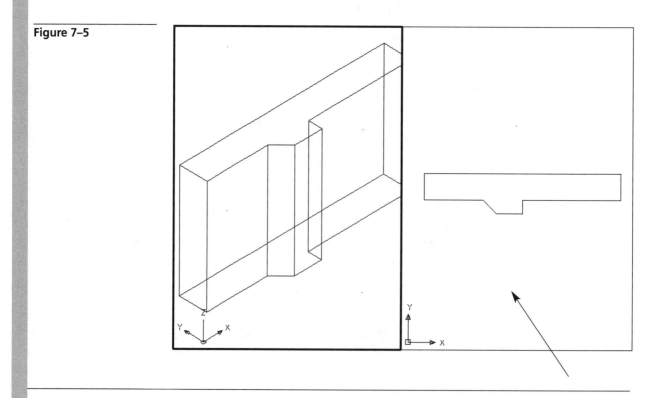

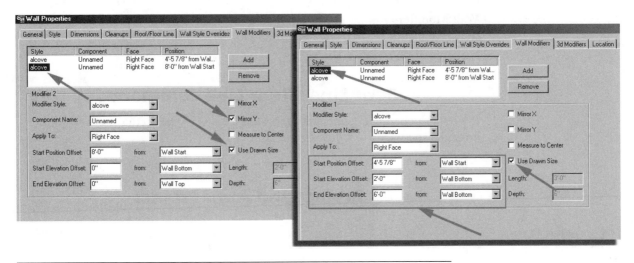

Figure 7–6

Modifying the Wall Modifiers

1. Select the wall, RMB on the wall and choose <u>Wall Properties</u> from the Contextual menu.

2. At the Wall Properties dialog box select the <u>Wall Modifiers</u> tab.

3. Press the <u>Add</u> button to create a new modifier.

4. Change the new modifier's <u>Style</u> to <u>alcove</u> by selecting alcove from the <u>Modifier Style</u> dropdown list.

5. Set the settings as shown in Figure 7–6, and press the OK button to create the second modifier (Figure 7–7).

Figure 7–7

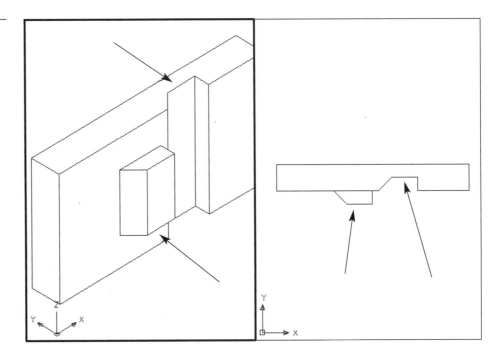

Wall Modifiers can be modified in almost unlimited ways. Experiment with all the settings under the <u>Wall Modifiers</u> tab.

Roof Line, Floor Line commands

Roof and Floor Line commands are useful for quickly projecting walls to roofs and ground planes. Try the following exercises.

Project and Auto Project

Hands On

1. Activate the <u>Wall</u> and <u>Wall Tools</u> toolbars and place them in a convenient place.
2. Using the Aec arch [imperial-intl].dwt template, select the Work-3D Layout tab.
3. Change the left viewport to Front View.
4. Activate the Top viewport.
5. Select the <u>Add Wall</u> icon, and create a 15′ <u>Standard</u> wall.
6. Activate the Front viewport, and draw polylines as shown in Figure 7–8. The polylines do not have to be on the wall, only parallel to it.
7. Select the <u>Roof Line</u> icon from the <u>Wall Tools</u> toolbar, choose <u>P</u> for <u>Project</u> from the Command line, and press the <u>Enter</u> key.
8. Select the wall, and then select the top polyline.

Figure 7–8

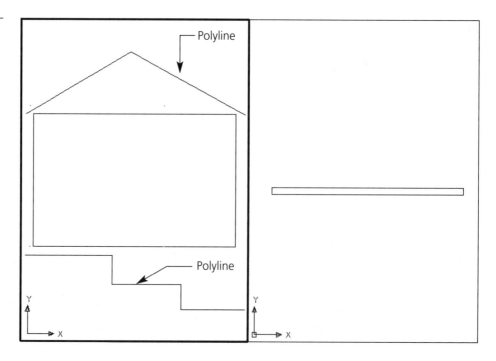

Figure 7–9

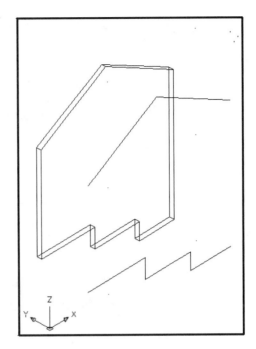

9. Repeat this same process with the <u>Floor Line</u> icon and the lower polyline.

10. Change the viewport to SW Isometric View (Figure 7–9).

<u>Auto Project</u> works in the same manner as <u>Project</u> except that <u>Project</u> is used for projecting walls to polylines while <u>Auto Project</u> is used for projecting walls to AEC Objects such as slabs, other walls, stairs, etc.

Interference Condition

Hands On

Setting Up the Exercise

1. Activate the <u>Wall</u> and <u>Wall Tools</u> toolbars and place them in a convenient place.

2. Using the Aec arch [imperial-intl].dwt template, select the Work-FLR Layout tab.

3. Activate the Top viewport.

4. Select the <u>Add Wall</u> icon, and create a 15′ <u>CMU-X Rigid-1.5 Air-2 Brick-4</u> wall.

5. Zoom extend.

6. Select the wall, RMB, and select <u>Entity Display</u> from the Contextual menu to bring up the <u>Entity Display</u> dialog box.

7. At the Entity Display dialog box select the Display Props tab.

Figure 7–10

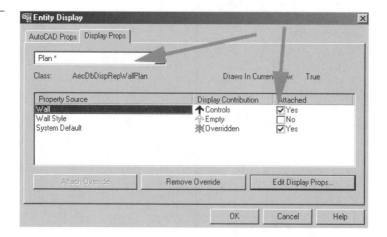

8. Make sure the drop down list is set to <u>Plan*</u>.
9. Check the checkbox for wall to attach an Override (Figure 7–10).
10. Press the <u>Edit Display Props</u> button to bring up the <u>Entity Properties</u> dialog box.
11. At the Entity Properties dialog box select the <u>Lineweight</u> button for Shrink Wrap to bring up the Lineweight dialog box, select the 2.00 mm lineweight, and press the OK button in both dialog boxes to complete the command (Figure 7–11).
12. Turn the <u>LWT</u> button on at the bottom of the screen to display <u>Lineweights</u>.

Shrink Wrap is the line forming the border of the wall in plan view.

13. Copy the wall twice as shown in Figure 7–12.
14. Select <u>Design | Structural Members | Add Column</u> from the main tool-bar to bring up the <u>Add Columns</u> toolbar.
15. At the Add Columns toolbar select <u>Concrete 16x16</u> as the style, and set its length to <u>8'-0"</u>.

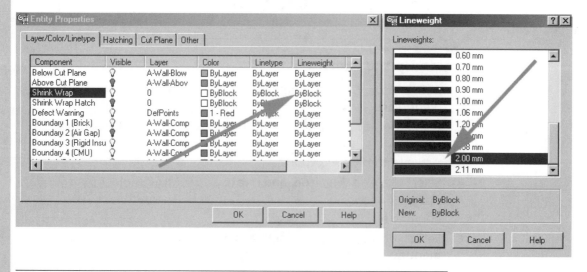

Figure 7–11

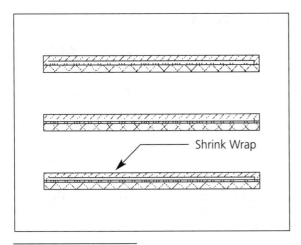

Figure 7–12

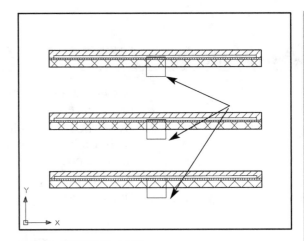

Figure 7–13

16. Press the <u>Enter</u> key (the command line says Return, but it means Enter), and place 3 columns in the walls as shown in Figure 7–13.

Additive, Subtractive and Ignore Interference Conditions

17. Select the <u>Interference Condition</u> icon from the <u>Wall Tools</u> toolbar.

18. Enter <u>A</u> for <u>Add</u> at the Command line, press the <u>Enter</u> key, select the top wall, press the <u>Enter</u> key, enter <u>A</u> for <u>Additive</u>, and press the <u>Enter</u> key twice to complete the command.

19. Repeat steps 17 and 18 for the following two walls and columns selecting the <u>Subtractive</u> and <u>Ignore</u> options respectively (Figure 7–14).

Interference Conditions are excellent when you have columns that meet with walls.

Figure 7–14

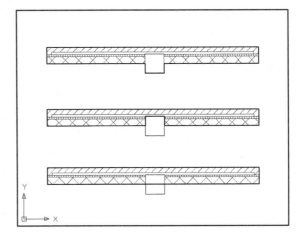

Sweep Profile

1. Activate the Wall and Wall Tools toolbars and place them in a convenient place.
2. Using the Aec arch [imperial-intl].dwt template, select the Work-3D Layout tab, and create 3 viewports; Top view, Right view, and SW Isometric view.
3. Activate the Top view viewport, select the Polyline icon from the Draw menu, and create the closed polyline shown in (Figure 7–15).

Creating the Profile

4. Select Desktop | Profiles | Profile Definitions from the Main toolbar to bring up the Style Manager dialog box.
5. In the Style Manager dialog box, press the New Style icon to create a new profile style.
6. Rename the New Style Coffered Wall.
7. In the Style Manager dialog box, select the newly created Coffered Wall icon, RMB, and select Set From from the Contextual menu.
8. Select the closed polyline you created in step 3, and accept N at the Command line by pressing the Enter key.
9. With the endpoint object snap set, select the lower left corner of the closed polyline (the Style Manager dialog box will now re-appear).

Figure 7–15

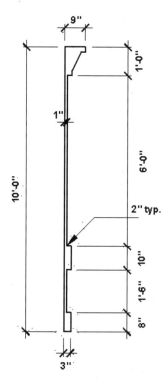

10. At the Style Manager dialog box, press the <u>OK</u> button to complete the command.

11. <u>Erase the closed polyline</u>.

You have now created a <u>Profile</u> called <u>Coffered Wall</u>.

Modifying the Wall Style

12. Select the <u>Add Wall</u> icon and create an <u>8' long, 10' high Concrete - 8 Furring</u> wall in the <u>Top</u> view.

13. Select the wall you created, RMB, and select <u>Edit Wall Style</u> from the Contextual menu to bring up the <u>Wall Style Properties</u> dialog box for that wall.

14. At the Wall Style Properties dialog box select the <u>Components</u> tab.

15. At the Components tab select index <u>3</u> (GWB -gypsum wallboard) and change the <u>Edge Offset to 9-7/8″</u> and <u>Width to 1″</u> (Figure 7–16).

16. Press the <u>OK</u> button to complete the command.

You have now made the gypsum wallboard component 1″ wide for the <u>Concrete - 8 Furring</u> wall.

Using the Profile

17. Select the <u>Sweep Profile</u> icon from the <u>Wall Tools</u> toolbar.

18. Select the wall you created and press the Enter key to bring up the <u>Profile Definitions</u> dialog box.

19. At the Profile Definitions dialog box select <u>Coffered Wall</u> and press the <u>OK</u> button.

20. Press the <u>F2</u> (function key) key to bring up the <u>AutoCAD text Window</u> (here you will find the index numbers for your wall—if you don't remember them from step 15).

Figure 7–16

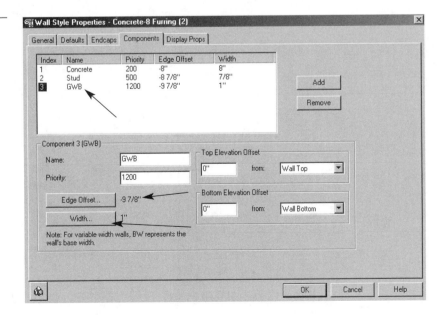

Figure 7–17

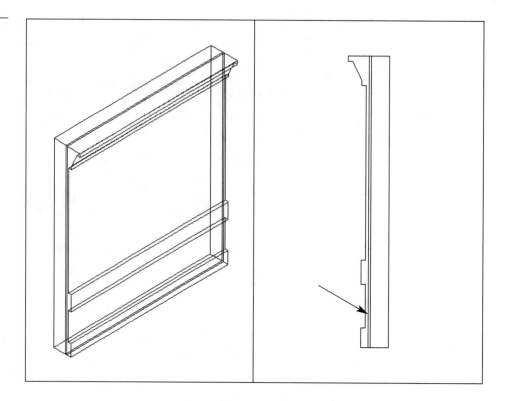

21. Enter 3̲ (for GWB) at the Command line, and press the Enter key to create the Sweep Profile (Figure 7–17).

Notice that the Sweep Profile only affects the GWB because Index 3 was selected in step 21. Experiment with other profiles and wall types.
Good Luck.

Section 8

Curtain Walls and Curtain Wall Units

When you finish this section, you should be able to do the following:

- ✔ Use the Curtain Wall.
- ✔ Understand the relationship between Curtain Walls and Curtain Wall Units.
- ✔ Edit Curtain Walls and Curtain Wall Units.
- ✔ Convert Linework and Layout Grids to Curtain Walls and Curtin Wall Units.

You can access Curtain Walls from the Curtain Walls toolbar.

You can also access **Curtain Walls** by selecting the Design | Curtain Walls menu from the Main toolbar.

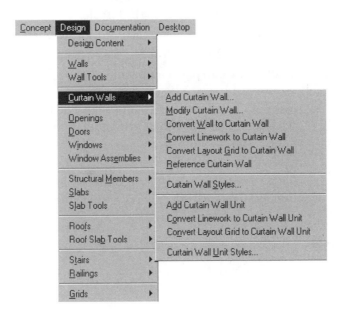

You can also get the Curtain Walls menu by RMB in any viewport. Curtain Walls are a twentieth-century building innovation. Typically, they are as the name implies, lightweight curtains of glass, steel, or even stone and concrete. One common factor is that they are usually made up of repetitive units and are not load bearing.

Autodesk Architectural Desktop Release 3 recognizes the need for this type of component and has a very complete Curtain Wall System. In Autodesk Architectural Desktop Release 3, **Curtain Walls** have many similarities to AEC walls, but they are made from parametric grids, which may also include Curtain Wall Units. **Curtain Wall Units** are separate assemblies that do not consume as much computer resources as Curtain Walls. Although they are edited in the same manner as Curtain Walls, Curtain Wall Units cannot contain doors or other AEC objects or be based on a curve. Because Curtain Wall Units use less computer resources, they are excellent for insertion in Curtain Walls or for specialized areas.

Curtain Walls are different from wall objects in that they are made up of <u>grids</u>. The grids in curtain walls have either horizontal or vertical divisions. Nesting grids inside grids allows for a wide variety of patterns.

Adding Curtain Walls

You add Curtain Walls in a similar manner as you did with regular walls.

Hands On

1. Activate the <u>Walls</u>, <u>View</u>, and <u>Curtain Walls</u> toolbars, and place them in a convenient spot.
2. Using the Aec arch [imperial-intl].dwt template, select the Work-3D Layout tab.
3. Set the left viewport to ½"=1'-0" scale.
4. Select the <u>Add Curtain Wall</u> icon from the <u>Curtain Walls</u> toolbar.
5. Add a 20-ft × 20-ft enclosure (Figure 8–1).
6. In the Front view, place a polyline as shown in Figure 8–2. (The polyline does not have to be on the Curtain Wall, just parallel to it.)
7. Select the Curtain Wall parallel to the polyline, RMB, and select <u>Tools | Floor Line</u> from the Contextual menu.
8. Type **P** for Project on the command line, and press the space bar or Enter key.
9. Select the polyline and press the space bar or Enter key to end the command (Figure 8–3).

Figure 8–1

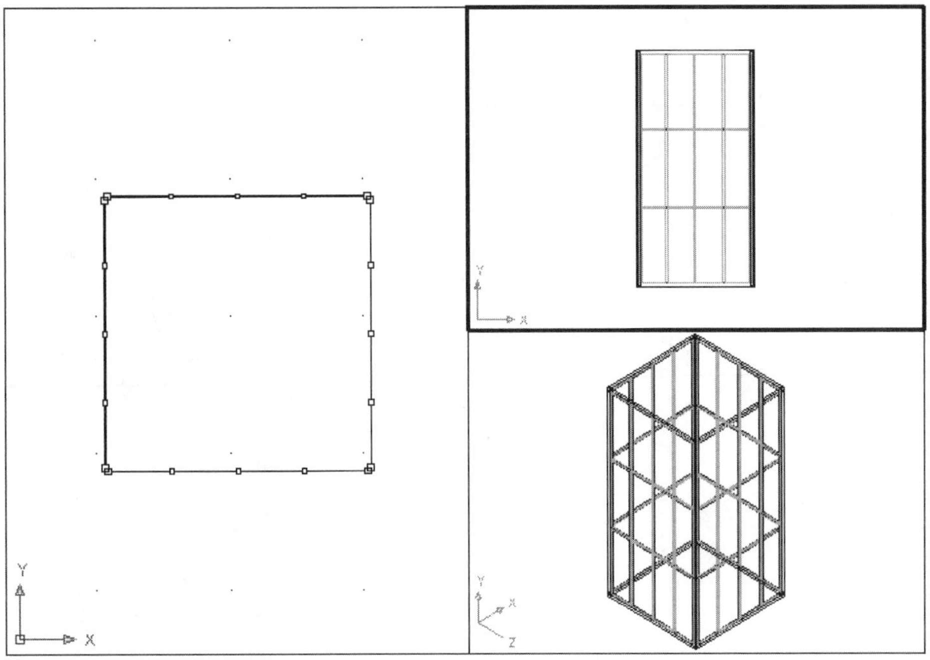

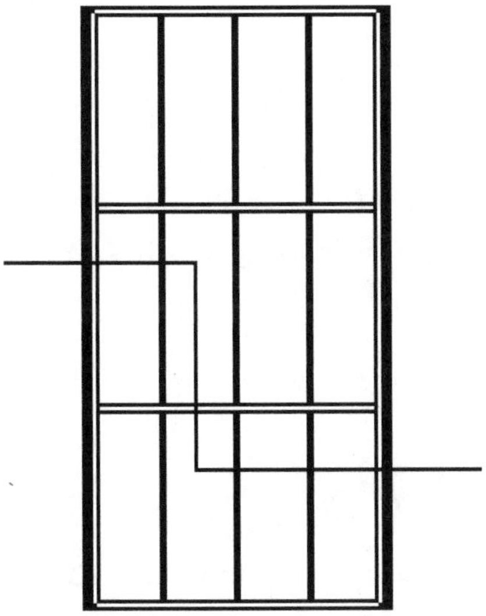

Figure 8–2

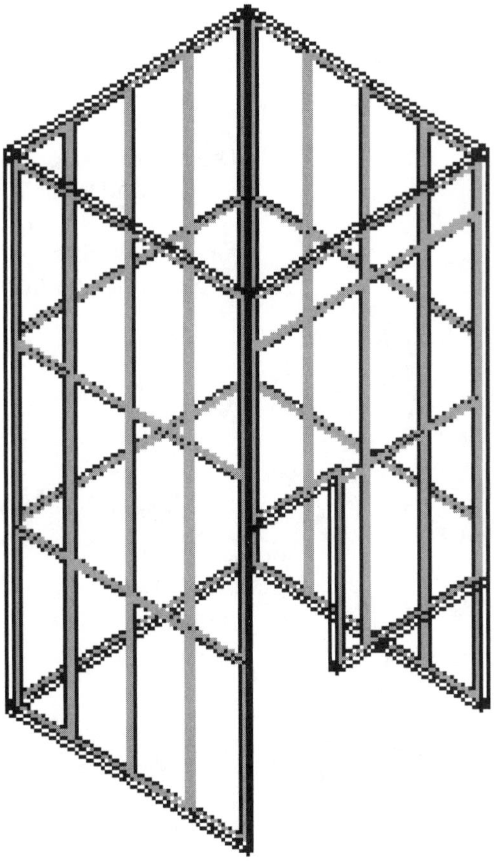

Figure 8–3

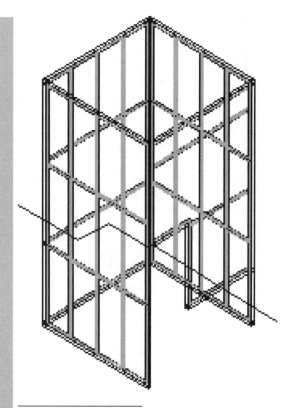

Figure 8–4

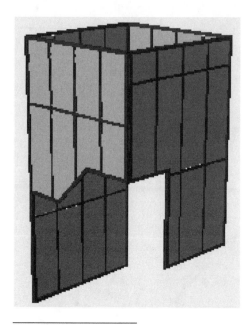

Figure 8–5

10. Draw another polyline, as shown in Figures 8–4 and 8– 5, and repeat Steps 8 and 9 for the sidewalls.

Using Floor Line and Roof Line from the Tools menu is an easy and quick way to modify Curtain Wall objects.

Converting Linework to Curtain Wall

You can customize Curtain Walls for special openings. Architectural Desktop 3 uses the Convert Linework to Curtain Wall and Curtain Wall Units to give you unlimited customization.

Hands On

1. Using the Aec arch [imperial-intl].dwt template, select the Work-3D Layout tab.
2. Select the Top View viewport, and create the line drawing shown in Figure 8–6.

Figure 8–6

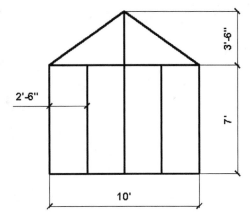

3. Select the <u>Convert Linework to Curtain Wall</u> icon from the <u>Curtain Walls</u> toolbar.

4. Select the line drawing you made in the previous step, and press the Enter key twice.

5. Accept N when asked to Erase the Geometry by pressing the Enter key.

Your line work will now create a curtain wall perpendicular to the top view (Figure 8–7).

6. Erase the original line drawing you drew in Step 2.

7. Select the new Curtain Wall, RMB, and select <u>Cell Markers > All Visible</u> from the Contextual menu.

Figure 8–7

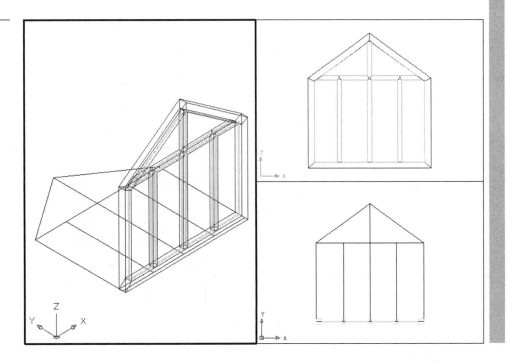

Figure 8–8

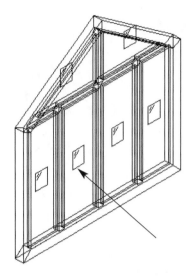

The Cell Markers now become visible (Figure 8–8).

8. Select the new Curtain Wall again, RMB, and select <u>Overrides ></u> <u>Merge Cells</u> from the Contextual menu.

9. When the command line reads "Select cell A," select the leftmost cell marker, and press the Enter key.

10. When the command line reads "Select cell B," select the next cell marker, and press the Enter key.

The two Curtain Wall divisions merge into one cell.

11. Repeat Steps 8, 9, and 10 to merge the upper cell. Select the curtain wall, RMB, and select <u>Cell Markers > Off</u> from the Contextual menu (Figure 8–9).

Figure 8–9

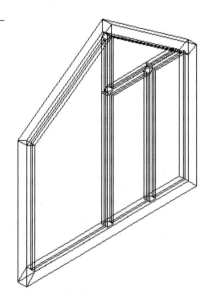

Figure 8–10

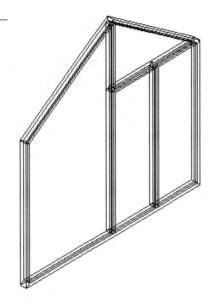

Adjust the Frame and Mullions

12. Select the <u>Curtain Wall Styles</u> icon from the <u>Curtain Walls</u> toolbar.
13. Create a new style called Custom Curtain Wall.
14. Select the <u>Design Rules</u> tab, and then select the <u>Frames</u> icon in the Tree View.
15. Change the Width to 2″ and the Depth to 4″.
16. Select the <u>Mullions</u> icon from the Tree View, and change the width to 2″ and depth to 4″. Then press the <u>OK</u> button.
17. Select the <u>Modify Curtain Wall</u> icon from the <u>Curtain Wall</u> toolbar.
18. Select the Curtain Wall, and change it to the <u>Custom Curtain Wall</u> style (Figure 8–10).

Converting Layout Grid to Curtain Wall

Hands On

1. Activate the <u>Layout Tools</u> and <u>Curtain Walls</u> toolbars, and place them in a convenient spot.
2. Using the Aec arch [imperial-intl].dwt template, select the Work-3D Layout tab.
3. Select the <u>Add Layout Grid (2D)</u> icon from the Layout Tools toolbar.
4. Place a 30-ft-wide by 15-ft-high grid in the Top View viewport. Set the grid to be divided by 6 in the X direction and 3 in the Y direction (Figure 8–11).

Figure 8–11

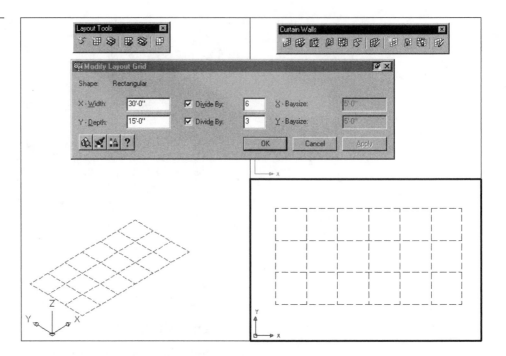

5. Select the layout grid, RMB, and select <u>2D Layout Grid Properties</u> from the Contextual menu to bring up the <u>Layout Grid Properties</u> dialog box.

6. At the Layout Grid Properties dialog box, select the <u>Dimensions</u> tab and uncheck the <u>Automatic Spacing</u> checkboxes for the X and Y axes. Press the <u>OK</u> button.

7. Select the layout grid in the Top view to activate its grips.

8. With the object snaps turned off, grip and move the layout grid to match Figure 8–12.

9. Select the <u>Convert Layout Grid to Curtain Wall</u> icon from the <u>Curtain Walls</u> toolbar.

10. Select the layout grid, and press the Enter key. Press the Enter key again to accept N at the command line question "Erase layout geometry?"

11. Accept the <Horizontal> Primary Division by pressing the Enter key, and name the Curtain Wall <u>Layout Curtain Wall</u>. Erase the layout grid to complete the exercise (Figure 8–13).

Figure 8–12

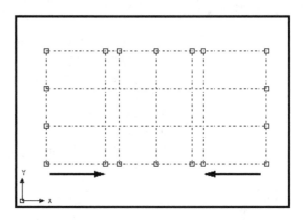

Figure 8–13

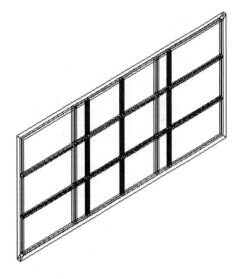

Curtain Wall Styles

Hands On

1. Activate the <u>Walls</u>, View, and Curtain Walls toolbars, and place them in a convenient spot.
2. Using the Aec arch [imperial-intl].dwt template, select the Work-FLR Layout tab.
3. Select the Add Curtain Wall icon from the Curtain Walls toolbar.
4. Add a 20-ft-long <u>Standard</u> Curtain Wall, 20 ft high.
5. Change the view to SW Isometric View (Figure 8–14).
6. Select the curtain wall, RMB, and select <u>Edit Curtain Wall Style</u> from the Contextual menu to bring up the <u>Curtain Wall Style Properties</u> dialog box.
7. At the Curtain Wall Style Properties dialog box, select the <u>General</u> tab.
8. Change the name of the Curtain Wall from <u>Standard</u> to <u>Standard2</u>.

Figure 8–14

This creates a new Curtain Wall style called Standard2 with the same properties as Standard.

9. Select the <u>Defaults</u> tab, check the <u>A-Base Height</u> checkbox, and change it to 20'-0".

10. Select the <u>Design Rules</u> tab, and activate the <u>Viewer</u> icon at the lower left of the tab. Place the Viewer so both the Design Rules tab and the Viewer can be seen at the same time.

11. In the Design Rules tab, select the <u>Divisions</u> icon to open up the divisions page. RMB, select the <u>New</u> button, and create a new division called <u>2.5' vertical division</u>. Select the vertical <u>Orientation</u> button, and set all settings as shown in Figure 8–15.

12. Repeat the process, creating a new horizontal division called <u>10' horizontal divisions</u>, setting the Orientation button to horizontal and cell dimension to 10'-0".

13. Select the <u>Primary Grid</u> icon to return to the main page in the <u>Design Rules</u> tab.

14. At the Design Rules tab, select the Element dropdown list, and select 10' horizontal.

The curtain wall in the viewer now shows the horizontal divisions to be 10 ft apart (Figure 8–16).

15. Change the Element dropdown list to <u>*Nested Grid*</u> for the <u>Secondary Grid</u> under <u>Cell Assignments</u>.

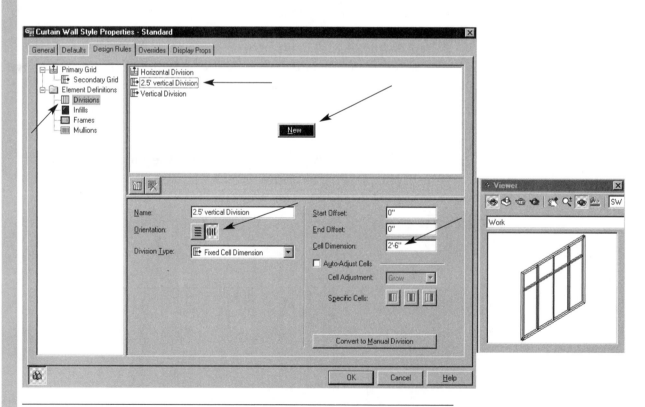

Figure 8–15

Figure 8–16

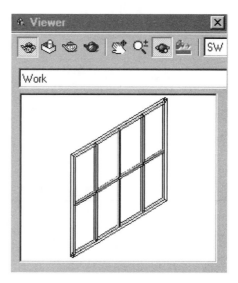

16. Select the Secondary Grid in the Tree View, and change the Element to 2.5' vertical from the dropdown list. Change the Element dropdown list for the Default Cell Assignment to *Nested Grid*. The Default cell name will change to New Nested Grid. Change that name to Third Grid (Figure 8–17).

17. Select Third Grid from the Tree View.

18. Create a new division called 5' Horizontal Divisions, set its Orientation to Horizontal, and set Cell Dimension to 5'-0".

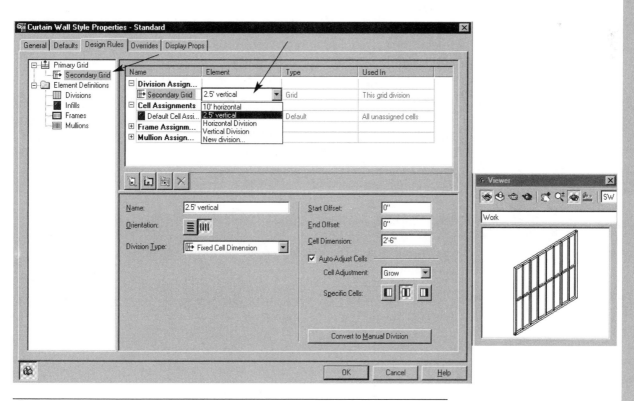

Figure 8–17

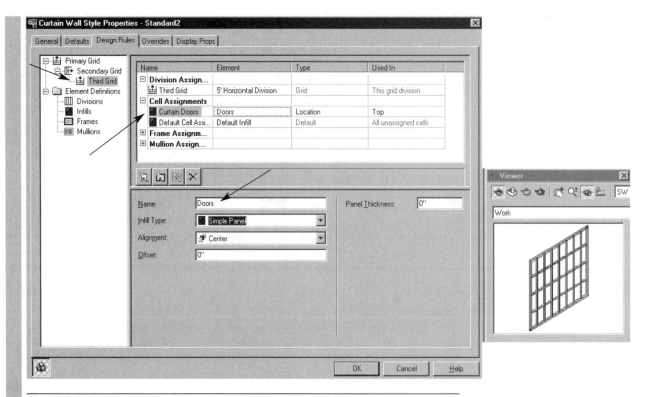

Figure 8–18

19. Select the New Cell Assignment icon to create a new cell assignment, and rename it <u>Curtain Doors</u>.

20. Select <u>New Infill</u> from the Element dropdown list.

21. In the lower name list, change the name from New Infill to <u>Doors</u> (Figure 8–18).

22. Select the curtain wall again, RMB, and again select <u>Edit Curtain Wall Style</u> from the Contextual menu.

23. Change the <u>Infill Type</u> dropdown list to <u>Style</u>, pick a Standard door from <u>Style</u>, and select top from <u>Used In</u> (Figure 8–19).

   You have now created a Curtain Wall with door infill panels (Figure 8–20).

   You can place any door, window, or window assembly into your Curtain Wall using this exercise.

24. Change the Doors <u>Infill Type</u> to <u>Hinged Single Center 3-0x6-8 + Sidelights + Transom</u> under Window Assembly (Figure 8–21).

Figure 8–19

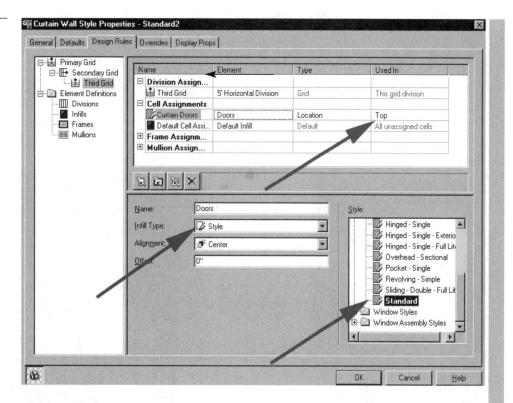

Figure 8–20

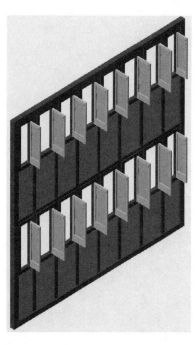

Figure 8–21

25. Change the <u>Used In</u> dropdown to <u>Bottom</u> for the doors in the Third Grid (Figure 8–22).

26. Select any window in the curtain wall, RMB, and select <u>Door Modify</u> from the Contextual menu.

27. At the Modify Doors dialog box, change Opening to 0% (Figure 8–23).

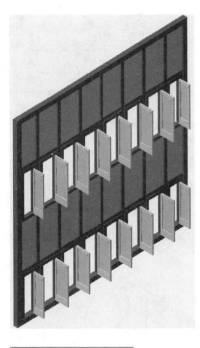

Figure 8–22

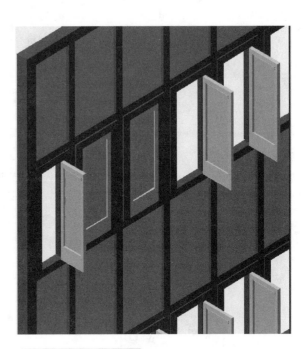

Figure 8–23

The exercises in this section can be used for both Curtain Walls and Curtain Wall Units. The Curtain Wall Units are placed as repetitive units within the Curtain Walls.

Section 9

Doors, Windows, and Openings

When you finish this section, you should be able to do the following:

- ✔ Add and Modify Doors, Windows, Window Assemblies, and Openings.
- ✔ Use Door, Window and Window Assembly Anchors.
- ✔ Use Profiles to customize Doors, Windows, and Openings.
- ✔ Set Door Thresholds and Window Sills.

Doors, Windows, Window Assemblies, and Openings are all similar AEC objects. You input them all into walls and modify them in the same manner. You can select them all from the same Doors-Windows-Openings toolbar.

Doors and Windows

You can input doors and windows into a drawing by selecting the <u>Add Door</u> icon or <u>Add Window</u> icon from the <u>Doors-Windows-Openings</u> toolbar.

You can also input doors and windows into a drawing by selecting the Design | Doors | Add Door or Design | Windows | Add Window menus from the Main toolbar.

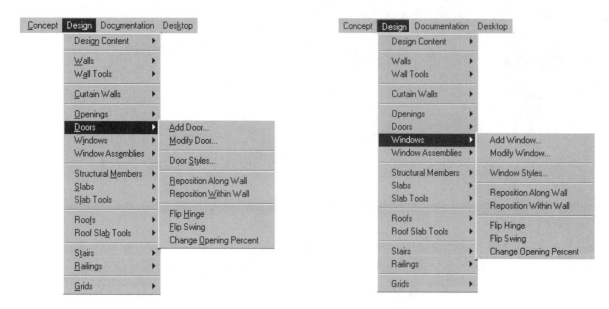

The **Add Doors** and **Add Windows** dialog boxes are very similar to the **Modify Doors** and **Modify Windows** dialog boxes (Figure 9–1).

Try the following lesson to experience using the Add Doors and Modify Doors dialog boxes.

Figure 9–1

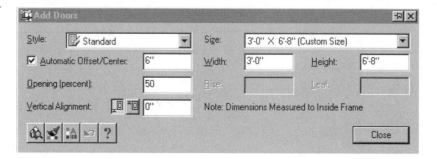

Hands On

1. Using the Aec arch [imperial-intl].dwt template, select the Work-FLR layout tab.

2. Place a 25′ long wall in the Plan viewport, make it a 6″ wide Standard Style.

3. Turn the **Objects Snaps** off.

4. Select the Add Doors icon from the Doors-Windows-Openings dialog box to bring up the Add Doors dialog box.

5. At the Add Doors dialog box check the Automatic Offset/Center checkbox and set its dimension to 1′, and leave all the other dimensions at their default.

6. Click on the wall approximately at its midpoint (Figure 9–2).

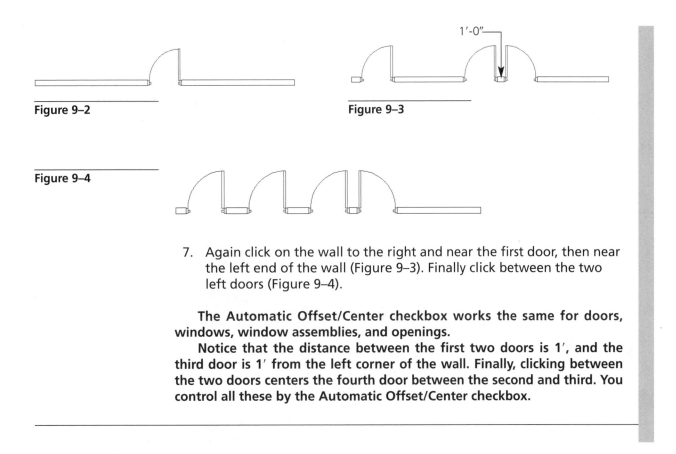

Figure 9–2

Figure 9–3

Figure 9–4

7. Again click on the wall to the right and near the first door, then near the left end of the wall (Figure 9–3). Finally click between the two left doors (Figure 9–4).

The **Automatic Offset/Center** checkbox works the same for doors, windows, window assemblies, and openings.

Notice that the distance between the first two doors is 1′, and the third door is 1′ from the left corner of the wall. Finally, clicking between the two doors centers the fourth door between the second and third. You control all these by the **Automatic Offset/Center** checkbox.

Modifying Doors, Windows, and Openings

Hands On

1. Use the previous exercise RMB on one of the doors, and select <u>Door Properties</u> from the Contextual menu to bring up the <u>Door Properties</u> dialog box.

2. At the Door Properties dialog box select the <u>Anchor</u> tab (Figure 9–5).

Figure 9–5

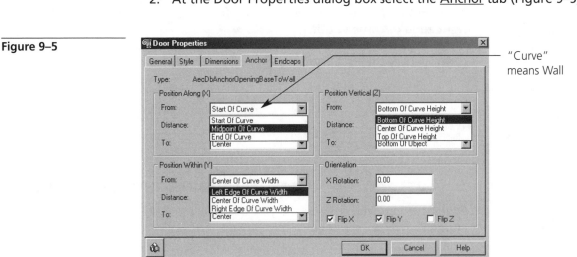

"Curve" means Wall

Figure 9–6

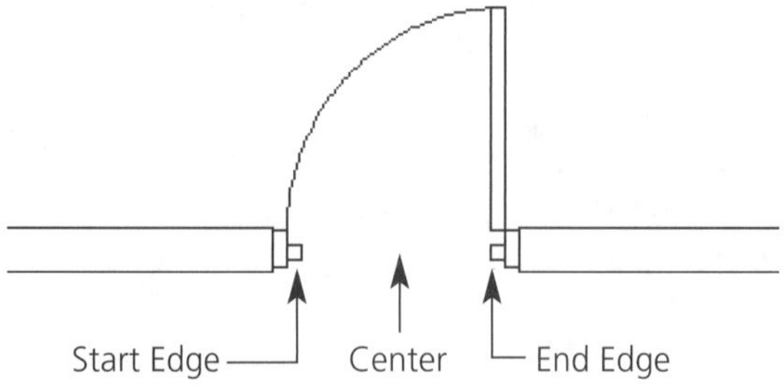

Start Edge —| ↑ Center   └— End Edge

Figure 9–7

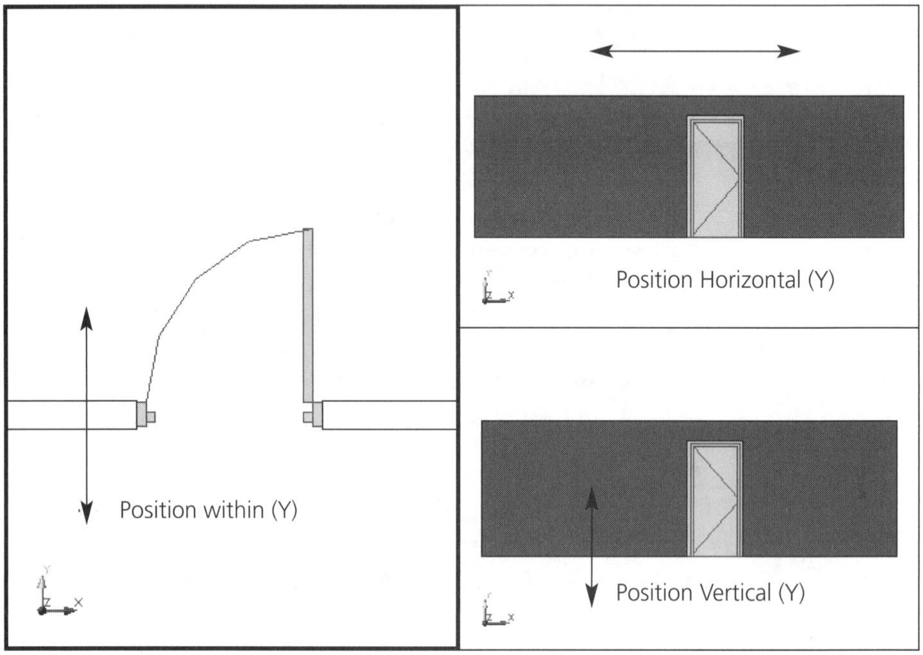

Position within (Y)

Position Horizontal (Y)

Position Vertical (Y)

Here you will find all the controls to accurately position your door in relationship to its wall.

Figure 9–6 illustrates the parts of the door in relationship to the start, midpoint, and end-of-the-curve (wall), and the left edge, center of, and right edge of curve width.

In Figure 9–7 the three positions of doors, windows, and openings controlled by the Properties dialog box are shown.

Customized Doors, Windows, and Openings

Doors, windows, and openings are very easy to customize using profiles. Try the following exercise to experience customizing these AEC objects.

Hands On

Making the Polyline for the Profile

1. Draw the following entities in Figure 9–8 and convert them into a closed polyline. If you don't know how to create a closed polyline, do the following exercise, then go to Step 2.

   a. After drawing the entities in Figure 9–8, select <u>Modify | Polyline</u> from the main toolbar.

   b. Select one of your entities, and at the command line accept <u>Y</u> at the question "Object selected is not a polyline do you want to turn it into one?"

   c. At "Enter an Option" in the command line, choose **Join**.

Select all the entities. Then press the <u>Enter</u> key to end the command. Your entities will now be a closed Polyline.

Defining the Profile

2. Select <u>Desktop | Profiles | Profile Definitions</u> from the <u>Main</u> toolbar dropdown.

3. At the <u>Style Manager</u> dialog box, select the <u>New Style</u> icon. Name the new style **Test Door Profile**, and click the <u>Apply</u> button.

4. Select the <u>Set From</u> icon, and select the closed polyline. Accept <u>N</u> from the command line; then accept <u>Centroid</u>.

5. When the <u>Style Manager</u> dialog box appears again click the <u>OK</u> button.

6. Select <u>Design | Doors |Door Styles</u> from the Main toolbar to bring up the <u>Style Manager</u> dialog box.

7. At the Style Manager dialog box, select the <u>New Style</u> icon. Name the new style - <u>Rounded Door</u>, and click the <u>Apply</u> button.

8. Double-click on the icon next to <u>Rounded Door</u> in the Explorer tree and bring up the <u>Door Style Properties</u> dialog box.

9. Select the <u>Design Rules</u> tab.

Figure 9–8

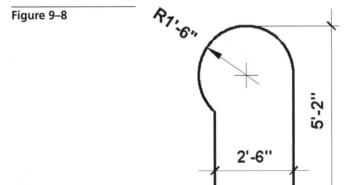

Figure 9–9

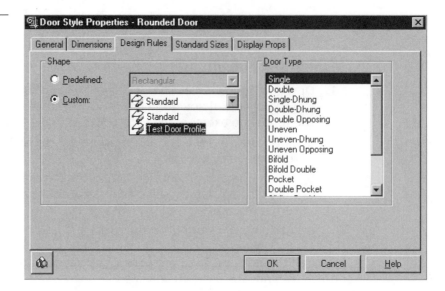

10. Select the <u>Custom</u> radio button, and select the <u>Test Door Profile</u> from the dropdown list. Select <u>OK</u>, and close all dialog boxes (Figure 9–9).

   To test your new custom door, window, or opening, insert a wall, and place your new object in it.

11. Using the <u>Work-3D Layout</u> tab, add a new 6″ wide <u>Standard</u> Wall in the <u>Top View</u> viewport.

12. Select <u>Design | Door | Add Door</u> from the <u>Main</u> toolbar to bring up the <u>Add Doors</u> dialog box.

13. At the <u>Add Doors</u> dialog box set the <u>Style</u> to <u>Rounded Door</u>, and the Width to 3′-0″, and place the door in the wall (Figure 9–10).

Figure 9–10

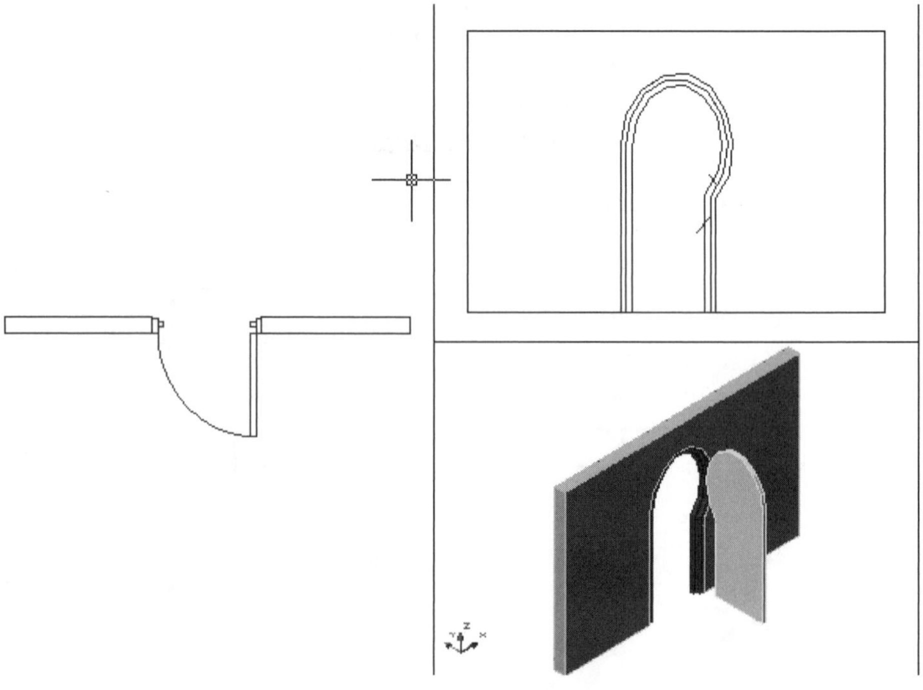

Add Opening

You can add openings to walls and space boundaries by selecting the <u>Add Opening</u> icon from the <u>Doors-Windows-Openings</u> toolbar.

You can add openings to walls and space boundaries by selecting <u>Design | Openings | Add Opening</u> from the <u>Main</u> toolbar.

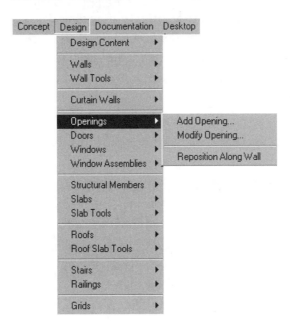

Predefined Shape and Custom Shape

Architectural Desktop Release 3 comes with 13 predefined opening shapes. You can also create custom shapes for openings using profiles (Figure 9–11).

Door Thresholds and Window Sills

Door thresholds and windowsills are only shown in plan view. Try the following exercise to see how they are displayed. Since doors and windows are so similar, only a door example is shown.

Figure 9–11

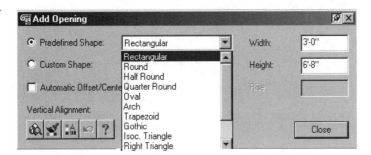

Hands On

1. Using the Aec arch [imperial-intl].dwt template, select the Work-FLR Layout tab.
2. Place a 25′ long wall in the Top viewport, and make it a 6″ wide Standard style.
3. Select the Add Doors icon from the Doors-Windows-Openings dialog box to bring up the Add Doors dialog box.
4. At the Add Doors dialog box, accept all defaults.
5. Click on the wall and insert a door.
6. Select the door, RMB, and choose Entity Display from the Contextual menu to bring up the Entity Display dialog box.
7. At the Entity Display dialog box select the Display Props tab.
8. Change the dropdown list to Threshold Plan* (Figure 9–12).
9. Check the checkbox shown in Figure 9–13 to attach an override on the door.

Attaching an Override to a door only affects that door. Attaching an Override to a Door Style affects all doors of this style, and Attaching an Over-

Figure 9–12

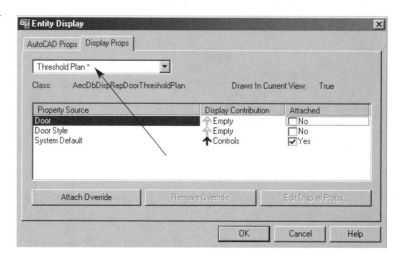

Figure 9–13

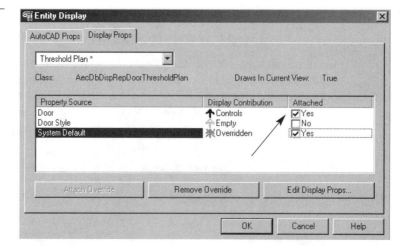

Figure 9–14

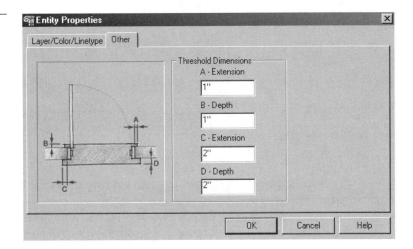

ride to the System Default affects all doors except those with door styles or door overides.

10. Click the Edit Display Props dialog box, and select the Other tab.

11. Set the dimensions in the dialog box to the following (Figure 9–14):

- A- Extension = 1″
- B- Depth = 1″
- C- Extension = 2″
- D- Depth = 2″

12. Select the Layer/Color/Linetype tab.

13. Select the light bulbs under the Visible category for both Threshold A and Threshold B. They should both turn yellow indicating that they are on (Figure 9–15).

14. Press the OK button to return to the Display Props tab, and press the OK button again to complete the command.

Figure 9–15

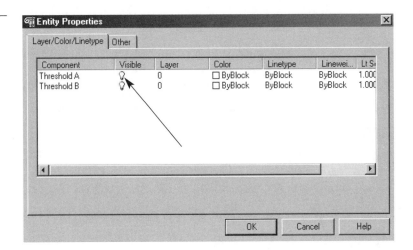

Figure 9–16

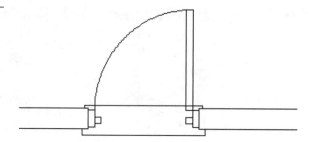

You have now set the size and displayed the door threshold (Figure 9–16).

By turning on the light bulbs in Step 13, you control the display of the inside and outside segments of the threshold. Try this same procedure for windowsills.

Section 10

Window Assemblies

When you finish this section, you should be able to do the following:

✔ Create and Edit Window Assemblies.

Window Assemblies provide a grid or framework for you to use in inserting windows or doors that are commonly used in the design of storefront windows. With this framework, you can create complex Window or Door Assemblies for insertion in a wall or as repetitive elements of a Curtain Wall.

Characteristics of the Window Assembly object include the following:

1. Is style based
2. Inserts like a door, window, or opening
3. Can be customized
4. Behaves parametrically like a Curtain Wall

You can input window assemblies into a drawing by selecting the <u>Add Window Assembly</u> icon from the <u>Doors-Windows-Openings</u> toolbar.

You can also input windows assemblies into a drawing by selecting the <u>Design |
Window Assemblies | Add Window</u> Assemblies menu from the <u>Main toolbar</u>.

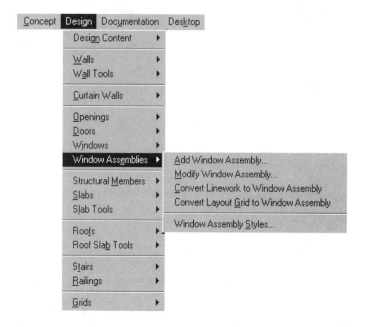

Grids

Grids are the basis of Window Assemblies. Each grid has four types of elements:

Divisions   define the horizontal or vertical direction of the grid.

Cell infills   contain nested grids, panels, or objects such as doors.

Frames   are outer edges of the primary and nested grids.

Mullions   are edges between cells.

You insert **window assemblies** like doors and windows. You customize them by
using the <u>Defaults</u>, <u>Shape</u>, <u>Design Rules</u>, and <u>Display props</u> tabs in the Window
Assembly Style Properties dialog box. The following exercise teaches you how to
customize a Window Assembly.

Tip   The following exercise is very important to the understanding of Window Assemblies and Curtain Walls. Do it several times until it becomes second nature.

Hands On

1.   Select the Window Assembly Styles icon from the <u>Doors</u> | <u>Windows</u> |
     <u>Openings</u> toolbar or the Style Manager icon from the **AEC Setup
     toolbar**.

Figure 10–1

2. At the Style Manager, select **Window Assembly Styles**; then click on the New Style icon. Name the new style Test, then click away from the name (Figure 10–1).

3. Double-click on the **Test** icon in the Style Manager to bring up the Window Assembly Style Properties dialog box.

4. Click on the **Viewer** icon at the lower left corner of the Window Assembly Style Properties dialog box, and resize and place it next to the Dialog box.

5. At the **Defaults** tab, change the Height to 6'0" and press the Enter key or space bar (notice that the change is reflected in the Viewer) (Figure 10–2).

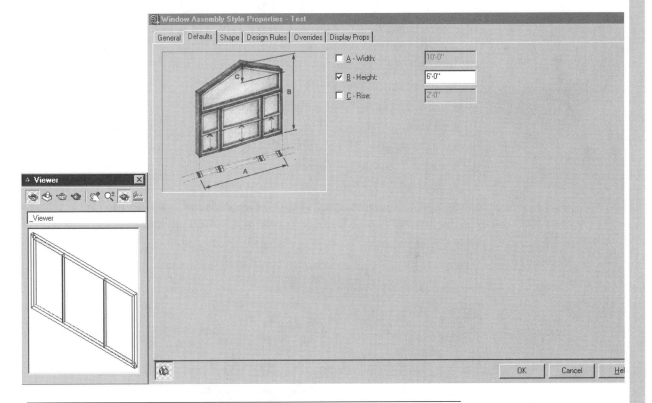

Figure 10–2

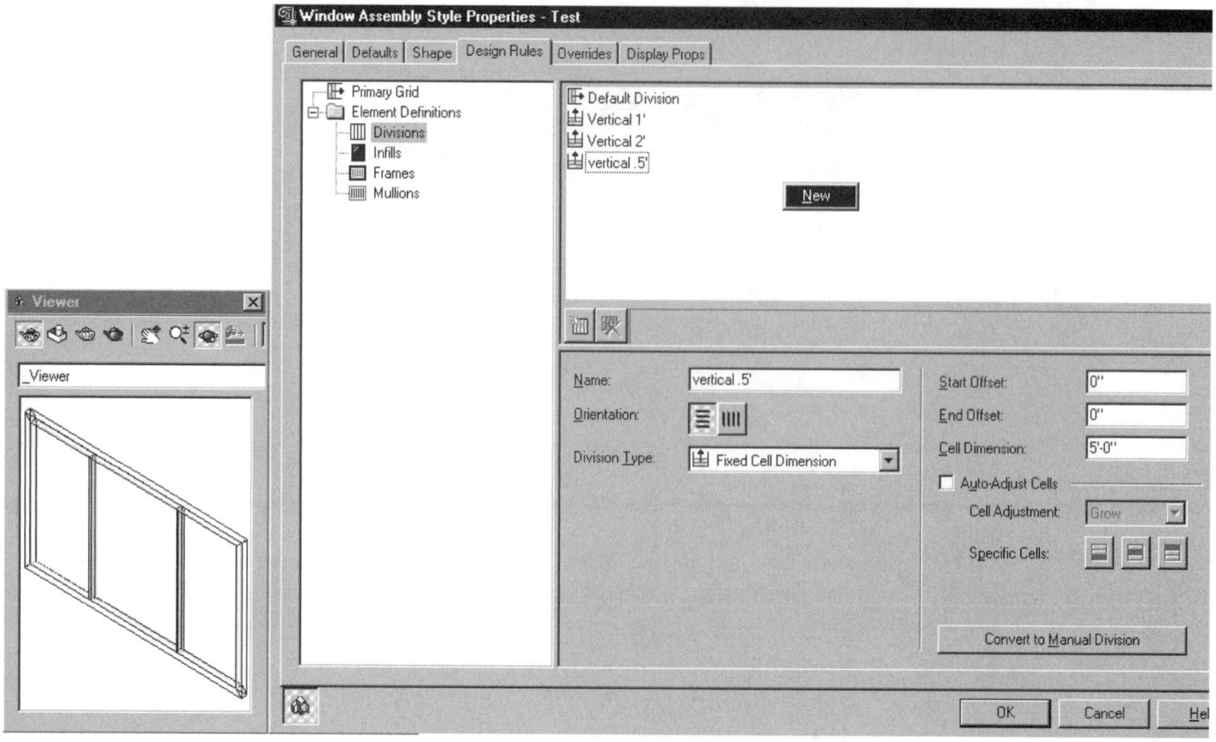

Figure 10–3

6. Select the <u>Design Rules</u> tab and click on the <u>Divisions</u> icon. RMB and create three new Divisions. Name the Divisions Vertical 1', Vertical 2', and Horizontal .5' (Figure 10–3).

7. Set the following for the Division called **Vertical 2'**:
   - *Orientation*—Vertical
   - *Division type*—Fixed Cell Dimension
   - *Cell Dimension*—2'-0"
   - *Auto-Adjust Cells*—(checked)
   - *Cell Adjustment*—(Grow)
   - *Specific Cells*—(center icon) (Figure 10–4)

8. Repeat this process for the other two divisions, making the Cell Dimensions for each the same as their name implies.

Figure 10–4

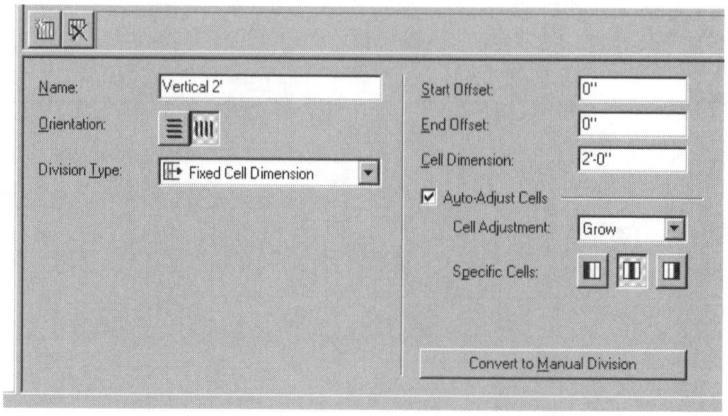

Figure 10–5

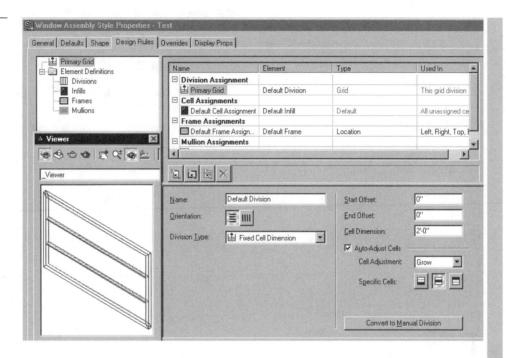

You have now named divisions for this style of windows, and you can use them in any grid.

9. Select the primary grid and set the settings per Figure 10–5. The Viewer should show the Window Assembly with three horizontal sections.

You are now going to place nested grids in each of the three window sections.

10. Under Cell Assignment, RMB and select New or click on the **New Cell assignment** icon. Under the **Element** section, select **Nested Grid**. Under the **Used In** section, click on the selection and select **Top** (Figure 10–6).

Figure 10–6

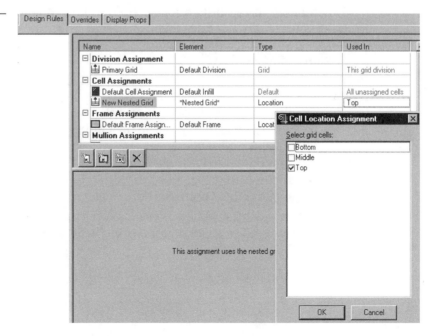

Figure 10–7

11. Rename the New Nested Grid to **Top Section**.

12. Double click Top Section in the main explorer tree; then choose **Vertical 2'** under Element for Top Section. The top section of the Window Assembly in the Viewer should now be divided into 2-ft-wide vertical divisions (Figure 10–7).

13. Repeat Steps 10–12, naming the new nested grid Bottom Section, setting Used In to Bottom, and setting its element to **Vertical 1'**. The bottom section of the Window Assembly in the Viewer should now be divided into 1-ft vertical divisions (Figure 10–8).

You now have finished a primary grid with one level of nested grids. Next you will do a second level of nested grids. In the final part of this exercise, you will add a nested grid to another nested grid in the middle section of the window.

14. Create a new Division called 3 Divisions in Center (see Step 6) and set Orientation to vertical, Division type to Fixed Number of Cells, and Number of Cells to 3. This will divide the center section into three equal parts.

15. Activate the Primary Grid in the Explorer tree, and create a new cell Assignment. Set its **Element** to Nested Grid and **Used In** to Middle. Rename the Cell Center Section.

16. Activate Center Section in the Explorer tree, and set its element to 3 Divisions in Center that you created in Step 14 (Figure 10–9).

Figure 10–8

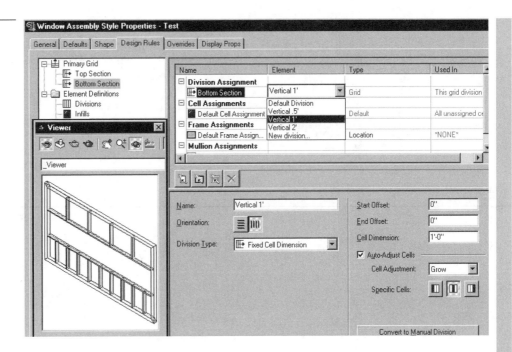

Figure 10–9

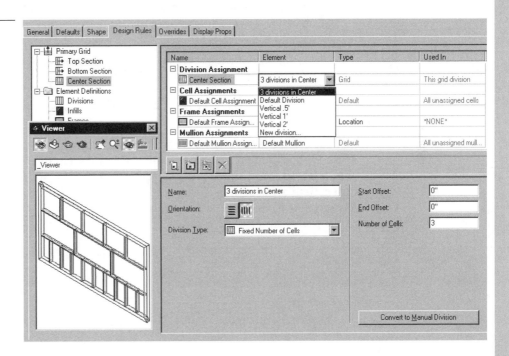

Figure 10–10

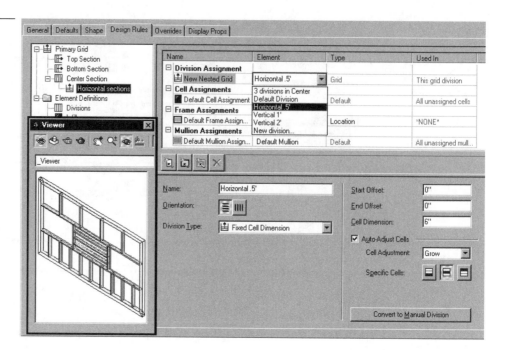

17. Create a new Cell Assignment (similar to Step 10), make it a <u>Nested Grid</u>, and use it in the middle of the grid called <u>Center Section</u>. Name it <u>Horizontal Sections</u>.

18. Activate Horizontal Sections in the Explorer tree, and set its element to Horizontal .5 (Figure 10–10).

You have now created a new Window Assembly Style called Test. Because of its versatility, you can create any type of Assembly. Once you are comfortable with the concept, try changing the profiles under the Shape tab, and experiment with adding doors, etc., using the Infill dropdown when the Cell Assignment Element is set to Infill.

Section 11

Structural Members

When you finish this section, you should be able to do the following:

- ✔ Add and Modify Structural Columns, Braces, and Beams.
- ✔ Use the Structural Member Catalog to add structural members to your program.
- ✔ Create composite Structural Members.

All buildings have a structural system. In the design of commercial buildings, the understanding and documentation of the structural system is of utmost importance. In Architectural Desktop 3, the Structural Members give control over this phase of construction.

You can input Structural Members into a drawing by selecting the appropriate member icon from the <u>Structural Members</u> toolbar.

You can also input Structural Members into a drawing by selecting the Design | <u>Structural Members</u> menu from the Main toolbar. The Structural Members menu can also be accessed by RMB in any viewport.

Structural systems for buildings usually follow a grid. The next exercise illustrates how to use Structural Members of Architectural Desktop 3 to construct a simple metal storage building.

Hands On

1. Activate the <u>Grids</u>, <u>Structural Members</u>, <u>UCS</u>, and <u>UCS II</u> toolbars, and place them in a convenient spot.
2. Using the Aec arch [imperial-intl].dwt template, select the <u>Work-3D</u> Viewport tab.
3. Activate the Top View viewport.
4. Select the <u>Add Column Grid</u> from the Grids toolbar.
5. At the Add Column Grid dialog box, set the following:

   - Shape = Rectangular
   - X-Width = 60'-0"
   - Y-Depth = 40'-0"
   - X-Baysize = 20'-0"
   - Y-Baysize = 20'-0"

6. Press the Column button, and set the following:

   - Style = <u>Standard</u>
   - Length = 10'
   - Justify = Middle Center

7. Insert the Grid in the Top View viewport at 0.00 rotation, and exit the command.

Figure 11–1

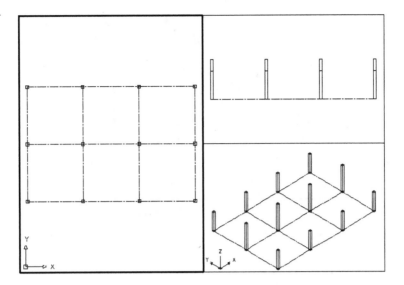

You have now placed a column grid, with Temporary Style columns automatically placed at all the Grid nodes (Figure 11–1).

8. Select the all the middle columns, RMB, and select <u>Member Properties</u> from the Contextual menu.
9. At the Structural Members dialog box, select the <u>Dimensions</u> tab, and set the length to 14'-0".
10. Set the osnap to <u>Node</u>.
11. Select the <u>Add Beam</u> icon from the <u>Structural Members</u> toolbar, set the Style to <u>Standard</u>, and Justify to <u>Bottom Center</u>.

Bottom Center is the location of the grips now set for the beam.

12. Click at the top of the first center column and then at the top of the second center column.
13. Repeat this process with the end columns (Figure 11–2).

Figure 11–2

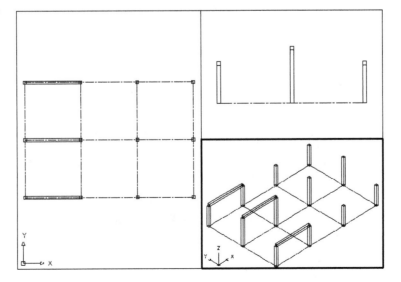

Figure 11–3

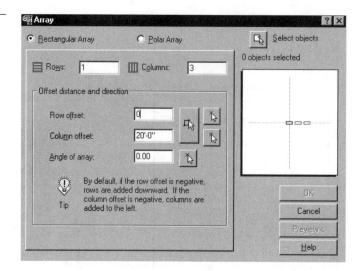

14. Select and Array the beams. Set the Array for 1 row, 3 columns with a column offset of 20′0″ (Figures 11–3 and11–4).

15. Select the end beams on the left side, RMB, and select Member Properties from the Contextual menu.

16. At the Structural Member Properties dialog box, select the <u>Dimensions</u> tab.

17. Set the <u>Start Offset</u> to <u>-6″</u>. Repeat this process with the right end beams, and set <u>End Offset</u> to <u>6″</u> (Figure 11–5).

18. Select the <u>Structural Member Catalog</u> icon from the Structural Members toolbar.

19. Select <u>Imperial | Steel | AISC | Channels | MC, Miscellaneous Channels</u>.

20. Double-click the <u>MC 12×10.6</u> channel.

21. When the Structural Member Style dialog box appears, name the channel <u>Channel</u> (Figure 11–6).

22. Select the all the outer beams in, RMB, and select <u>Member Properties</u> from the Contextual menu. At the <u>Structural Member Properties</u> dialog box, select the <u>Style</u> tab, and change the style to <u>Channel</u> (Figure 11–7).

Figure 11–4

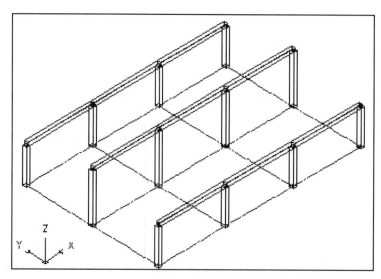

Figure 11–5

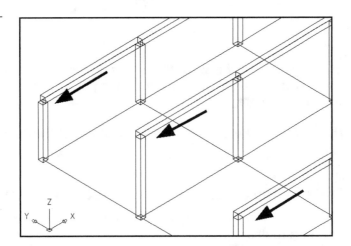

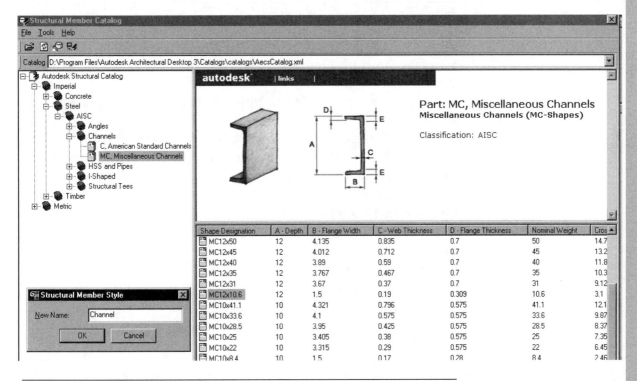

Figure 11–6

Figure 11–7

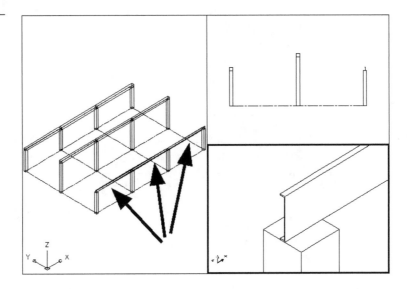

23. Repeat this process for the beams on the other side. This time also select the Dimensions tab and change E-Roll to <u>180</u> and Justification to <u>Top Center</u>.

This will cause the other Channels to rotate 180° with the grip on the bottom.

Create a Round, Composite Concrete-and-Steel Column

24. Select the <u>Structural Member Catalog</u> icon from the <u>Structural Members</u> toolbar.
25. Select **Imperial | Concrete | Circular Columns**.
26. Double click the 14″ diameter, and name it <u>14″ Diameter</u>. Then close the catalog.
27. Select the <u>Structural Member Catalog</u> icon from the <u>Structural Members</u> toolbar.
28. Select **Imperial | Steel | AISC | Channels | I Shaped, Wn Wide-Flange Shapes**.
29. Double-click <u>W6×25</u>, name it <u>W6×25</u>, and then close the catalog.
30. Select the <u>Member Styles</u> icon from the <u>Structural Members</u> toolbar.
31. At the Style Manager dialog box, select the <u>New</u> icon, and name it <u>Composite Column</u>.
32. Double-click on <u>Composite Column</u>.
33. At the <u>Structural Member Style Properties</u> dialog box, select the <u>Design Rules</u> tab.
34. Rename the Unnamed Component to <u>Concrete</u>.
35. Click the Add button, and rename the next component <u>W6×25</u>.
36. Select <u>14″ Diameter</u> under Start Shape.
37. Select <u>W6×25″ Diameter</u> next under Start Shape (Figure 11–8).

Figure 11–8

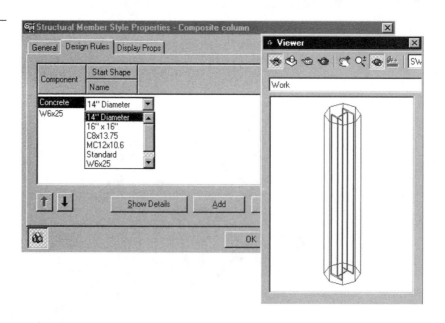

You have now created a composite, round concrete column with a steel shape inside.

38. Select all the columns, RMB, and select <u>Member Properties</u>.
39. At the <u>Structural Member Properties</u> dialog box, select the <u>Style</u> tab.
40. Select the <u>Composite</u> column.

All the columns change to composite columns.

Adding Bar Joists

Hands On

1. Select the <u>Member Styles</u> icon from the <u>Structural Members</u> toolbar.
2. At the Style Manager, select the <u>Open Drawing</u> icon.
3. At the <u>Open Drawing</u> dialog box, open the Bar Joist Styles (Imperial) drawing.
4. Drag the <u>Steel Joist 24</u> from the content drawing into your drawing (Figure 11–9).

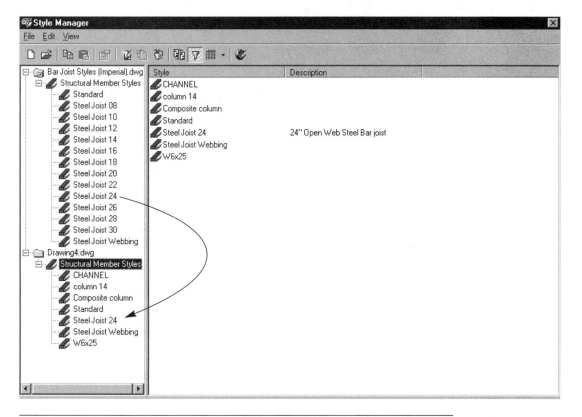

Figure 11–9

Figure 11–10

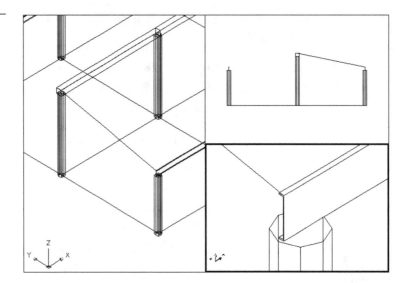

5. Using the previous exercise, place a line from the middle beam to the channel (Figure 11–10).

6. Select the <u>Convert to Beam</u> icon from the <u>Structural Members</u> toolbar.

7. Select the line you place in Step 5, erase the geometry, and select the <u>Steel Joist 24</u>. The line changes into the 24-in.-deep steel joist (Figure 11–11).

8. Select the Bar joist, RMB, and select <u>Member Properties</u> from the Contextual menu.

9. Select the <u>Dimensions</u> tab, and change the <u>End offset</u> to <u>6″</u> (Figure 11–12).

Figure 11–11

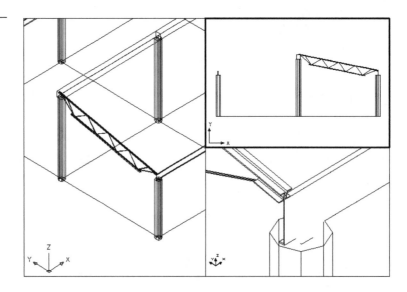

Figure 11–12

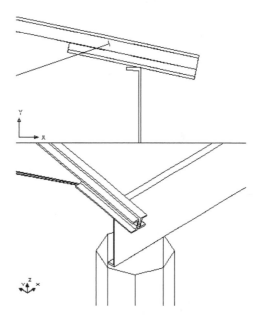

Figure 11–13

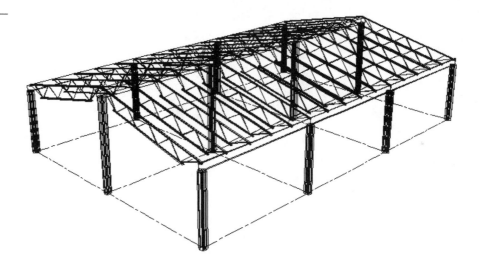

10. <u>Mirror</u> the Steel joist to the opposite side, and array the joists using
     the <u>Array</u> command (Figure 11–13).

Section 12 | Slabs

When you finish this section, you should be able to do the following:

✔ Add, Modify, and Convert Slabs and Slab Edges.

AEC Slab Objects can act as floors and roofs. You can input, modify, and convert slabs or edit their edges by selecting the appropriate slab icon from the Slabs toolbar.

You can also input, modify, or convert slabs or edit their edges by selecting the Design | Slabs menu from the Main toolbar. You can get the Slabs menu by RMB in any viewport.

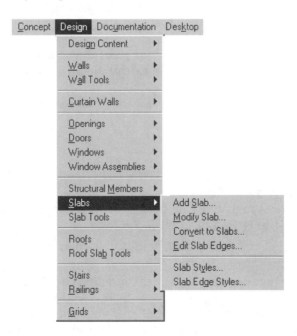

Direct and Projected Modes

Direction

Slabs can be either Direct or Projected modes. Direct Mode allows you to place a Flat slab, and Direct Projected Mode allows you to place a slab at a location in space with a given slope. You use **Direction** with **Ortho Close**.

Hands On

The first point establishes slab origin and pivot point. The first line establishes the base line.

1. After starting Architectural Desktop with the default imperial template Aec arch [imperial-intl].dwt, select the Work -3D Layout tab, and create 3 viewports.
2. Activate the <u>Slabs</u> toolbar, and place it in a convenient place.
3. Activate the Top View viewport, and choose the <u>Add Slab</u> icon from the Slab toolbar.
4. At the <u>Add Slab</u> dialog box, change
   a. Style to <u>Standard</u>
   b. Thickness to 12"
   c. Overhang to 0"
   d. Mode to **Direct**
   e. Justify to <u>Bottom</u>
5. Select the <u>Left</u> Direction arrow, and set the first point of your slab.
6. Moving clockwise, set the second point at 10 ft to the right.
7. Select <u>Ortho Close</u> from the Add Slab dialog box.
8. Repeat Steps 5, 6, and 7 slightly below the first slab in the top viewport, **but** change the Direction arrow to the Right Direction arrow.

<u>Ortho Close</u> works differently for slabs than for walls. For Slabs only one line is drawn, so the direction arrow dictates which direction the slab is cast (Figures 12–1 and 12–2).

Directed Mode

9. Erase everything.
10. Again activate the Top View viewport, and choose the <u>Add Slab</u> icon from the <u>Slab</u> toolbar.
11. At the Add Slab dialog box, leave all settings the same, but change Mode to **Projected**.
12. Set <u>Rise</u> to <u>6.0</u> and <u>Base Height</u> to <u>0</u>; then select the Right direction arrow.
13. Moving clockwise, set the second point at 10 ft to the right.

Notice that the Pivot symbol is at your starting point. Also notice that selecting the projected mode causes the slope option to be available.

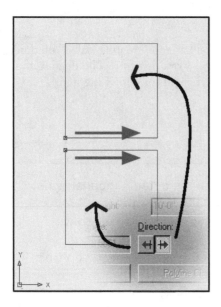

Figure 12–1

Figure 12–2

14. Repeat Steps 5, 6, 7, and 8 (Figure 12–3).
15. Select the <u>Modify Slab</u> icon from the Slabs toolbar.
16. Change the <u>Rise</u> to <u>12.0</u>, and press the <u>Apply</u> Button.

   You change only the Rise numbers. Leave Run at 12.000 and Angle at automatically calculate.

17. Experiment with the other settings in the Modify Slab dialog box, and watch the slab changes.

Figure 12–3

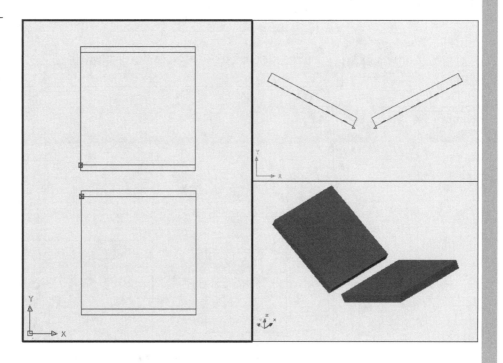

Convert to Slabs

Convert to Slabs uses closed polylines or walls as a basis for creating slabs. You don't need closed walls to convert to slabs; one wall will work just fine. The default location for slabs created by Convert to Slabs using walls is at the top of the wall.

Hands On

1. After starting Architectural Desktop with the default imperial template Aec arch [imperial-intl].dwt, select the Work-3D Layout tab.

2. Activate the <u>Slabs</u> and <u>Walls</u> toolbars, and place them in a convenient place.

3. Activate the Top View viewport, and choose the <u>Add Wall</u> icon from the Walls toolbar.

4. Starting at the bottom left and moving clockwise, place an 8-ft × 8-ft enclosure plus a single 15-ft-long wall that are both 8 ft high, as shown in Figure 12–4.

5. Select the <u>Convert to Slab</u> icon from the <u>Slabs</u> toolbar, and select all the walls of the 8-ft × 8-ft enclosure starting at the bottom wall and moving counterclockwise. Press the space bar or Enter key to accept the selection.

6. At the Command line, accept N to leave the Walls in place.

7. For slab justification, select <u>Bottom</u>. For wall justification, select <u>Right</u>. Select slope direction "<u>Right</u>" of "Left" (doesn't matter), and accept the <u>Standard</u> Slab Style.

   You have now placed a <u>Standard</u> Slab Object at the top of the wall enclosure.

Tip   The First wall you pick becomes the pivot wall!

Figure 12–4

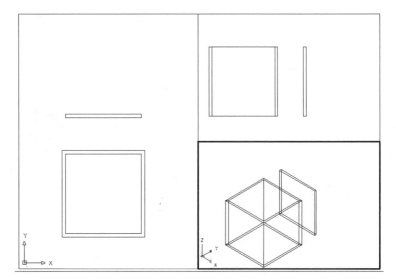

Figure 12–5

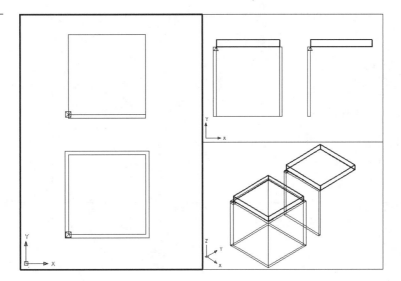

Tip | The single wall was inserted from left to right.

8. Select the <u>Convert to Slab</u> icon from the <u>Slabs</u> toolbar, and select the single 8-ft wall. Press the space bar or Enter key to accept the selection.
9. At the Command line, accept N to leave the Wall in place.
10. For slab justification, select <u>Bottom</u>, for wall justification, select <u>Left</u>, and for slope direction choose <u>Left</u> (Figure 12–5).
11. Repeat these exercises, changing the wall justification, slab justification, and slope direction until you feel comfortable with the controls.
12. Save your exercise.

Modifying the Slab Object and Editing Edges

Once you have placed a Slab Object, there are many controls for manipulating the Object.

Hands On

1. Using the previous exercise, erase the single wall and slab.
2. Zoom in on the Right View.
3. Select the Slab Object, RMB, and select <u>Slab Properties</u> from the Contextual menu.

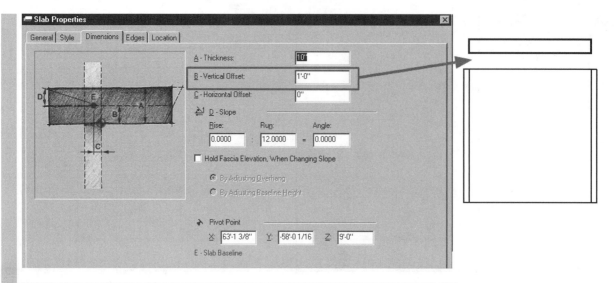

Figure 12–6

4. Change the <u>Vertical Offset</u> to 1'-0", and apply it (Figure 12–6).

5. Return the Slab Object to its original position by changing the <u>Vertical Offset</u> to 0.00.

6. Select the <u>Modify Slab</u> icon from the <u>Slabs</u> toolbar, and select the Slab Object.

7. Change the <u>Rise</u> to 12.0, and press the <u>Apply</u> button (Figure 12–7).

8. Select the Slab Object, RMB, and select <u>Edit Edges</u> from the Contextual menu.

9. Select the raised edge of the Slab Object, and press the space bar or Enter key.

Figure 12–7

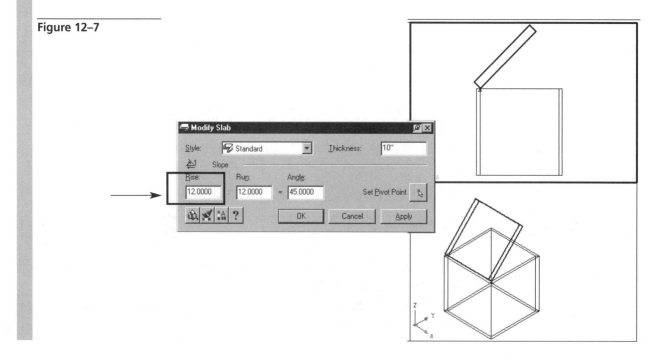

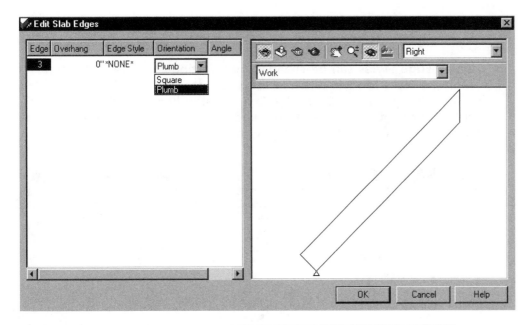

Figure 12–8

10. Change the Orientation to <u>Plumb</u> (Figures 12–8 and 12–9).

11. Return the Slab Object to its original position by changing the <u>Rise</u> to 0.00, and change the edge Orientation back to <u>Square</u>.

12. Select the Slab Object, RMB, and select <u>Edit Edges</u> from the Contextual menu.

13. Select three of the edges when requeted at the command line, and press the space bar or Enter key on your keyboard.

Figure 12–9

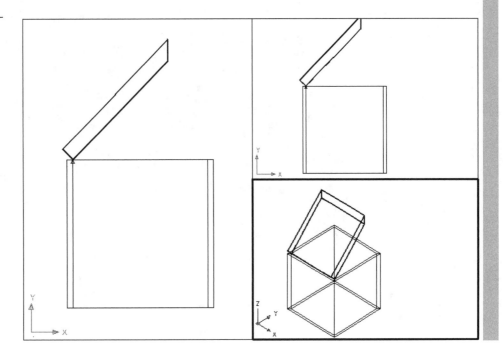

14. At the <u>Edit Slab Edges</u> dialog box, change the <u>Edge Style</u> to <u>Curb</u>, and apply it (Figure 12–10).

Slab Edge Styles can be changed by selecting the Slab Edge Styles icon in the Slabs toolbar. When in the Style manager, double-clicking on the Style brings up the Slab Edge Styles dialog box. This dialog box is identical for Roof Slab Edge Styles. Here you can use profiles (polylines) to create custom edges and soffits (Figure 12–11).

Figure 12–10

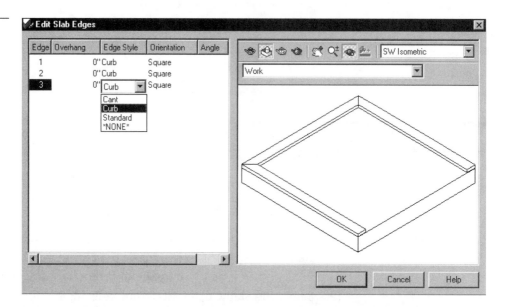

Figure 12–11

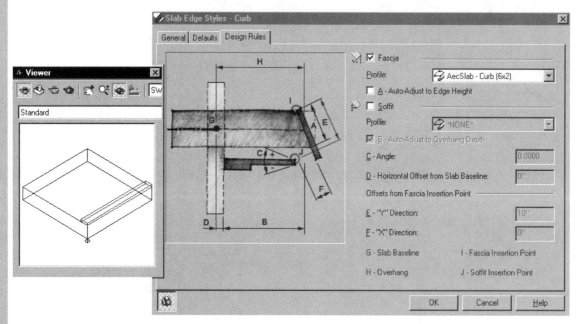

Section 13 | Slab Tools

When you finish this section, you should be able to do the following:

- ✔ Trim and miter Slab Objects.
- ✔ Add and remove Slab Object vertices, and use Slab grips.
- ✔ Use the Object Slab Boolean command.

Slab Objects are very versatile. Use Slab tools to manipulate these objects in innumerable ways. With these tools, almost any Slab Object configuration can be created.

You can input, modify, or convert <u>Slab Tools</u> or edit their edges by selecting the appropriate slab icon from <u>Slabs</u> toolbar.

You can also input, modify, or convert Slab Tools or edit their edges by selecting the <u>Design | Slab Tools</u> menu from the <u>Main</u> toolbar. You can get the Slab Tools menu by RMB in any viewport.

Tip Although the Slab Tools and Roof Slab Tools toolbars look very similar, Slab Tool commands work only for slabs, and Roof Slab tools work only for roof slabs.

Trim Slab

You can trim a Slab Object by another slab, a wall, or a polyline. Trimming can also produce new vertices.

Hands On

1. After starting Architectural Desktop with the default imperial template Aec arch [imperial-intl].dwt, select the Work-3D Layout tab, and create 3 viewports.

2. Activate the <u>Slab Tools</u> and <u>Slabs</u> toolbars, and place them in a convenient place.

3. Activate the Top View viewport, and create a 10-ft x 10-ft x 12-in.-thick slab.

4. Draw a polyline similar to that in Figure 13–1. The polyline does not have to touch the slab; it only has to be parallel to it.

Figure 13–1

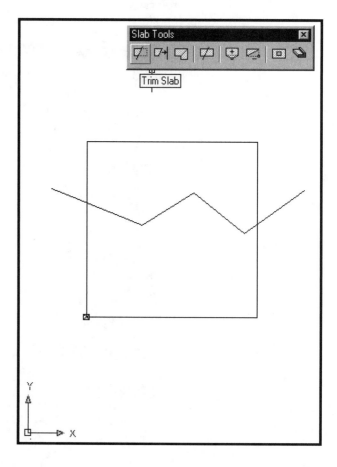

Figure 13–2

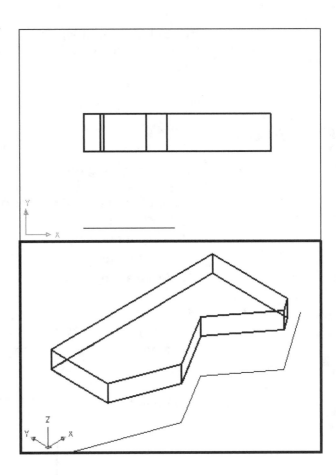

5. Select the <u>Trim Slab</u> icon from the <u>Slab Tools</u> toolbar. Select the polyline, then the slab, and then the side of the slab to be trimmed (Figure 13–2).

6. Select the slab to activate its grips. Hold down the <u>CTRL</u> key on your keyboard, and pull on the vertex as shown in Figure 13–3.

Experiment by pulling on various vertices both while holding the CTRL key and not holding the CTRL key.

Figure 13–3

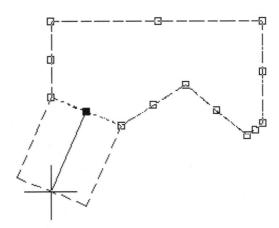

Trim Slab with Another Slab
Do you need an angled slab face? Try this trick that works only when trimming slabs with slabs.

Hands On

1. After starting Architectural Desktop with the default imperial template Aec arch [imperial-intl].dwt template, select the Work-3D Layout tab, and create 2 horizontal viewports.

2. Activate the <u>Slabs tools</u> and <u>Slabs</u> toolbars, and place them in a convenient place.

3. Create a 10-ft × 10-ft × 12-in.-thick slab.

4. Make a copy of the slab, and rotate and place it as shown in Figure 13–4.

5. Select <u>Trim Slab</u> from the <u>Slab Tools</u> toolbar, and trim the first slab by using the copy as the cutting object (Figure 13–5).

6. Modify the slab, and change its thickness to 5 ft (Figure 13–6).

Figure 13–4

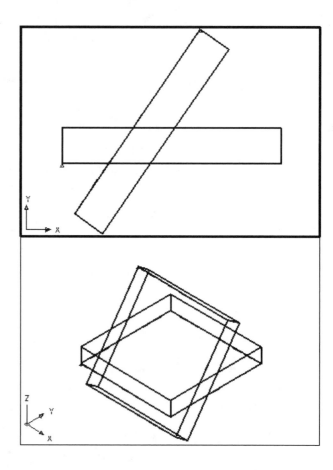

Figure 13–5

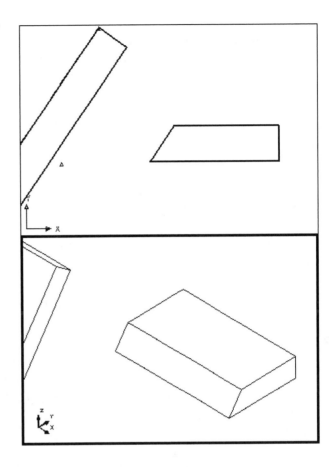

Figure 13–6

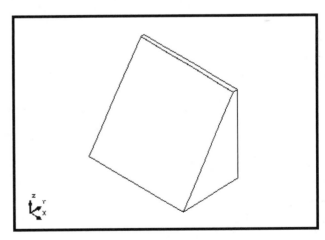

Miter Slab

The two mitering methods are by **Intersection** and by **Edges**.

Hands On

Miter Slab by Edges

1. After starting Architectural Desktop with the default imperial template Aec arch [imperial-intl].dwt template, select the Work-3D Layout tab and create 2 horizontal viewports.

2. Activate the <u>Slabs Tools</u> and <u>Slabs</u> toolbars, and place them in a convenient place.

3. Create a 10-ft × 10-ft × 12-in.-thick slab.

4. Make a copy of the slab, and rotate and place it as shown in Figure 13–7.

5. Select the <u>Miter Slab</u> icon from the <u>Slab Tools</u> toolbar.

6. Select the <u>Edges</u> option at the command line; pick the two <u>edges</u> shown in Figure 13–7. (It is best to do this in the 3D viewport.)

   The slabs are now mitered (Figure 13–8).

Miter Slab by Intersection

1. Erase everything.

2. Again create a 10-ft × 10-ft × 12-in.-thick slab.

3. Make a copy of the slab, and rotate and place it as shown in Figure 13–9.

4. Select the <u>Miter Slab</u> icon from the Slab Tools toolbar.

5. Select the Intersection option at the command line; pick the two <u>sides</u> shown in Figure 13–9. (It is best to do this in the 3D viewport.)

Figure 13–7

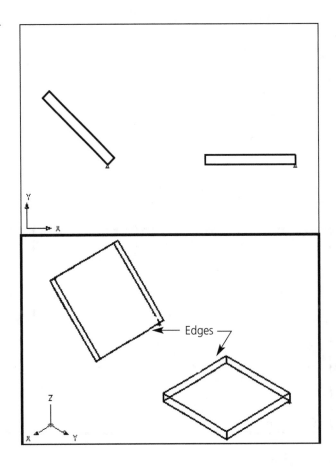

Figure 13–8

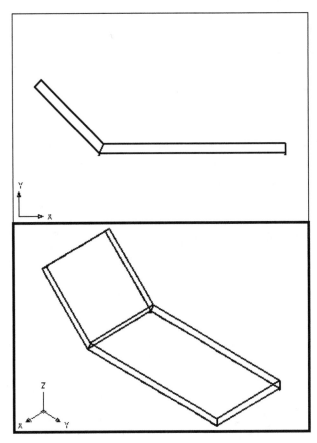

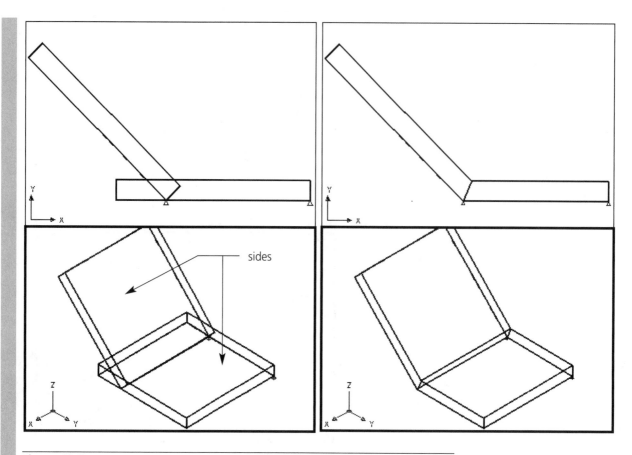

Figure 13–9

Section 14

Roofs

When you finish this section, you should be able to do the following:

- ✔ Use the Add and Modify Roof commands.
- ✔ Add, modify, and convert to Roof Slabs.
- ✔ Understand the Surfu and Slab modify edges commands.

You can input roofs into a drawing by selecting the icon from the **Roofs - Roof Slabs** toolbar.

You can also input roofs into a drawing by selecting the <u>Design | Roofs | Add Roof</u> menu from the Main toolbar.

You can get the Roofs menu by RMB in any viewport, choosing <u>Design | Roofs,</u> or selecting a Roof and RMB.

Adding Roofs

Roofs are intelligent AEC Objects. There are several ways to place them, and many controls to modify them. It is probably easiest to place a roof and then modify it rather than set the roof controls before placement.

Do the following lesson to experience how to add, convert, and modify roofs.

Hands On

1. Activate the <u>Roofs-Roof Slabs</u>, <u>Walls</u>, and <u>Wall Tools</u> toolbars.
2. Using the Aec arch [imperial-intl].dwt template, select the Work-3D Viewport tab, and create 3 viewports.
3. Activate the Top View viewport.
4. Using the Walls toolbar, create the floor plan shown in Figure 14–1. Make the walls 4" wide and 8'-0" high.
5. Set object snap to <u>End Point</u>.
6. RMB in the top viewport and select <u>Design | Roofs | Add Roof</u>.

   You can also select the <u>Add Roof</u> icon from the <u>Roofs</u> toolbar or <u>Design | Roofs | Add Roof</u> from the Main toolbar.

7. Starting at the corner shown in Figure 14–2, move clockwise until you get to point 6; then press the Enter key.
8. Select the roof, RMB, and select <u>Modify Roof</u> from the Contextual menu.
9. At the <u>Modify Roof</u> dialog box, check the <u>Overhang</u> checkbox, set the distance to 1'-0", and Apply it (Figure 14–3).

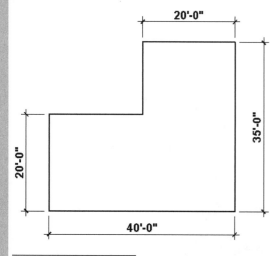

Figure 14–1

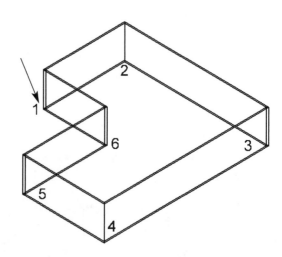

Figure 14–2

Figure 14–3

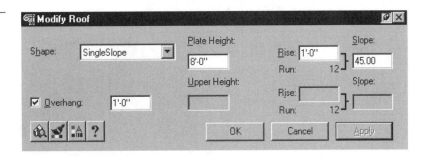

10. Select the <u>Edit Roof Edges /Faces</u> icon from the <u>Roofs-Roof Slabs</u> tool-bar, and select the edge shown in Figure 14–4.

11. At the <u>Edit Roof Edges</u> dialog box, set the slope to 90° (Figure 14–5). This will create a gable end roof (Figure 14–6).

12. Select the <u>Roof Line</u> icon from the Wall Tools toolbar.

13. At the command Line, choose the <u>Auto Project</u> option, and choose the wall shown in Figure 14–6. After selecting the wall, press the space bar or Enter key.

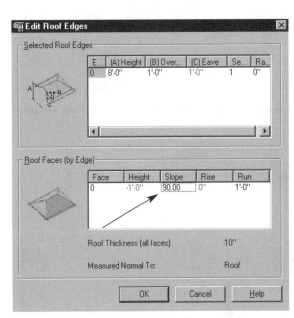

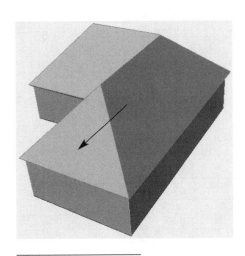

Figure 14–4

Figure 14–5

Figure 14–6

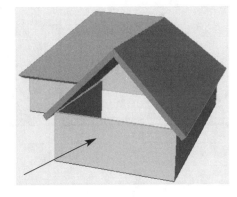

Figure 14–7

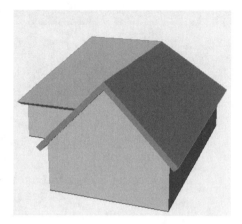

14. At the Select Entities request in the command line, pick the roof near the wall.

   You will now have created the gable end wall in your building (Figure 14–7).

15. In the Top View viewport, select the roof and pull on the vertex shown in Figure 14–8.

   You have now created a simple house with roof and carport overhang.

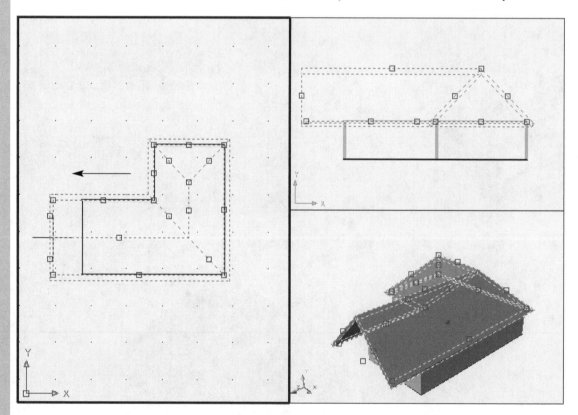

Figure 14–8

Convert to Roof and Surfu

Another way to create a roof is to use <u>Convert to Roof</u>. The following exercise uses Convert to Roof because of the curved walls.

Hands On

1. Activate the <u>Roofs-Roof Slabs</u>, <u>Walls</u>, and <u>Wall Tools</u> toolbars.
2. Using the Aec arch [imperial-intl].dwt template, select the Work-3D Viewport tab.
3. Activate the Top View viewport.
4. Create the floor plan shown in Figure 14–9.
5. Select the <u>Convert to Walls</u> icon from the <u>Walls toolbar</u>, select all the floor plan entities, and at the Command prompt, select Y to the Erase Layout Geometry? question.
6. Select Standard Wall when the Wall Properties dialog box appears.

You should now have the building walls shown in Figure 14–10.

7. Type **<u>surfu</u>** on the command line, and press the space bar or Enter key.
8. Set the new value to **<u>4</u>** on the command line and press the space bar or Enter key.

<u>Surfu</u> is the variable that controls the smoothness of the roof curves. This variable must be set before the roofs are placed.

9. Select the <u>Convert to Roof</u> icon from the <u>Roofs-Roof Slabs</u> toolbar, and select all the walls.
10. Type N at the command line question Erase layout geometry?

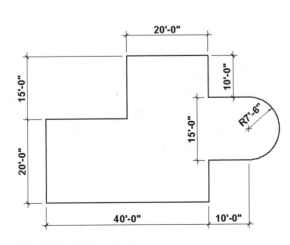

Figure 14–9

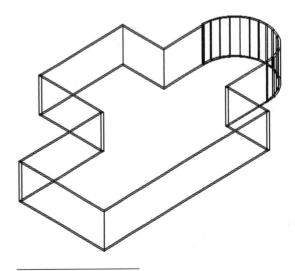

Figure 14–10

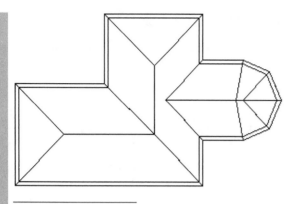

Figure 14–11

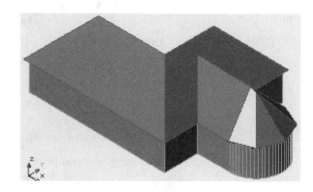

Figure 14–12

11. When the Modify Roof dialog box appears, check to make sure the Plate Height is the same as the Base Height of the walls, and press the OK button. **Save this exercise.**

   You have now created a roof with one command. This technique is very useful when you have rounded roofs (Figures 14–11 and 14–12).

12. Erase the roof.
13. Type **surfu** on the command line, and press the space bar or Enter key.
14. Set the new value to **24** on the command line and press the space bar or Enter key.
15. Again use Convert to Roof to make a roof.

Figures 14–13 and 14–14 show the effects of increasing the surfu variable to 24 (more facets).

16. Save this exercise.

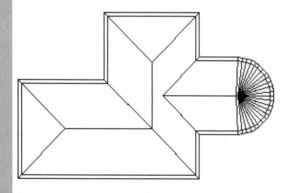

Figure 14–13

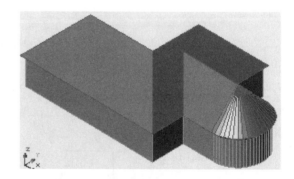

Figure 14–14

Tip Roofs can also be created by adding roof slab objects. This system is identical to that for creating slabs (see Section 12 for exercises on creating, modifying, and editing slabs).

Convert to Roof Slabs

Converting roofs to slabs allows you the flexibility inherent in slabs. Often it is best to start with a standard Roof Object and then convert it to Roof Slabs.

Hands On

1. Use the previous exercise.
2. Select the **Convert to Roof Slabs** icon from the Roofs-Roof Slabs toolbar.
3. Select the Roof Object, and press the space bar or Enter key.
4. Type Y at the command line question Erase layout geometry? and press the space bar or Enter key. Accept the Standard roof, and again press the space bar or Enter key.

   The roof color should now change, and the roof will now be made of Roof Slab objects. To check this select the individual roof panels.

roofslabmodifyedges

Although not documented in the manual, **roofslabmodifyedges** allows you to adjust all the roof edges at one time.

Hands On

1. Using the previous exercise.
2. Type **slabmodifyedges** in the command line.
3. Type **All** at the command line request to select slabs to modify, and press the space bar or Enter key.
4. Select the Baseline option at the command line, and press the space bar or Enter key.
5. Type **OV** for OVerhang, and press the space bar or Enter key.
6. Enter 2'-0" at the command line, and press the space bar or Enter key.

   You have now adjusted the overhang for all the Roof Slab objects. If a slab object edge fails to adjust, use the Edit Roof Slab Edges command to adjust that object.

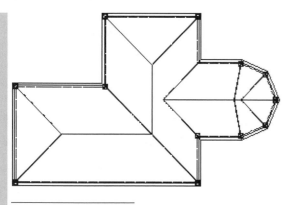

Figure 14–15

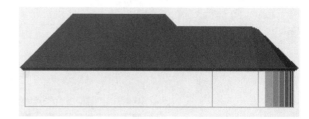

Figure 14–16

Figures 14–15 and 14–16 show overhang before. Figures 14–17 and 14–18 show overhang after being changed to 2 ft.

7. Again type **slabmodifyedges** in the command line.
8. Type **All** at the command line request to select slabs to modify, and press the space bar or Enter key.
9. Select the <u>Baseline</u> option at the command line, and press the space bar or Enter key.
10. Type **O** for Orientation, and press the space bar or Enter key.
11. Enter **P** for Plumb at the command line, and press the space bar or Enter key. **Save your exercise** (Figure 14–19).

You have now changed the fascia orientation. There are many more Roof Slab and Roof Slab Edge options. See the Architectural Desktop 3 User's Guide for help with those options.

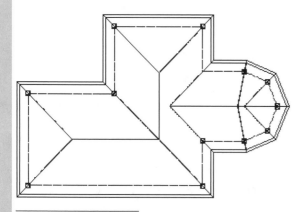

Figure 14–17

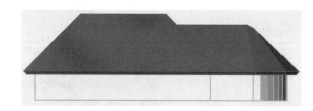

Figure 14–18

Figure 14–19

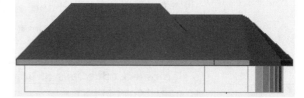

Section **15** | Roof Slab Tools

When you finish this section, you should be able to do the following:

✔ Use the Roof Slab Hole tool and be able to add a skylight.

✔ Use the Roof Dormer tool.

You can get the <u>Roof Slab tools</u> from the <u>Roof Slab Tools</u> toolbar.

    You can also get the Roof Slab tools by selecting the <u>Design | Roof Slab</u> Tools menu from the <u>Main</u> toolbar. You can get the Roof Slab Tools menu by RMB in any viewport, choosing Design | Roof Slab Tools, or selecting a Roof Slab and RMB.

> **Tip**
>
> Because roof slabs are similar to other slabs, the Roof Slab tools work in an almost identical manner as Slab tools, except that these tools include a Roof Dormer tool. Although the tools work the same, Slab tools will work only with slabs, and Roof Slab tools will work only with roof slabs. Check the Slab tools section of this book for exercises on using Slab tools.

Roof Slab Hole

Creating a Skylight Hole and Skylight

The Roof Slab Hole tool is very useful when you are creating skylights, etc. The roofs that they are in, though, are typically pitched. The following exercise explains how to use this tool effectively.

Hands On

1. Activate the Walls, Roofs-Roof Slabs, Roof Slab Tools, UCS, and UCS II toolbars, and place them in a convenient spot.
2. Using the Aec arch [imperial-intl].dwt template, select the Work-3D Viewport tab, and create 3 viewports.
3. Activate the Top View viewport.
4. Place a 36-ft × 24-ft rectangle in the viewport.
5. Select the Convert to Walls icon from the Walls toolbar.
6. Select the rectangle, and convert the rectangle to standard walls (Figure 15–1).
7. Select the Convert to Roof icon from the Roofs-Roof Slabs toolbar, and select the walls you have just created.
8. Enter N at the command line question Erase Layout Geometry? to maintain the walls.
9. At the Modify Roof dialog box, change the Overhang to 12", make sure the Plate Height is the same as the Wall Base Height, and press the Apply button (Figure 15–2).
10. Select the Convert to Roof Slabs icon from the Roofs-Roof Slabs toolbar.
11. Select the Roof, and type Y at the command line question Erase Layout Geometry? This will erase the original roof and leave the roof slabs.
12. Accept the Standard Roof Slab option at the command line.

Now locate the hole for the skylight.

13. Select the Object UCS icon from the UCS toolbar, and select the left roof slab.

This aligns the UCS with the roof slab.

14. Place a line from the apex of the roof slab to its midpoint, select the Move UCS Origin icon from the UCS II toolbar, and move it to the midpoint of the line you just placed.

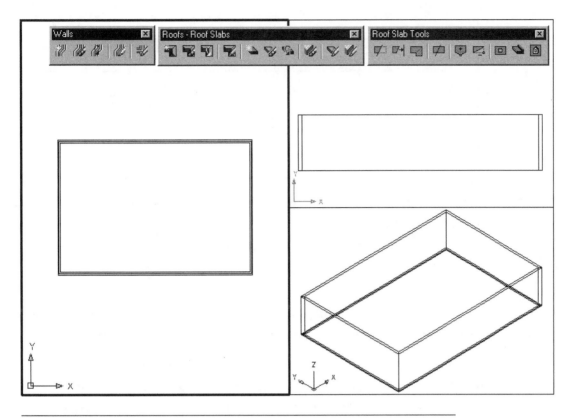

Figure 15–1

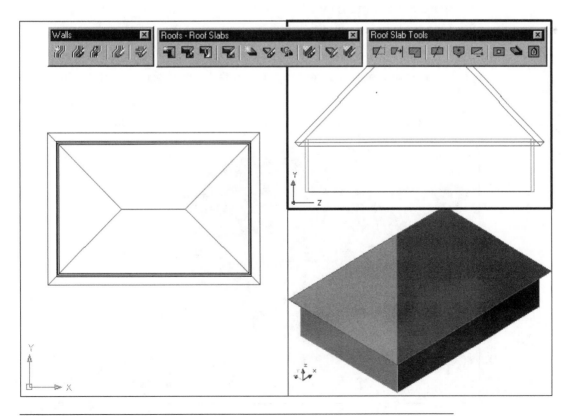

Figure 15–2

Figure 15–3

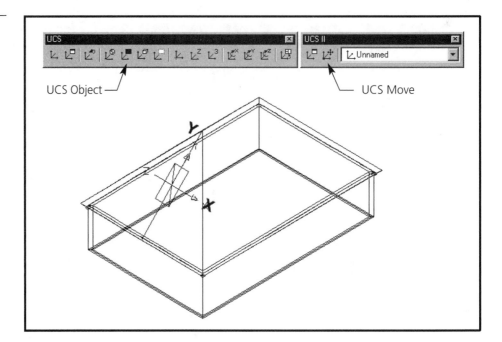

UCS Object ⎯   ⎯ UCS Move

15. Place a 3-ft x 6-ft rectangle as shown in Figure 15–3.
16. Select the <u>Roof Slab Hole</u> icon from the <u>Roof Slab Tools</u> toolbar.
17. Type A for Add at the command line; press the space bar or Enter key.
18. Select the left roof slab; then select the left rectangle, and press the space bar or Enter key.
19. Type Y at the command line question Erase Layout Geometry? and press the space bar or Enter key. **Save this exercise.**

You have now created a rectangular hole in the left roof slab (Figure 15–4).

Figure 15–4

Creating the Skylight

For this you will make a skylight and WBLOCK it, bring it into our original drawing, and place it in the roof.

1. Start a new drawing.
2. Place a 6-ft × 3-ft rectangle.
3. <u>Convert to Walls</u> the rectangle.
4. Set the walls to 1-in. Width with a Height of 4 in.
5. <u>Convert to Roof</u>; don't erase the walls.
6. Set the roof to no overhang and a 4-in. Rise.
7. Select the Roof properties and set the roof thickness to ½ in.
8. WBLOCK the skylight, and call it SKYLITE.

You have now made the skylight (Figure 15–5).

Figure 15–5

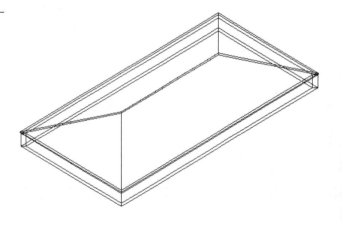

Placing the Skylight in the Roof

1. Open the house drawing from the previous exercise.
2. With the Insert Block command insert the skylight drawing in the hole in the right roof slab (Figures 15–6, 15–7, 15–8, and 15–9).

Figure 15–6

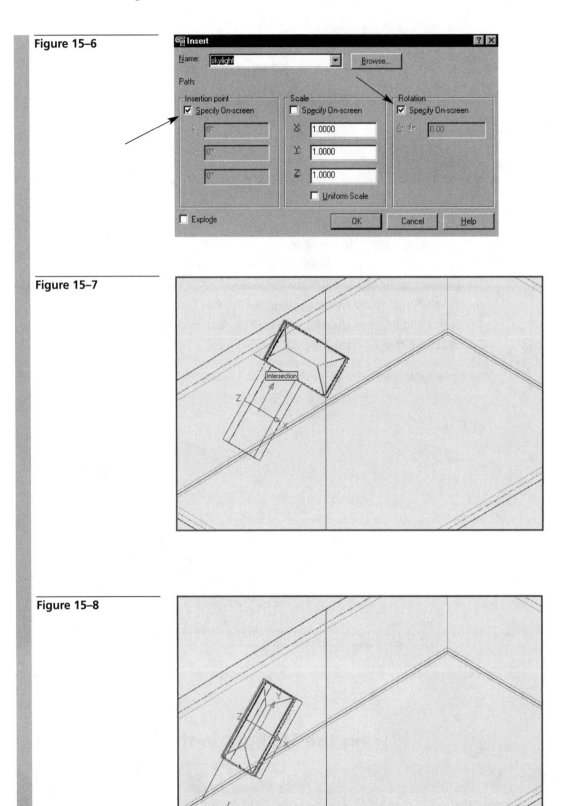

Figure 15–7

Figure 15–8

Figure 15–9

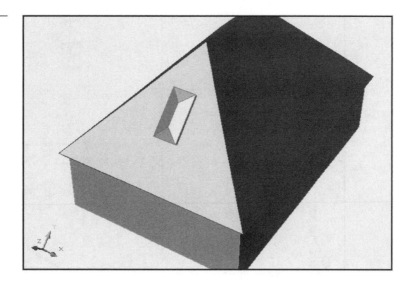

Dormers

Dormers are in vogue today. Architectural Desktop 3 has a command that aids in the creation of these objects.

Use the previous exercise for the next one.

Hands On

1. Place two 8-ft-high × 12-ft-6-in.-long standard walls as shown in Figure 15–10.
2. Activate the Right View. Select both walls, RMB, and select <u>Wall Properties</u> from the Contextual menu.

Figure 15–10

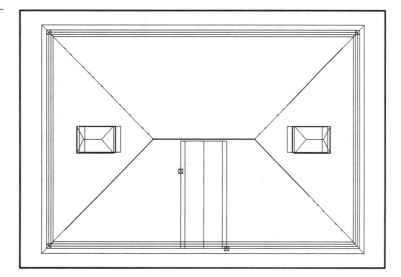

Figure 15–11

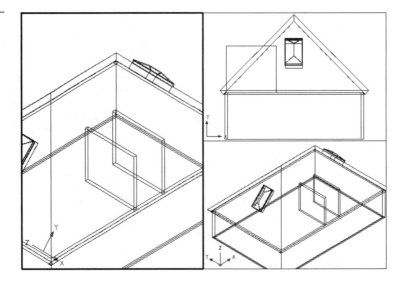

3. At the Wall Properties dialog box, select the <u>Dimensions</u> tab, and change the Y insertion point to 8'-0" (Figure 15–11). **If the edges of the dormer walls are not on the same plane as the front wall, move them with the move and perpendicular OSNAP.**

   You have now created the dormer walls.

4. Select the <u>Convert to Roof Slabs</u> icon from the <u>Roof Slab Tools</u> toolbar, and select the sidewalls of the future dormer. Don't erase the layout geometry; it is the sidewalls!

5. Specify <u>slab justification</u> to **Bottom**, <u>wall justification for edge alignment</u> to **Right**, and slope direction to **Left**.

6. When the <u>Roof Slab Properties</u> dialog box appears, select the <u>Dimensions</u> tab and set the <u>Thickness</u> to 6". (If the roof slabs don't match (Figure 15–12), reverse one of the dormer walls, and repeat the command on that wall.)

If <u>Convert to Roof Slabs</u> fails to work, check to make sure that the UCS is placed as shown in Figure 15–12 with Z in the up position.

Figure 15–12

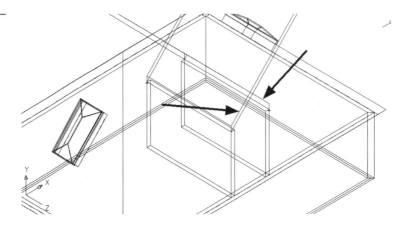

7. Select the <u>Miter Roof Slab</u> icon from the Roof Slabs Tools toolbar and miter by **Intersection**.

8. Select the two Dormer roof slabs as shown to miter the dormer roof (Figure 15–12).

9. Select the front wall of the building, and select <u>Model Tools | Roof Line</u> from the Contextual menu.

10. Select <u>Auto project</u>. When the command line says Select Entities, select the two Dormer roof slabs and press the space bar or Enter key.

This makes the front wall of the building continue up the front of the dormer.

11. Select the <u>Roof Dormer</u> icon from the Roof Slab Tools toolbar.

12. Select the roof slab of the building, and then select all the walls plus the roof slabs of the future dormer. <u>(Don't forget the front wall.)</u>

13. Slice the wall with the roof slab Y, and press the OK button.

14. Select the <u>Modify Roof Slab</u> icon from the Roof Slab Tools toolbar.

15. Select the <u>Properties</u> icon on the Modify Roof Slab dialog box.

16. Select the <u>Edges</u> tab.

17. Select the two front edges of the Dormer Roof Slabs, and set their overhang to 12"; also set the side edge overhangs to 12" (Figure 15–13).

The dormer is complete. Now add a window.

Tip   If you are using an early version of Architectural Desktop Release 3 and you do not select the dormer walls, the program crashes. This has been fixed, and there is a patch available.

Figure 15–13

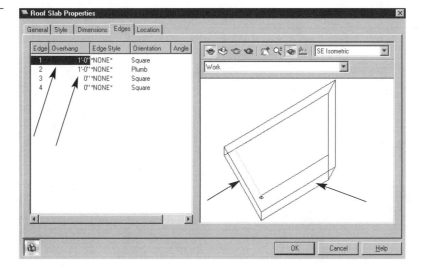

Figure 15–14

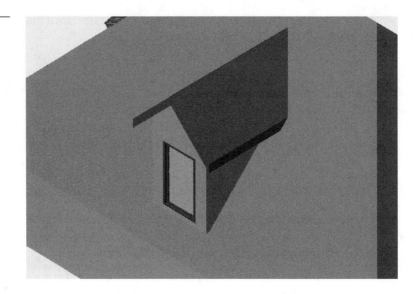

18. Select the front wall again, RMB, and select <u>Insert | Window</u> from the Contextual window (Figure 15–14).

Section 16 | Stairs

When you finish this section, you should be able to do the following:

✔ Create and edit AEC Stair Object Styles.
✔ Create and modify AEC Stair Objects.
✔ Understand and customize AEC Stair Edges.
✔ Place a stair rail.

Stairs are an important part of almost every project, and it is here that designers often make mistakes. AutoCAD Architectural Desktop Release 3's stair and railing systems aid in the productivity and accuracy of these objects.

In AutoCAD Architectural Desktop Release 3, much refinement has been done to the stair system. Stairs are controlled by three factors, style, shape, and turn type. The AEC Arch Imperial and Metric templates come preset by the developers with seven different styles. They are cantilever, concrete, standard, steel-opened, steel pan, wood-housed, and wood saddle. As with the other styles in this program, there are many controls available for the styles in the Stair Styles dialog box. By creating your own styles, you can quickly and efficiently place stairs into a project.

Tip Although Architectural Desktop Release 3 features an automatic stair calculating system that does the work for you, it is important to understand the underlying concepts pertaining to Stairs. There are basically two different systems to be concerned with, residential and commercial, and understanding the terms tread, riser, and stringer is essential. Treads refer to the horizontal plane of a stair, the riser is the distance vertically between each horizontal plane, and a stringer is the support on which the horizontal and vertical planes rest. Until recently, in the United States, there was a difference in the tread and riser requirements for commercial and residential stairs. Now BOCA, the basic building code, requires that all stairs have a maximum 7" rise and 11 inch tread. By code, the riser height can vary to a minimum of 4", but must be the same throughout the stair run. BOCA also restricts Flight limits to 12', and stair headroom height to 6'-8".

You can also input AEC Stairs into a drawing by selecting the Add Stair icon from the Stairs - Railings toolbar. And, you can input stairs into a drawing by selecting the Design | Stairs | Add Stair menu from the Main toolbar.

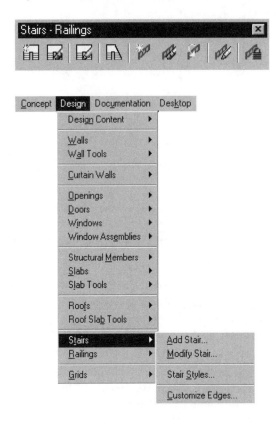

Stair Defaults

Stair defaults are set in the **AEC Stair Defaults** dialog box. You can reach it by going to Tools | Options from the Main toolbar or by RMB in any layout, selecting Options from the Contextual menu, and then selecting the AEC Stair Defaults tab. It is important that you understand the building code and stair construction, because many of the settings must be set according to code and construction. Headroom clearance, riser height, and tread depth are just some of the code-dictated inputs. Tread and riser thickness as well as nosing length depend on the materials used in the stair construction (Figure 16–1).

Stair Styles

As noted earlier, Autodesk Architectural Desktop 3 ships with seven pre-configured stair styles. Modifications to these configurations can be made by modifying the stair styles.

Figure 16–1

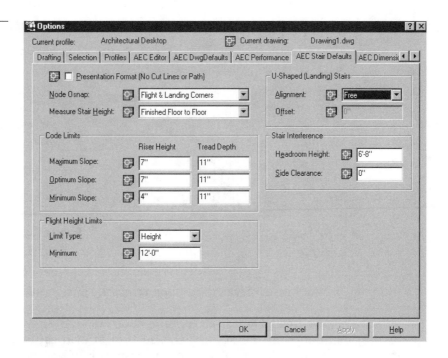

Modifying Stair Styles

Hands On

1. Select the <u>Style Manager</u> icon on the <u>AEC Setup</u> toolbar to bring up the <u>Style Manager</u> dialog box (Figure 16–2).

2. At the Style Manager dialog box, click on the <u>Standard</u> stair icon.

3. Select <u>Edit</u> from the <u>Main</u> toolbar in the Style Manager dialog box, <u>Copy</u> then <u>Paste a Copy</u> of the Standard Stair. (It will paste as Standard (2).)

4. Select <u>Standard(2)</u>, RMB and rename it to <u>TEST 1</u>.

5. Double click on the <u>TEST 1</u> icon to bring up the <u>Stair Styles</u> dialog box.

Figure 16–2

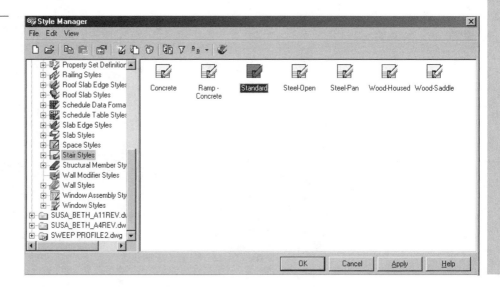

Figure 16–3

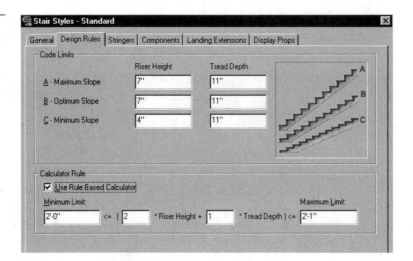

6.   At the Stair Styles dialog box, select the Design Rules tab (Figure 16–3).

The Design Rules tab contains code limits set in the AEC Stair Defaults mentioned at the start of this section. It also contains controls for the automatic stair calculator. Leave these as is. If you need odd riser/ treads for lawns, etc., turn the calculator off.

7.   Select the Stringers tab.
8.   At the Stringers tab, press the Add button twice (Figure 16–4).

   ■ Set the first stringer Type to: housed, set the second stringer Type to: saddled.

   ■ Set the first stringer Alignment to align left, set the second stringer Alignment to: align right.

   ■ Set the first stringer A-Width to: 2″, set the second stringer A-Width to: 2″.

   ■ Set the second stringer B- Offset to 2″ (the first stringer is a "housed" stringer, and thus can't be offset.

   ■ Set the Flight and Landing Waists.

Figure 16–4

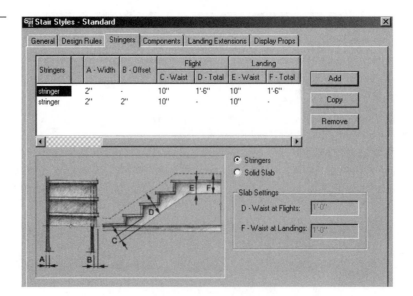

Figure 16–5

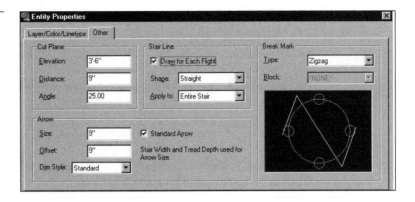

9. Select the <u>Components</u> tab.
10. At the Components tab:
    - Set A-Tread Thickness to 1-1/4" (5/4 pine).
    - Set B-Riser thickness to 3/4".
    - Set C-Nosing Length to 1".
    - Make sure the Sloping Riser checkbox is not checked (only metal pan and concrete stairs need sloped risers).
    - Set the Landing Thickness to 4".
11. Press the <u>OK</u> button to close the dialog box.
12. Select the <u>Display</u> props tab.
13. Select the <u>Edit Display Props</u> button to bring up the <u>Entity Properties</u> dialog box.
14. At the Entity Properties dialog box, select the <u>Other</u> tab. Here you can set the height of the stair Cut Plane, Break Mark type, Arrow size, etc. (Figure 16–5).

You have now set the settings for TEST 1 stair style, and are ready to use it.

Making a U-shaped Stair

Hands On

1. Activate the <u>Stairs-Railings</u>, and <u>Walls</u>, toolbars, and place them in a convenient place.
2. Start a new drawing using the Aec arch [imperial-intl].dwt template.
3. Select the <u>Work-3D Layout</u> tab and make sure the left viewport is SW Isometric View, and the right viewport is in Top View.
4. Create an enclosure 20 ft. by 10 ft. using 4 standard walls 9 ft. high.
5. Check <u>Perpendicular</u>, and <u>Nearest</u> snaps in the object snap dialog box, and make sure that Osnap is turned on (F3).
6. Activate the Top View; select the <u>Add Stair</u> icon from the <u>Stair - Railings</u> toolbar to bring up the <u>Add Stairs</u> dialog box.
7. At the Add Stairs dialog box set the <u>Style</u> to TEST 1, <u>Shape</u> to U-shaped, and <u>Turn Type</u> to 1/2 landing, and **Height to 12'**.

8. Set the height for 9'-0" (the height of the wall), and set Justify to Left.

9. Click a spot on the left wall, (the Nearest object snap should appear), and then drag the cursor in the direction of 90 degrees to the opposite wall and the perpendicular snap appears. Click the mouse to complete the command.

You now have created your first stair, close the add stairs dialog box (Figure 16–6).

Your landing is 3'0" wide, but you have just learned that you need it to be 4' wide to make provision for a standpipe.

10. Select the stair to turn on its grips.

11. Select the center grip at the rear face of the landing and move your cursor in the direction of 90 degrees, then enter 1' in the command line and press the Enter key.

Your landing is now 4' wide, but the stair is not against the rear wall.

12. Select the stair again, and then select the <u>Move</u> icon from the <u>Modify</u> toolbar.

13. Using the Endpoint object snap move the stair into position (Figure 16–7).

Try building this same stair, but change the Turn Type to 1/2 Turn. This setting cannot be modified after the stair has been placed (Figure 16–8).
      Stair objects can also be modified by moving their grips (Figure 16–9).

Figure 16–6

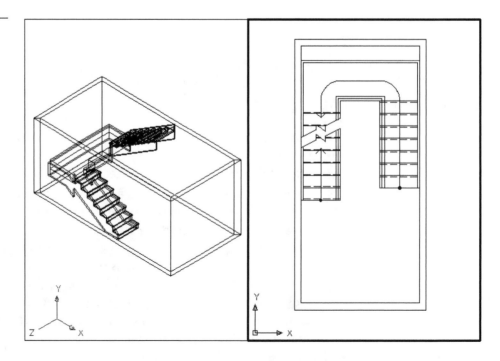

Figure 16–7

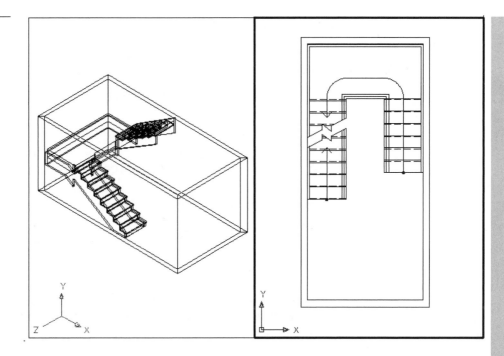

Figure 16–8

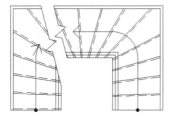

Figure 16–9

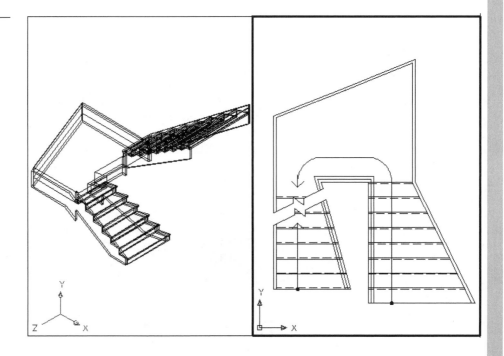

Making a Multi-Landing Stair

1. Activate the <u>Stairs-Railings</u>, toolbars, and place them in a convenient place.

2. Start a new drawing using the Aec arch [imperial-intl].dwt template.

3. Select the <u>Work-3D Layout</u> tab and make sure the left viewport is <u>SW Isometric</u> view, and the right viewport is the <u>Top</u> view.

4. Select the <u>POLAR</u> button at the bottom of the screen, RMB to bring up its Contextual menu.

5. Select <u>Settings</u> to bring up the <u>Drafting Settings</u> dialog box.

6. At the Drafting Settings dialog box select the <u>Polar Tracking</u> tab.

7. Under the Polar Tracking tab set the <u>Polar Angle Setting</u> to <u>30.00</u>, and press the <u>OK</u> button.

8. Activate the <u>Top</u> view; select the <u>Add Stair</u> icon from the <u>Stair-Railings</u> toolbar to bring up the <u>Add Stairs</u> dialog box.

9. At the Add Stairs dialog box set the <u>Style</u> to TEST 1, <u>Shape</u> to Multi-landing, and <u>Turn</u> to 1/2 Landing.

10. Click in <u>Top</u> view to start the stair.

11. Drag your cursor in the direction of 90 degrees, enter 9' in the command line, and then press the Enter key.

12. Move the cursor in the direction of 30 degrees, enter 4' in command line, and then press the Enter key. This creates a landing.

13. Move the cursor in the direction of 90 degrees, enter 6' in command line, and then press the Enter key. This creates a second stair run.

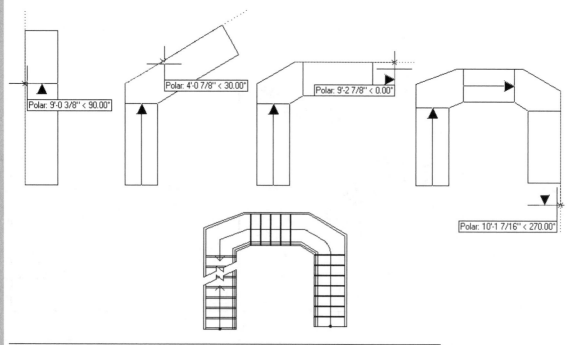

Figure 16–10

14. Move the cursor in the direction of 330 degrees, enter 4' in command line, and then press the Enter key. This creates a second landing.

15. Drag the cursor in the direction of 270 until the red cursor arrow is beyond the stair, and then click the mouse to complete the command.

You now have created a Multi-landing stair (Figures 16-10 and 16-11).

Try building a Multi-landing stair, but change the Turn Type to 1/4 Landing, 1/4 Turn, and 1/2 Turn. This setting cannot be modified after the stair has been placed (Figure 16–12).

Figure 16–11

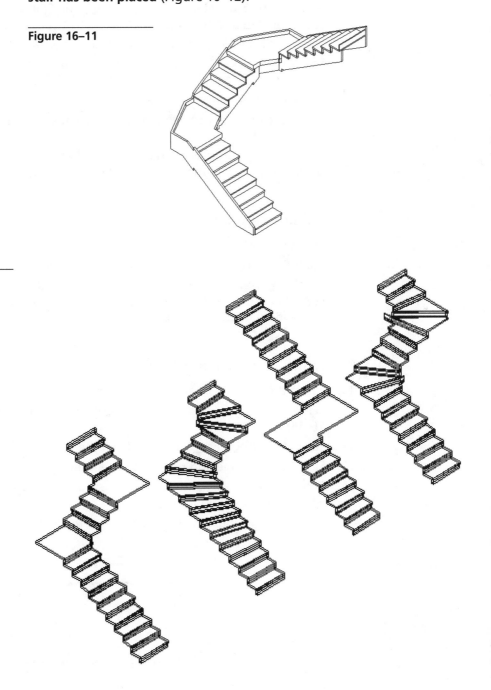

Figure 16–12

Customize Edges

This series of commands include <u>Project</u>, <u>Offset</u>, <u>Remove</u> customization, and <u>Generate</u> <u>polyline</u>. Use these commands when you need to modify stairs to fit unusual conditions.

Projecting an Edge

Hands On

1. Activate the <u>Stairs-Railings</u>, <u>Walls</u>, <u>Slabs</u>, and <u>Slab Tools</u> toolbars, and place them in a convenient place.
2. Start a new drawing using the Aec arch [imperial-intl].dwt template.
3. Select the <u>Work-3D Layout</u> tab and make sure the left viewport is <u>SW</u> <u>Isometric</u> view, and the right viewport is in <u>Top</u> view.
4. Activate the <u>Top</u> view viewport.
5. Select the <u>Polyline</u> icon from the <u>Draw</u> toolbar and draw the shape shown in (Figure 16–13).
6. Select the <u>Add Stair</u> icon from the <u>Stairs-Railings</u> toolbar and add a U-shaped stair 8' high inside the polyline as shown in (Figure 16–14).

Projecting to a polyline

7. Select Customize <u>Edges</u> from the <u>Stair-Railings</u> toolbar.
8. Enter <u>P</u> for <u>Project</u> in the command line and press the <u>Enter</u> key.
9. In the <u>Top</u> view select the front of the stair landing, then select the curved part of the polyline, and then press the Enter key to project the landing (Figure 16–15).

Projecting to a wall or AEC object

10. Select the polyline to activate its grips.
11. Select an end grip, and modify the polyline as shown in (Figure 16–16).
12. Select the <u>Convert to Walls</u> icon from the <u>Walls toolbar</u>.
13. Select the Polyline and press the Enter key.
14. Enter Y in the command line, and press the Enter key to bring up the <u>Wall Properties</u> dialog box.
15. At the Wall Properties dialog box select the <u>Style tab</u>.

Figure 16–13

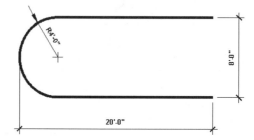

Figure 16–14

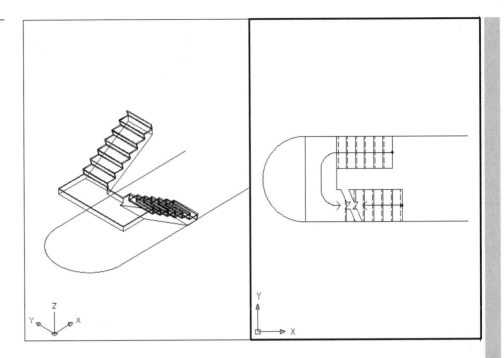

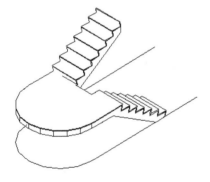

Figure 16–15

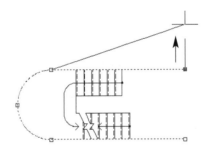

Figure 16–16

16. At the Style tab select the <u>CMU-8 Rigid-1.5 Air-2 Brick-4</u> wall.

17. Select the walls, RMB and select <u>Wall Modify</u> from the Contextual menu to bring up the <u>Modify Walls</u> dialog box.

18. At the Modify Walls dialog box change <u>Justify</u> to <u>Right</u>.

You now have a stair within a masonry enclosure (Figure 16–17).

Figure 16–17

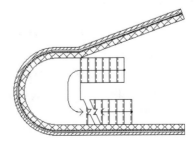

Figure 16–18

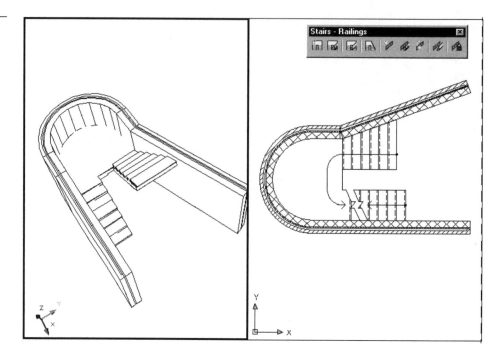

19. Select the <u>Customize Edges</u> icon from the <u>Stairs-Railings</u> toolbar.
20. Enter <u>P</u> for <u>Project</u> in the command line and press the <u>Enter</u> key.
21. Select the right hand edge of the stair run, then select the wall opposite it, and then press the Enter key to complete the command.
22. Save this exercise.

The stair run projects itself to the wall (Figure 16–18).

Generate Polyline

The generate polyline command is very useful when you have created a stair, and need a polyline to create walls, or to create an opening in a slab.

Hands On

1. Use the previous exercise.
2. Activate the <u>Walls</u>, <u>Slabs</u>, and <u>Slab Tools</u> toolbars, and place them in a convenient place.
3. Erase the walls leaving just the stair.
4. Select the <u>Add Slab</u> icon from the <u>Slabs</u> toolbar to bring up the <u>Add Slab</u> dialog box.

Figure 16–19

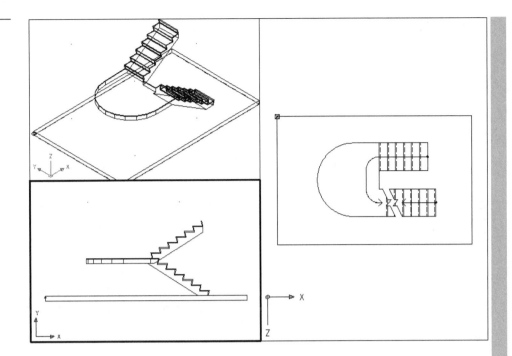

5. At the Add Slab dialog box create a <u>Standard 6"</u>, <u>Direct Mode</u>, <u>Top Justify</u> slab underneath the stair as shown in (Figure 16–19).

6. Select the <u>Customize Edges</u> icon from the <u>Stairs-Railings</u> toolbar.

7. Enter <u>G</u> for <u>Generate polyline</u> at the command line and press the <u>Enter</u> key.

8. Select the outer edge of the stair, and then repeat step 7, and touch the front of the lower stair run. Press the Enter key to complete the command, and then place a line at the inner edge of the lower stair run (Figure 16–20).

9. Select the <u>Layers</u> icon from the <u>Object Properties</u> toolbar and <u>Freeze</u> the Stair layer (A-Flor-Strs) to hide the stair.

Figure 16–20

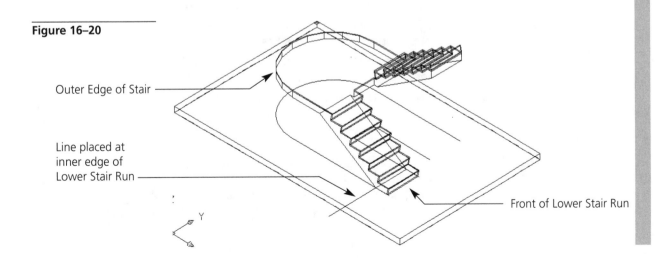

Outer Edge of Stair

Line placed at inner edge of Lower Stair Run

Front of Lower Stair Run

Figure 16–21

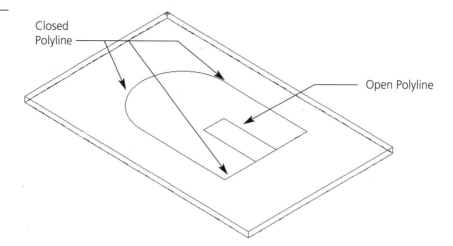

Closed Polyline

Open Polyline

10. Using <u>Extend</u> and <u>Trim</u>, cleanup the polylines created by the Generate polyline option of Customize Edges in Steps 7 and 8. Next, select the Edit Polyline icon from the Modify II toolbar and create two polylines (Figure 16–21).

11. Select the <u>Slab Hole</u> icon from the <u>Slab Tools</u> toolbar.

12. Press the <u>Enter</u> key to accept the <Add> option in the command line.

13. Select the <u>slab</u>, then the <u>closed polyline</u>, enter <u>Y</u> for Yes in the command line, and press the <u>Enter</u> key to create the hole in the slab.

You have now made a hole in the slab exactly matching the stair through the use of the Generate poly option of the Customizing Edges command.

Finishing the Stairway

14. Un-Freeze the stair layer to un-hide the stair.

15. Select the <u>Convert to Walls</u> icon from the <u>Walls</u> toolbar.

16. Select the open polyline, enter <u>Y</u> for Yes in the command line, and press the <u>Enter</u> key to bring up the <u>Wall Properties</u> dialog box.

17. At the Wall Properties dialog box select the <u>Style</u> tab.

18. At the Style tab select the <u>Standard</u> Wall, and press the <u>Enter</u> key to convert the open polyline to a <u>Standard</u> wall.

19. Select the new walls, RMB and select <u>Wall Modify</u> from the Contextual menu to bring up the <u>Modify Walls</u> dialog box.

20. At the Modify Walls dialog box set <u>Justify</u> to <u>Left</u>.

You have now created a stair, slab, and walls (Figure 16–22).

21. Select the <u>Add Railing</u> icon from the <u>Stairs-Railings</u> toolbar to bring up the <u>Add Railing</u> dialog box.

22. At the Add Railing dialog box select the <u>Guardrail-Pipe + Rod Balusters + Handrail</u> Style, Attached to: <u>Stair</u>, Offset <u>2"</u>, and check the Automatic check box (Figure 16–23).

23. Select the stair, and press the Close button.

24. Array 2 more copies of the stairway in the Y direction to create the final stairway (Figure 16–24).

Figure 16–22

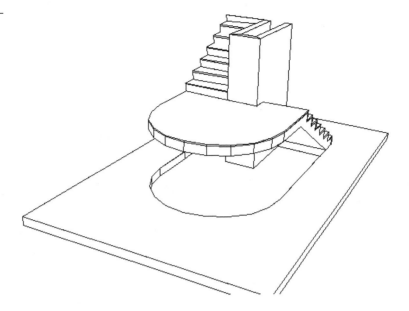

Figure 16–23

Figure 16–24

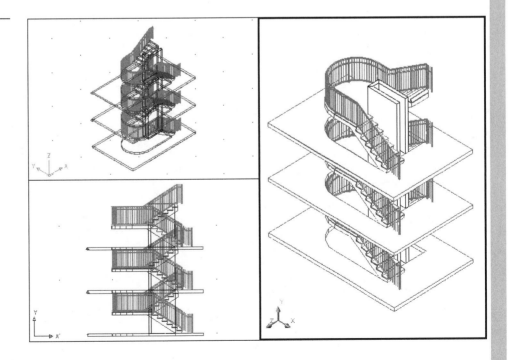

Section 17

Railings

When you finish this section, you should be able to do the following:

- ✔ Create and modify Railings.
- ✔ Attach and apply Railings.

You can input railings into a drawing by selecting the <u>Add Stair</u> icon from the <u>Stairs-Railings</u> toolbar.

You can also input railings into a drawing by selecting the <u>Design | Stairs | Add Railings</u> menu from the <u>Main</u> toolbar.

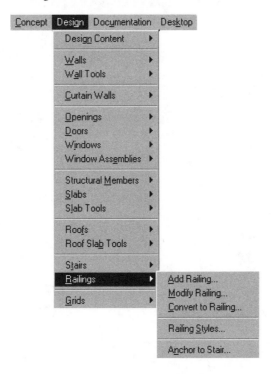

Setting Railing Defaults

Hands On

1. Select the Railing Styles icon from the <u>Stairs-Railings</u> toolbar to bring up the <u>Style Manager</u> dialog box.
2. At the Style Manager dialog box select the <u>Standard</u> icon (standard railing), RMB, and select <u>Edit</u> from the Contextual menu to bring up the <u>Railing Styles-Standard</u> dialog box.
3. At the Railing Styles-Standard dialog box select the <u>Rail Locations</u> tab (Figure 17–1).

Here you set the amount and height locations of the rails within each railing style. Typical BOCA code height is 3'-6".

4. Select the <u>Post Locations</u> tab (Figure 17–2).

Here you set the posts and balusters as well as the extension height of the posts above the rails. BOCA requires a <u>maximum</u> 4" opening between balusters.

5. Select the <u>Components</u> tab (Figure 17–3).

Here you set the shape of all the railing components as well as their width, depth, and rotation.

The shapes are derived from <u>Profiles</u> that are stored in the <u>Style Manager</u> under the profiles section. They can be accessed through dropdown lists (Figure 17–4).

Figure 17–1

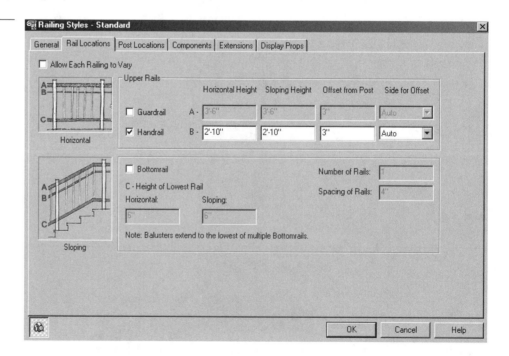

Figure 17–2

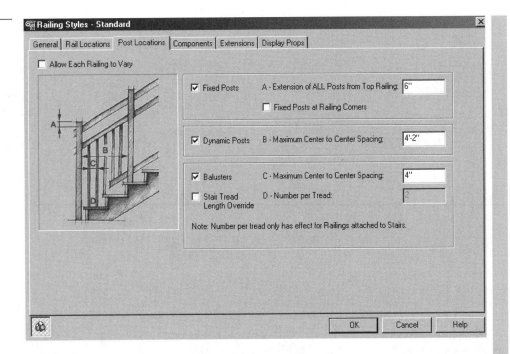

Figure 17–3

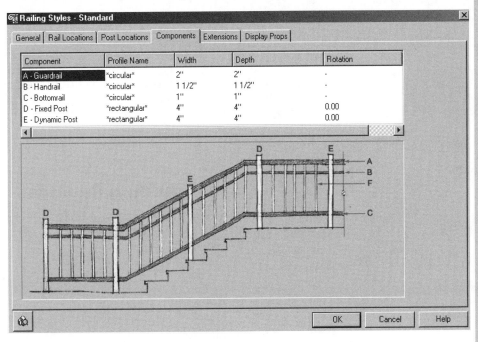

Figure 17–4

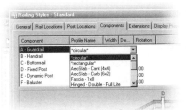

Figure 17–5

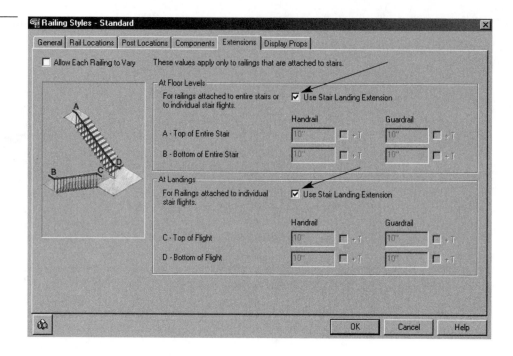

6. Select the <u>Extensions</u> tab (Figure 17–5).

Here you can set the railing extensions at floor levels and landings.

Adding Railings

Stair railings can be attached by four methods; <u>Attached to Stair (Automatic)</u>, <u>Attached to Stair (not Automatic)</u>, <u>Attached to Stair Flight (Automatic)</u>, and <u>Attached to None</u>.

Tip

Because of the need for backward compatibility with Architectural Desktop Release 2, the programmers included the <u>Use Stair Landing Extension</u> checkboxes. Only the <u>Standard</u> Style Railing has this checkbox checked. All other railing styles figure the extension in relation to the rail, so the <u>Use Stair Landing Extension</u> checkboxes are turned off, and the extensions are set for the code required 1'-0" (Figure 17–6).

Attached to Stair (Automatic)

Hands On

1. Activate the <u>Stairs-Railings</u> toolbar, and place it in a convenient place.
2. Start a new drawing using the Aec arch [imperial-intl].dwt template.
3. Select the <u>Work-3D Layout</u> tab and make sure the left viewport is SW Isometric view, and the right viewport is in Top view.
4. Select the <u>Add Stair</u> icon from the <u>Stairs-Railings</u> and create a <u>Standard</u> U-shaped, 1/2 landing stair 8'-0" in height.
5. Select the <u>Add Railing</u> icon from the <u>Stairs-Railings</u> toolbar to bring up the <u>Add Railing</u> dialog box.
6. At the add railing dialog box, set the following (Figure 17–7):
   - Style = Guardrail-Pipe.
   - Attached to = Stair.

Figure 17-6

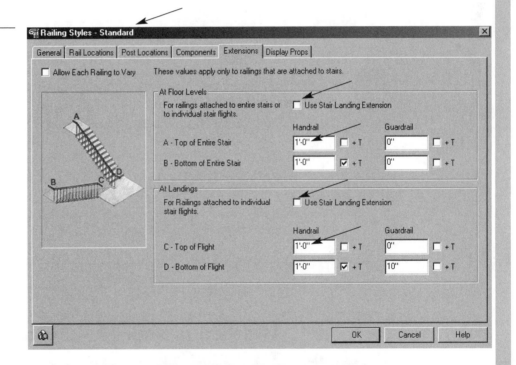

Figure 17-7

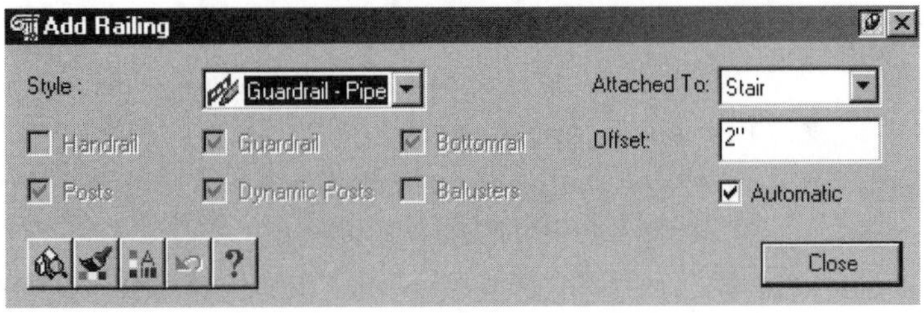

Figure 17–8

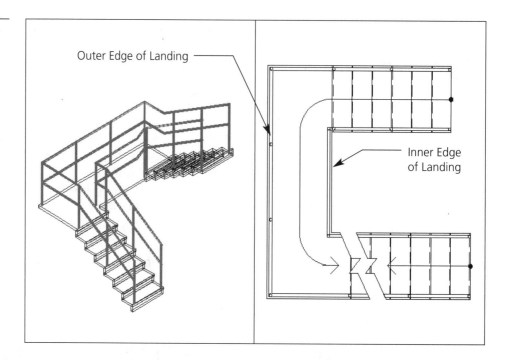

Outer Edge of Landing

Inner Edge of Landing

It is best to select stairs in plan rather than in any of the Isometric views because the selector doesn't always find the correct location on the stairs when selecting in 3D.

- Offset = 2″.
- Automatic = checked.

7. Being sure to be in the <u>Top View</u>, select the outer edge of the landing, than the inner edge to create both railings, and then press the <u>Close</u> button to complete the command (Figure 17–8).

Attached to Stair (Not Automatic)

Hands On

1. Erase the previous stair railing, leaving only the stair.
2. Turn all <u>Object Snaps</u> off.
3. Select the <u>Add Railing</u> icon from the <u>Stairs-Railings</u> toolbar to bring up the <u>Add Railing</u> dialog box.
4. Use the same settings as the previous exercise, but this time <u>uncheck</u> the <u>Automatic</u> checkbox.
5. Select anywhere on the outside of the stair.

Figure 17–9

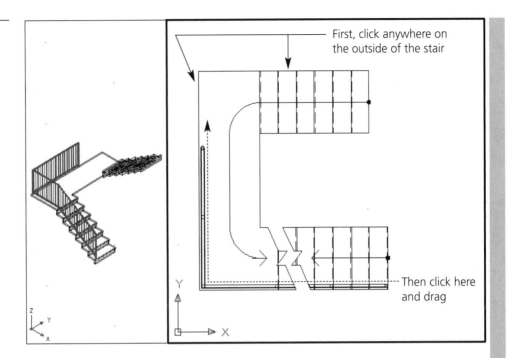

First, click anywhere on
the outside of the stair

Then click here
and drag

6. Select again anywhere near the outside of the lower stair flight, or
    on the landing and drag in the direction toward the upper stair
    flight (Figure 17–9).

    **Attached to Stair (not Automatic) allows one to drag a railing, and
    stop at any point.**

Attaching to Stair Flight (Automatic)

Hands On

1. Erase the previous stair railing, leaving only the stair.
2. Turn all <u>Object Snaps</u> <u>off</u>.
3. Select the <u>Add Railing</u> icon from the <u>Stairs-Railings</u> toolbar to bring
    up the <u>Add Railing</u> dialog box.
4. Keep the railing style, but this time, select <u>Stair Flight</u> in the drop-
    down list and check the <u>Automatic</u> checkbox.
5. Select both sides of the lower stair flight, and both sides of the upper
    stair flight.
6. Select again anywhere else except the stair flights and see that a rail
    does not appear (Figure 17–10).

Figure 17–10

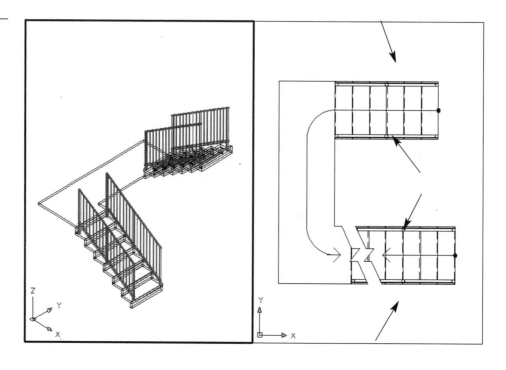

| Tip | Attach to Stair Flight (not Automatic) has no effect since Attach to Stair (Automatic) will attach rails on flights. |

Attach to None

<u>Attach to None</u> allows one to create segmented railings. This command is excellent for fences, porch railings, etc.

Hands On

1. Erase everything in the previous exercise.
2. Select the <u>Add Railing</u> icon from the <u>Stairs-Railings</u> toolbar to bring up the <u>Add Railing</u> dialog box.
3. Keep the railing style, but this time, select <u>None</u> in the dropdown list (the <u>Automatic</u> checkbox will gray-out, and become inactive).
4. Click anywhere in the Top View, clicking and dragging the mouse in different directions.
5. When you wish to stop, RMB and pick Enter from the Contextual menu (Figure 17–11).

Figure 17–11

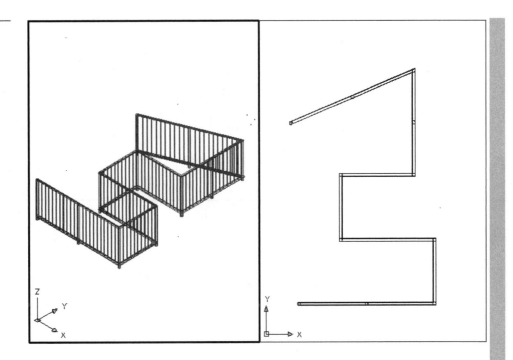

     The above railing can be adjusted by selecting it, and activating its grips.

Convert to Railing

1. Erase everything in the previous exercise.
2. In the Top View create the polyline shown in Figure 17–12.
3. Select the <u>Convert to Railing</u> icon from the <u>Stairs-Railings</u> toolbar.
4. Select the polyline created in the previous step, and press the <u>Enter</u> key.

Figure 17–12

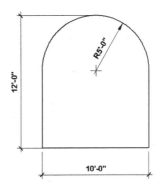

Figure 17–13

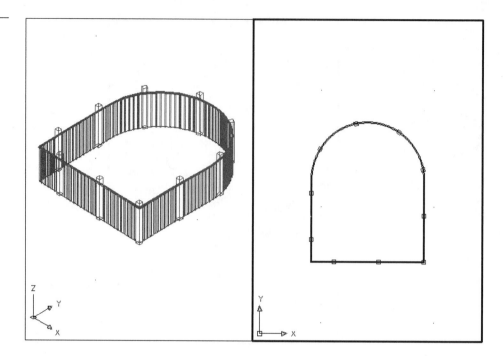

5. Enter <u>Y</u> for Yes to erase layout geometry, and press the <u>Enter</u> key to bring up the <u>Railing Properties</u> dialog box.

6. At the Railing Properties dialog box select the <u>Style</u> tab.

7. At the Style tab, select the <u>Standard</u> railing icon, and then press the <u>OK</u> button to complete the command and create the railing (Figure 17–13).

As with other AEC objects, you can change the railings to a different Style by selecting the railing, RMB, and selecting a different Style.

Section 18 | Grids

When you finish this section, you should be able to do the following:

✔ Add, Modify, Label, and Dimension Column Grids.
✔ Use grids for placing columns.

Architects and engineers commonly use column grids as the basis for their structures. Because of their importance, Architectural Desktop 3 has created the GRIDS routines.

You can input, modify, clip, label, and dimension Column Grids or input, modify, or clip Ceiling Grids by selecting the appropriate Grid icon from the Grids toolbar.

You can also input, modify, clip, label, and dimension Column Grids or input, modify, or clip Ceiling Grids by selecting the Design | Grids menu from the Main toolbar. Or, you can get the Grids menu by RMB in any viewport and selecting Design | Grids.

Creating Grids

Understanding how to control the Grid object will greatly improve your speed in creating structures.

X-Width and Y-Depth vs. X- and Y-Bay Sizes

The X Width and Y Depth are the sizes of the Grid. The X and Y bays are the sizes of the bays within the Grid (Figure 18–1).

Figure 18–1

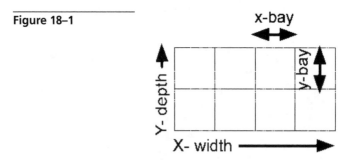

Hands On

1. Activate the <u>Grids</u> and <u>Structural Members</u> toolbars, and place them in a convenient spot.

2. Using the Aec arch [imperial-intl].dwt template, select the <u>Work-3D</u> Viewport tab.

3. Activate the Top View viewport.

4. Select the <u>Add Column Grid</u> icon from the Grids toolbar.

5. At the <u>Add Column Grid</u> dialog box, uncheck the <u>Divide By</u>, and <u>Specify on Screen</u> checkboxes.

6. First, set the X-Baysize and Y-Baysize to 10 ft, and then set the X-Width and Y-Depth to 10 ft (Figure 18–2). Click in the viewport and place the grid.

7. Select the grid you placed, RMB, and choose Modify Column Grid from the Contextual menu.

The <u>Modify Column Grid</u> dialog box appears. It is the same as the previous dialog box, except that it doesn't have a <u>Specify on Screen</u> checkbox. Instead, it has an Apply button (Figure 18–3).

Do the following exercises while paying attention to the change in the Grid.

8. a. Change the X-Baysize and Y-Baysize to 20', and press the Apply button.

The X-Width and Y-Width do not change because the width of the entire grid cannot be smaller than its bays.

   b. Change the X-Width to 60' and Y-Depth to 40', and place another grid.

   c. Check the <u>Divide By</u> checkboxes, and set the X direction to 5 and the Y direction to 3. Press the <u>Apply</u> button.

Figure 18–2

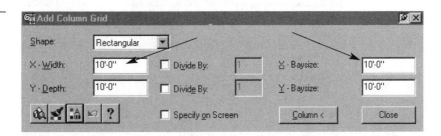

Figure 18–3

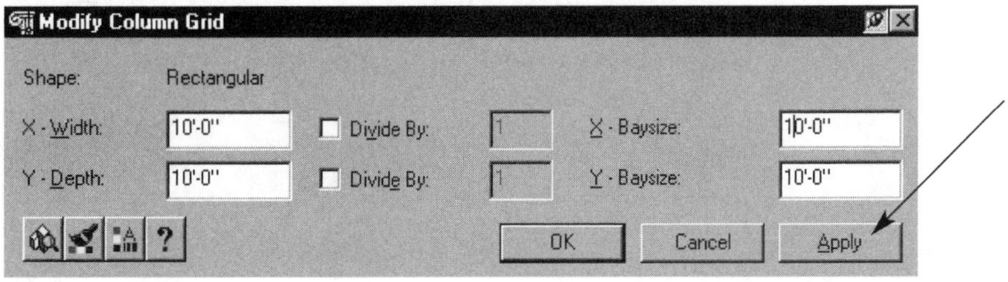

Figure 18–4

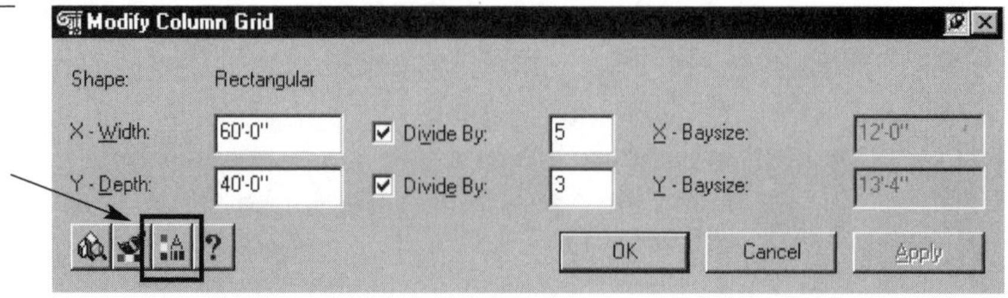

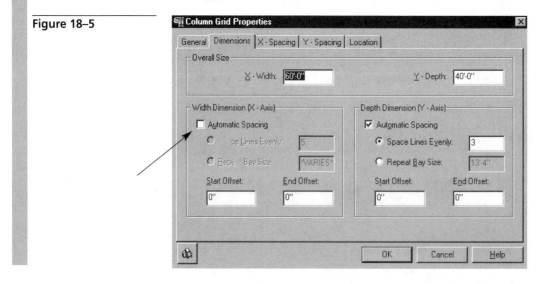

Notice that the grayed-out X- and Y-Baysize dimensions give the sizes of the bays.

9. Select the <u>Properties</u> icon at the bottom of the Modify Column Grid dialog box (Figure 18–4).

The Column Grid Properties dialog box now appears with five tabs. Explore each tab!

10. Open the X-Spacing and Y-Spacing tabs.

Notice that the numbers are grayed out and that they cannot be changed.

11. Open the <u>Dimension</u> tab, and uncheck the <u>Automatic Spacing</u> for the Width Dimension (X-Axis) (Figure 18–5).

12. Return to the X-Spacing tab.

Notice the numbers are active and you can now change them.

13. Click on the second <u>Distance to Line</u>, which should read 24'-0". Change it to 30'-0" and press the OK button (Figure 18–6). When you return to the <u>Modify Column Grid</u> dialog box, press the Apply button.

Figure 18–5

Figure 18–6

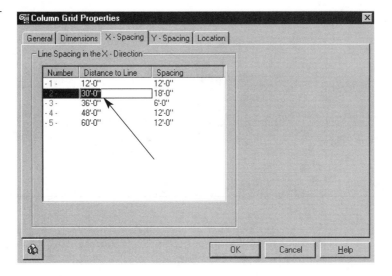

Figure 18–7

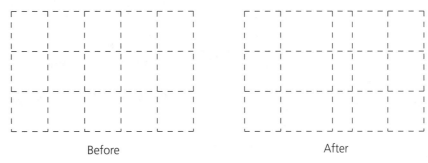

Before   After

The grid line moves over. See Figure 18–7 for before and after the change. Save this exercise.

Layout Mode

In the previous exercise you turned off the <u>Automatic Spacing</u> in order to adjust the grid lines. There are other ways to do this once you have the grid in place.

Hands On

Use the grid you created in the previous exercise.

1. RMB on the grid, go to <u>Column Grid Properties</u>, and make sure both <u>Automatic Spacing</u> checkboxes are checked in the <u>Dimensions</u> tab.

Notice that the grid has grips only at the corners (Figure 18–8).

Figure 18–8

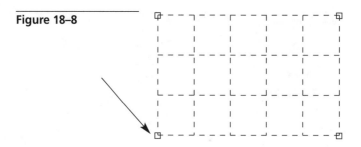

2. RMB again and select X-Axis from the Contextual menu (Figure 18–9).

   Here you will find controls to manually add, remove, and adjust grid lines in both the X- and Y-axes.

3. Select the <u>Layout Mode</u> selection (Figure 18–9).

   This will allow you to control all the controls in the Column Grid Properties-Dimensions Tab dialog box from the command line.

4. At the command line, select <u>Manual</u>, and press the space bar or Enter key.
5. Reselect the grid.

Figure 18–9

<u>R</u>epeat COLUMNGRIDPROPS
Cu<u>t</u>
<u>C</u>opy
Copy with <u>B</u>ase Point
<u>P</u>aste
Paste as Bloc<u>k</u>
Paste to Original Coordinates
<u>E</u>rase
<u>M</u>ove
Cop<u>y</u> Selection
Sc<u>a</u>le
R<u>o</u>tate
Notes...
Object Viewer...
Entity Display...
Edit Schedule Data...
X Axis ▶
Y Axis ▶
Dimensions
Labels...
Column Grid Modify...
Column Grid Properties...
Deselect <u>A</u>ll
<u>Q</u>uick Select...
<u>F</u>ind...
Propertie<u>s</u>

Add Grid Line
Remove Grid Line
Layout Mode

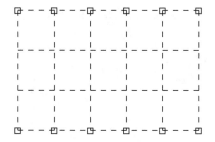

Figure 18–10

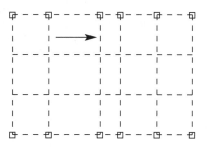

Figure 18–11

Notice that the grid now has grips at all X grid lines (Figure 18–10).

6.   Turn all object snaps <off>.

7.   Select one of the grips, drag it to the right, enter 5' at the keyboard, and press the Enter key.

You have now manually moved a grid line 5'-0" to the right (Figure 18–11).

8.   Explore all the <u>Layout Mode</u>, <u>Add Grid Line,</u> and <u>Remove Grid Line</u> options for both the X-Axis and Y-Axis. **Save this exercise.**

Dimensions and Labels

For grids to be valuable, they need to be labeled and dimensioned. Architectural Desktop 3 automates the standard grid annotation system.

Hands On

1.   Select the grid in the previous exercise, RMB, and select <u>Dimensions</u> from the Contextual menu.

2.   At the command line, accept the 4'-0" distance (the distance in scale from the grid to the first dimension string).

3.   Again, select the grid, RMB, and select <u>Labels</u> from the Contextual menu.

4.   At the <u>Column Grid Labeling</u> dialog box, select the X-Labeling tab.

5.   Select the first spot under <u>Number,</u> and enter the letter A. Then select another spot. (The other spots will fill with letters.) See Figure 18–12.

6.   Under <u>Bubble Parameters</u>, set the <u>Extension Distance</u> to 10'-0", and press the OK button (Figure 18–13). **Save this exercise.**

Figure 18–12

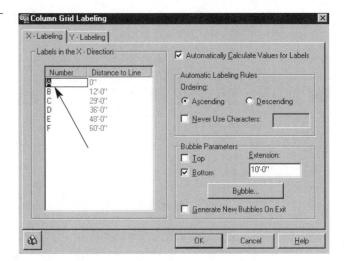

Figure 18–13

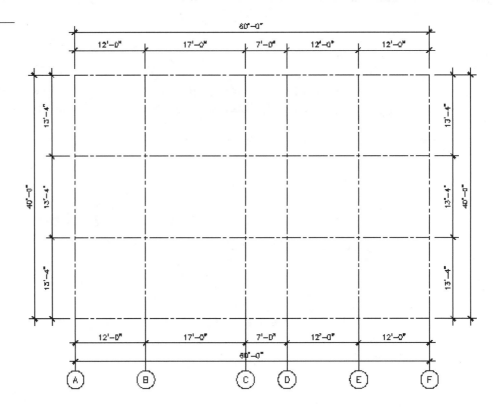

You have now dimensioned the grid and labeled it in the X direction. Explore the other labeling options.

Using the Grid

Placing Columns in the grid is a snap.

Hands On

1. Using the previous exercise, change the viewport to SW Isometric View.
2. RMB in the viewport, and select Design | Structural Members | Add Column from the Contextual menu.
3. Select Grid, and place the column at a grid point (Figure 18–14).

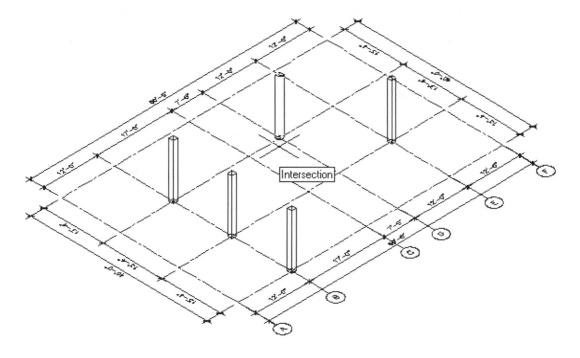

Figure 18–14

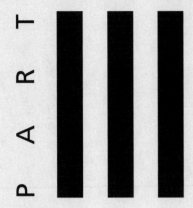

PART

III

Concept

Design

Documentation

Desktop

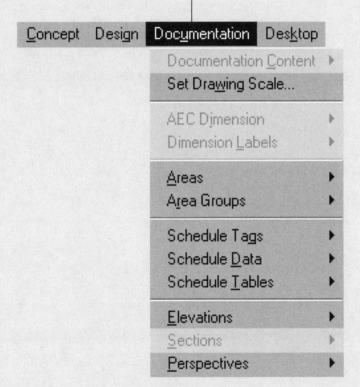

| Concept | Design | Documentation | Desktop |

Documentation Content ▶

Set Drawing Scale...

AEC Dimension ▶
Dimension Labels ▶

Areas ▶
Area Groups ▶

Schedule Tags ▶
Schedule Data ▶
Schedule Tables ▶

Elevations ▶
Sections ▶
Perspectives ▶

Section 19

Documentation Content

When you finish this section, you should be able to do the following:

✔ Add AEC documentation to a drawing.
✔ Customize document content.
✔ Understand the nuances of different types of documentation content.

You can input documentation by selecting the appropriate icon from the <u>Documentation - Imperial</u> or <u>Documentation - Metric</u> toolbars.

You can also input documentation by selecting it from the <u>Documentation | Documentation Content</u> menu from the <u>Main</u> toolbar.

Break Marks

You can use Break Marks when an object is too big for the page or when you want to show only part of an object. Seven different Break Marks come with the software (Figure 19–1).

Figure 19–1

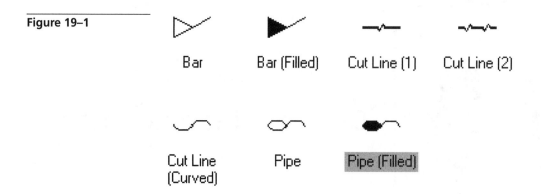

Bar   Bar (Filled)   Cut Line (1)   Cut Line (2)

Cut Line   Pipe   Pipe (Filled)
(Curved)

Trim, Scale, or Stretch

Hands On

1. Activate the <u>Documentation-Imperial</u> toolbar, and place it in a convenient spot.
2. Using the Aec arch [imperial-intl].dwt template, select the <u>Work-FLR</u> Viewport tab.
3. Place a 10-ft x 10-ft rectangle.
4. Select the <u>Break Marks</u> icon from the <u>Documentation-Imperial</u> toolbar.
5. At the <u>Design Center</u> dialog box, select the <u>Cut Line (1)</u> icon.
6. RMB and select <u>Insert</u> from the Contextual menu.
7. Select a starting point to the left of the rectangle, drag horizontally across your rectangle, and click again.
8. Select the rectangle below the break line, and it will trim.

The default for this command is trim.

9. Undo back to Step 4.
10. Again select the <u>Break Marks</u> icon from the <u>Documentation-Imperial</u> toolbar.
11. At the <u>Design Center</u> dialog box, select the <u>Cut Line (1)</u> icon.
12. RMB and select <u>Insert</u> from the Contextual menu.
13. Select a starting point to the left of the rectangle, drag horizontally across your rectangle, and click again.

Tip   Double-clicking or dragging will have the same effect of inserting all documentation content symbols.

Figure 19–2

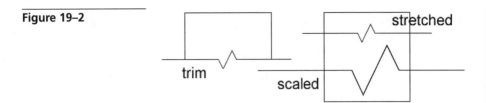

14. Again select the <u>Break Marks</u> icon from the <u>Documentation-Imperial</u> toolbar.

15. At the Design Center dialog box, select the <u>Cut Line (1)</u> icon.

16. RMB and select <u>Insert</u> from the Contextual menu.

17. Select a starting point to the left of the rectangle and below the previous break mark.

18. Type **T** for trim at the command line, and press the <u>Enter</u> key.

19. Type **SC** for Scaled, and press the <u>Enter</u> key.

20. Drag your mouse to the right, and click.

Notice the difference between the two break marks. The first is the default <u>Stretched</u>, the second is the Scaled option (Figure 19–2). Practice using all the Break symbols.

Detail Marks

Detail Marks are symbols that emphasize certain areas or features of a building. They often cross reference to other details. You can use them in plan, section, and elevation views (Figure 19–3).

Detail Boundary **A** has options for Symbol, Linetype, and Pline Width. Detail Boundaries **B** and **C** have options for Symbol, Linetype, Pline Width, and Radius.

Figure 19–3

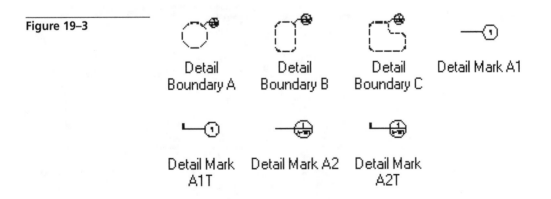

Hands On

1. Clear the previous exercise.
2. Select <u>Format | Linetype</u> from the <u>Main</u> toolbar to bring up the <u>Line-type Manager</u>.
3. At the Linetype Manager, select the Load button to load a new linetype.
4. At the Load or Reload Linetypes dialog box, scroll down and select the <u>ZIGZAG</u> linetype. Press the <u>OK</u> button, and close all the dialog boxes.

You have now loaded the ZIGZAG linetype for this exercise.

5. Turn <u>Ortho</u> on.
6. Select the <u>Detail Marks</u> icon from the Documentation toolbar to bring up the <u>Design Center</u>.
7. At the Design Center, select <u>Detail Boundary C</u>, RMB, and select <u>Insert</u> from the Contextual menu.
8. Click in your drawing, drag to the <u>right</u>, enter 20', and press the space bar. Drag <u>downward</u>, enter 30', and press the space bar. Drag to the <u>left</u> enter 10', and press the space bar. Drag <u>upward</u>, enter 10', and press the space bar. Drag to the <u>left</u> enter 10', and press the space bar. Press the space bar to close.
9. Click at a point on your detail boundary; drag to the right, click, and then press the Enter key to bring up the <u>Edit Attributes</u> dialog box.
10. At the Edit Attributes dialog box, enter a Detail Number and Sheet Number (Figure 19–4).

You have now placed a detail boundary with a cross-reference symbol. You control the size of the symbol and its text by the Set Drawing Scale command (Figure 19–5).

Tip   You can also drag the documentation symbol from the Design Center into your drawing; try it.

Figure 19–4

Edit Attributes   ? ×

Block name: Anno_Detail_A2

Detail Number | 2

Sheet Number | A-3

| OK | Cancel | Previous | Next | Help |

Figure 19–5

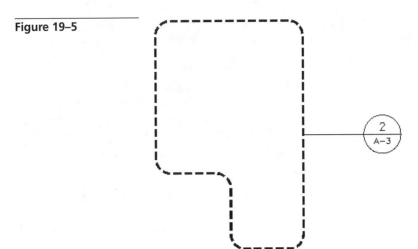

You can change the options for your Detail boundaries before insertion; note the warning message on the command line telling you that you have changed the default option. When you bring in the symbol again, it will revert to its defaults.

You can always change the linetype and linewidth after the boundary has been placed by selecting the boundary and selecting linetype and linewidth from the Object Properties toolbar. To change the radius of Detail Boundaries B and C, you must use the Options at the command line before insertion.

Elevation Marks

Architects use Elevation Marks to denote the direction or directions from which elevations are viewed. Autodesk Architectural Desktop 3 adds to these marks by allowing you to automatically create actual elevations linked to these marks (Figure 19–6).

 Tip | For this exercise, use the Kitchen drawing created in Section 5.

Figure 19–6

Elevation Mark Elevation Mark Elevation Mark Elevation Mark
A1   A2   B1   B2

Elevation Mark Elevation Mark
C1   C2

Hands On

1. Open the <u>Kitchen</u> drawing.
2. Select <u>Documentation | Set drawing Scale</u> from the <u>Main</u> toolbar to bring up the <u>Drawing Setup</u> dialog box.
3. At the Drawing Setup dialog box, select the <u>Scale</u> tab, and set <u>Drawing Scale</u> to 1/4"=1'-0"and the <u>Annotation plot Size</u> to 1/8".
4. Set the Viewport scale to 1/4"= 1'0", and lock the viewport (Figure 19–7).
5. Select the <u>Elevation Marks</u> icon from the <u>Documentation-Imperial</u> toolbar to open the <u>Design Center</u>.
6. At the Design Center, select <u>Elevation Mark B1</u>, RMB, and select Insert from the Contextual menu.
7. Place the elevation mark in the center of the kitchen.
8. Drag the cursor to the right, click to set the first elevation number, and bring up the <u>Edit Attributes</u> dialog box.
9. At the Edit Attributes dialog box, enter a <u>Sheet Number</u> (reference number), and press the <u>OK</u> button.

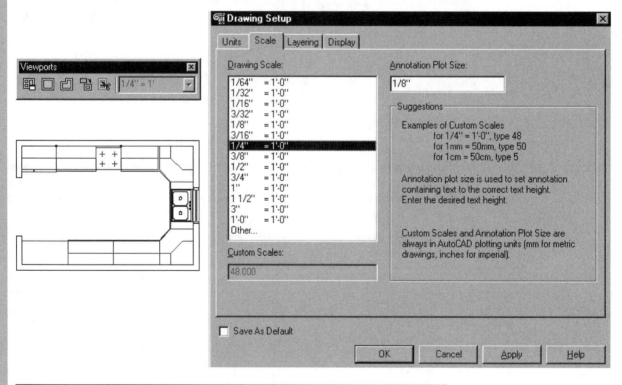

Figure 19–7

Figure 19–8

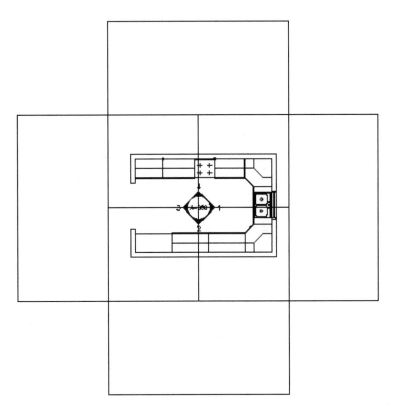

10. Type **Y** at the command line, and press the Enter key twice to complete the command.

   When you typed Y you added <u>AEC Elevation Lines</u> in all directions (Figure 19–8).

11. Select one of the <u>AEC Elevations Lines</u>, RMB, and select <u>Generate Elevation</u> from the Contextual menu to bring up the <u>Generate Section/Elevation</u> dialog box.

12. At the Generate Section/Elevation dialog box, select the <u>Select Objects</u> button, window-select the entire kitchen, and press the space bar or Enter key.

13. When you return to the <u>Generate Section/Elevation</u> dialog box, select the <u>2D Section/Elevation Object with Hidden Line Removal</u> radio button and <u>Pick Point</u> button; then pick a spot to the right of the kitchen.

14. Press the OK button to end the command.

15. Repeat Steps 11–14 for the other three <u>AEC Elevation Lines</u>.

   You have now automatically created all four elevations of the kitchen (Figure 19–9).

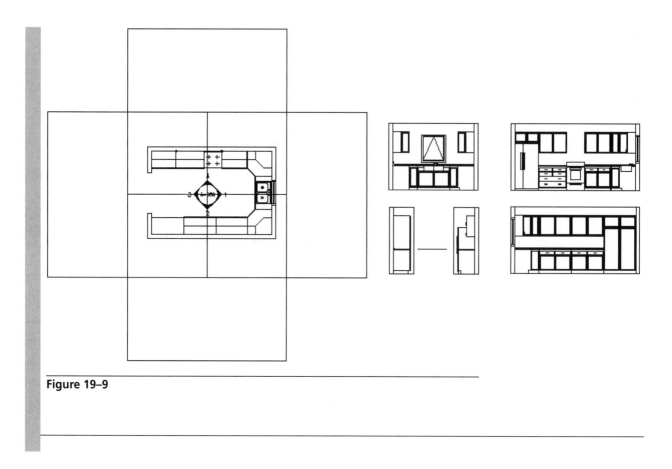

Figure 19–9

Figure 19–10

Section Mark
A1

Section Mark
A1T

Section Mark
A2

Section Mark
A2T

Section Marks

Architects use Section Marks to denote the direction or directions from which sections are viewed. As with Elevation Marks, Autodesk Architectural Desktop 3 adds to these marks by allowing you to automatically create actual linked sections (Figure 19–10).

See the section on Elevations for explanations on the use of section marks.

Making Custom Documentation Symbols

Although Autodesk Architectural Desktop 3 comes with a very comprehensive set of documentation symbols, you may want to make your own custom symbols. This is really quite easy within the program.

Hands On

1. Activate the <u>Refedit</u> and <u>Documentation-Imperial</u> toolbars, and place them in a convenient spot. (Refedit is an AutoCAD toolbar.)
2. Using the Aec arch [imperial-intl].dwt template, select the Work-FLR Viewport tab.
3. Select the <u>Title Marks</u> icon from the Documentation-Imperial toolbar to open the <u>Design Center</u>.
4. At the Design Center, select the <u>Title Mark A1</u> mark, RMB, and select <u>Open</u> from the Contextual menu (Figure 19–11).
5. Save the opened mark as <u>Custom Architect Mark</u>.
6. Select the <u>Edit block or Xref</u> icon from the <u>Refedit</u> toolbar.
7. Select the circle in the opened mark to bring up the <u>Reference Edit</u> dialog box. Because you are not changing the attributes, do not check the <u>Display attribute definitions for editing</u> checkbox (Figure 19–12).
8. Select the circle again when asked to <u>select nested objects</u> at the command line, and press the space bar or <u>Enter</u> key.

The mark will now gray out, and you are in edit mode.

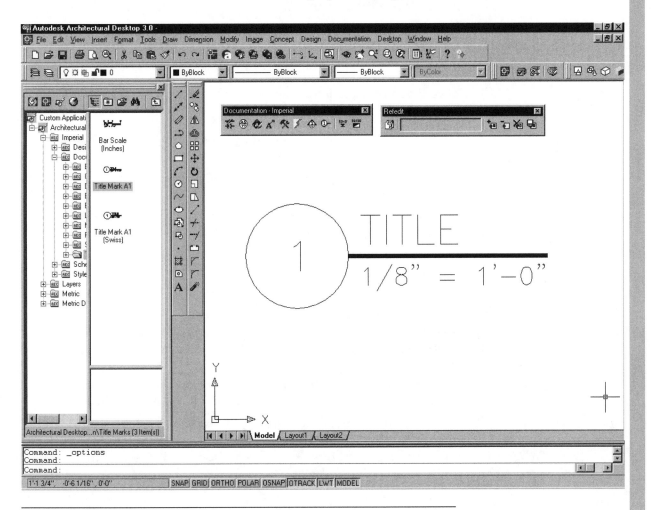

Figure 19–11

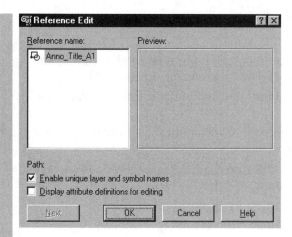

Figure 19–12

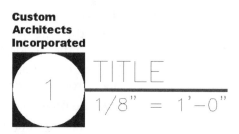

Figure 19–13

9.   Add a rectangle, solid hatch, and text as shown in Figure 19–13.

10. Select the <u>Save back changes to reference</u> icon from the <u>Refedit</u> toolbar, and press the <u>OK</u> button.

11. Close the Design center, save the custom mark, and close the drawing.

12. Start a new drawing, and again select the <u>Title Marks</u> icon from the <u>Documentation-Imperial</u> toolbar to open the <u>Design Center</u>.

Notice that a new mark now appears in the Design Center called <u>Custom Architect Mark</u>.

13. Select <u>Documentation | Set Drawing Scale</u> from the <u>Main</u> toolbar to bring up the <u>Drawing Setup</u> dialog box.

14. At the Drawing Setup dialog box, set the <u>Drawing scale</u> to **1"=1'-0"**, and press the <u>Apply</u> button.

15. Select the mark, RMB, and select <u>Insert</u> from the Contextual menu.

16. Select a location in the new drawing and apply the mark.

     The Custom Architect Mark is now placed with the scale of 1"=1'-0".

Changing the Type Style

17. Close the previous drawing, and open a new drawing.

18. Select <u>Format | Text Style</u> from the Main toolbar to bring up the Text Style dialog box.

19. At the Text Style dialog box create a new Style named <u>Stylus</u>, and using the <u>Stylus</u> True Type font that comes with the program.

20. Select the <u>Custom Architect Mark</u> in the Design Center, RMB, and select <u>Open</u> from the Contextual menu.

21. Again select the <u>Edit block or Xref</u> icon from the <u>Refedit</u> toolbar.

22. Select the word <u>Title</u> in the opened mark to open the <u>Reference Edit</u> dialog box.

23. At the Reference Edit dialog box, check the <u>Display attribute definitions for editing</u> checkbox (Figure 19–14).

Figure 19–14

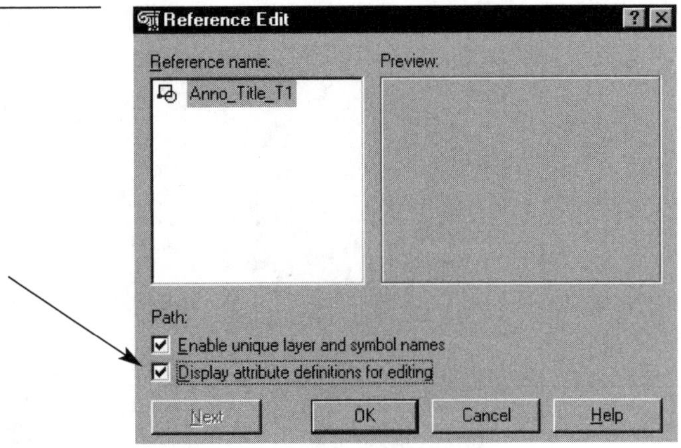

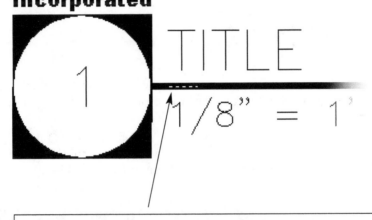

Figure 19–15

Custom
Architects
Incorporated

Tip

This line has been placed here because the Refedit command needs an entity to select in order to work.

24. When asked to select nested objects, select the little line placed behind the title line (Figure 19–15).
25. Select the attribute called TITLE, RMB, and select Properties from the Contextual menu to bring up the Properties dialog box.
26. In the Properties dialog box, select the Text Style dropdown list and choose Stylus.
27. Repeat this process for the SCALE attribute, select the Save back changes to reference icon from the Refedit toolbar, and press the OK button.

   You have now set the Attribute text style to Stylus.

28. Select Desktop | Create AEC Content from the Main toolbar to bring up the Create AEC Content Wizard.
29. At the Create AEC Content Wizard, select the Custom Command radio button and make sure the Content File list shows the Anno_Title_A1 and Anno_Title_T1 blocks. Press the Next button (Figure 19–16).

Figure 19–16

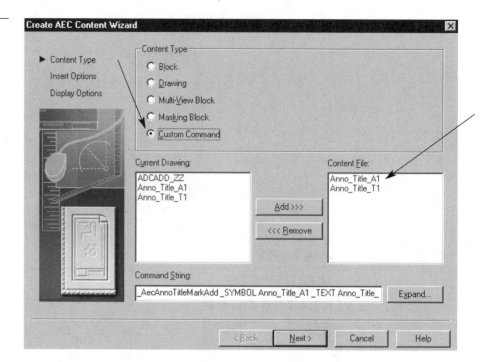

30. In the next screen of the Wizard (Insert Options), select the <u>As Defined by Content</u> radio button. Press the <u>Next</u> button (Figure 19–17).

31. In the next screen of the Wizard (Display Options), select the <u>Current Drawing</u> and Save Preview Graphics checkboxes. Press the <u>Finish</u> button to complete the command (Figure 19–18).

Figure 19–17

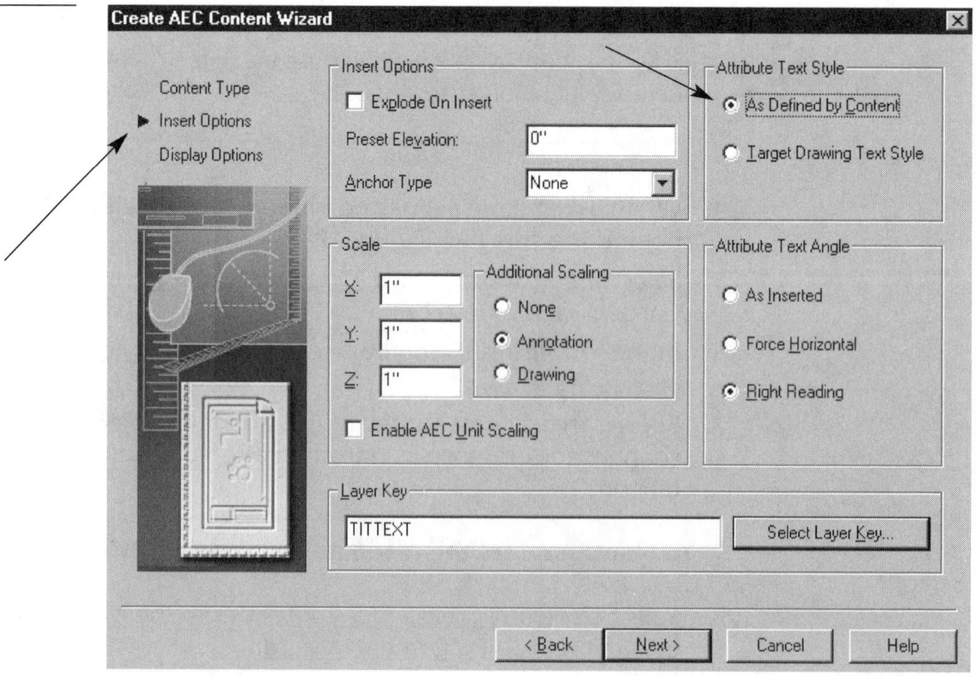

Figure 19–18

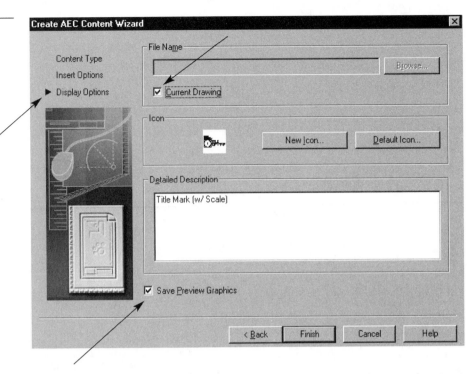

Again start a new drawing, open the Design center, and insert the Custom Architect Mark. The Stylus Type Style will now insert (Figures 19–19 and 19–20).

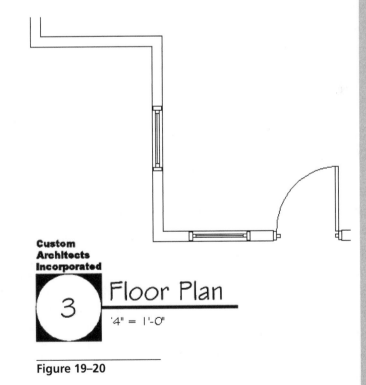

Figure 19–19

Figure 19–20

Section 20

Set Drawing Scale

When you finish this section, you should be able to do the following:

✔ Understand the relationship between the drawing scale, annotation plot size, and the documentation content.

The drawing scale and the documentation content work together. In order to have the documentation plot correctly, you need to know the scale factor of the viewport in which you are working. **(If you do not have a good understanding of the Model Space to Paper Space relationships, this would be a good time for you to read up on that subject.)** Architectural Desktop 3 makes this process easier through the use of the Set Drawing Scale dialog box.

In order to set the drawing scale, you first need to create viewports.

Hands On

1. Activate the <u>Walls</u>, <u>Viewports</u>, <u>AEC Setup</u>, <u>Documentation-Imperial</u>, and <u>Layer Management</u> toolbars, and place them in a convenient spot.
2. Using the Aec arch [imperial-intl].dwt template, select the Work-FLR Viewport tab.
3. Make sure you are in Paper Space.
4. Select <u>Erase</u>, and type <u>all</u> at the command line in response to Select objects.

   This will remove the existing viewports.

5. Select the <u>Display Viewports Dialog</u> icon from the Viewports toolbar.
6. At the Viewports dialog box, select the <u>New Viewports</u> tab, select <u>Two: Vertical</u>, and press the OK button.
7. Accept the <Fit> option at the command line.

   You have created two Paper Space viewports.

Figure 20–1

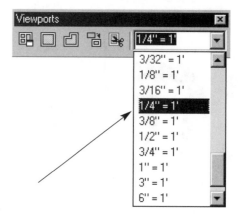

8. Double-click in the <u>left</u> viewport to change it to Model Space.

9. Select <u>1/4" =1'</u> from the Viewports dropdown (Figure 20–1).

10. Click in the <u>right</u> viewport and select <u>1/2" =1'</u> from the Viewports dropdown menu.

11. Return to the left viewport and using the <u>Add Wall</u> icon place a 20-ft x 20-ft enclosure using the standard wall. It will also appear at a different size in the right viewport. Using Pan, center the enclosure in both viewports (Figure 20–2).

The enclosure appears to be different sizes because it is being displayed at different scales.

Figure 20–2

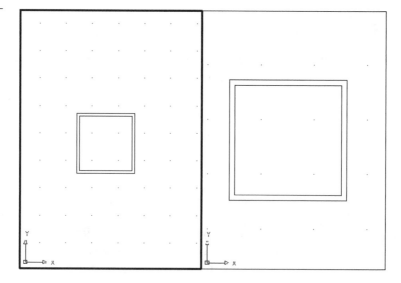

Tip You can also get the Drawing Setup, and Scale tab by selecting Documentation | Set Drawing Scale from the Main toolbar.

The scale for the Documentation Content must now be set.

Hands On

1. Activate the left viewport and select the <u>Drawing Setup</u> icon from the AEC Setup toolbar.
2. At the Drawing Setup dialog box, select the <u>Scale</u> tab.
3. Select 1/4" = 1'-0" as the Drawing Scale, <u>1/2"</u> as the Annotation Plot Size, and press the <u>Apply</u> button (Figure 20–3).
4. Activate the left viewport and the Detail Marks icon from the <u>Documentation-Imperial</u> toolbar.
5. When the Detail Marks explorer view appears at the left of your screen, select and drag the <u>Detail Mark A1</u> into your drawing. Click and drag the mark across the right wall of your structure, click again, and then press the Enter key (Figure 20–4).

Figure 20–3

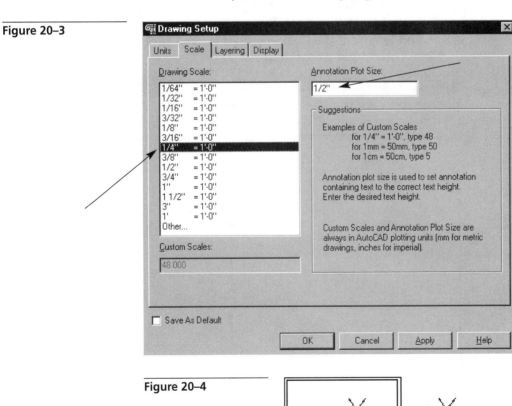

Figure 20–4

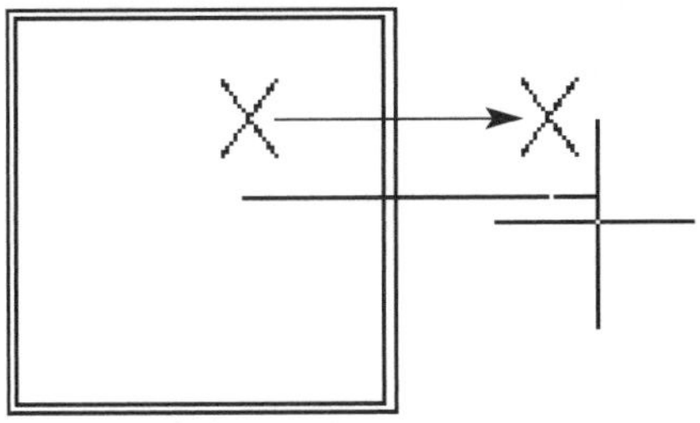

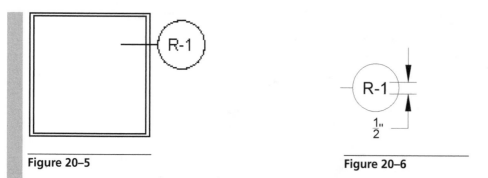

Figure 20–5

Figure 20–6

6.   At the Edit Attributes dialog box enter <u>R-1</u>, and select the OK button.

You have now added a detail mark into your 1/4"=1'-0" scale drawing (Figure 20–5).
If you change to Paper Space and measure the annotation, you will find that it is 1/2 in. high—the size you set for the Annotation Plot Size (Figure 20–6).
Everything seems fine, but when you look at the 1/2" = 1'-0" viewport next to the 1/4" = 1'0" viewport, you see the same annotation, but it is twice the size, and the <u>R-1</u> is 1/2 in. high (Figure 20–7).

7.   Activate the right viewport; set its drawing scale to <u>1/2"=1'0"</u> and its annotation plot size to <u>1/4"</u>.

8.   Place the same Detail Mark in the right viewport below the first Detail Mark, and label it R-2.

Notice that the Detail Marks <u>R-1</u> in the left viewport and <u>R-2</u> in the right viewport are the same size (Figure 20–8). The solution is to hide R-2 in the left viewport and R-1 in the right viewport.
To solve this problem you must use Layer Key Overides.

Figure 20–7

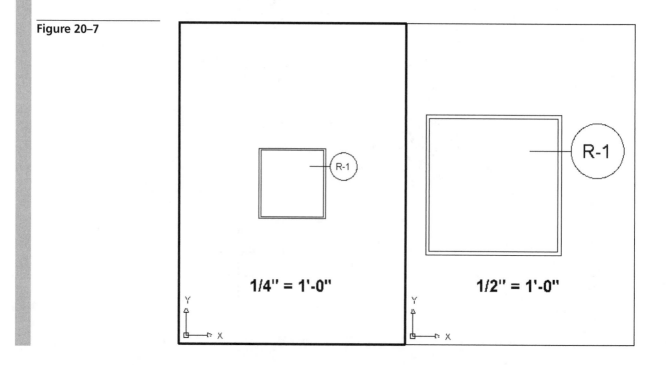

1/4" = 1'-0"   1/2" = 1'-0"

Figure 20–8

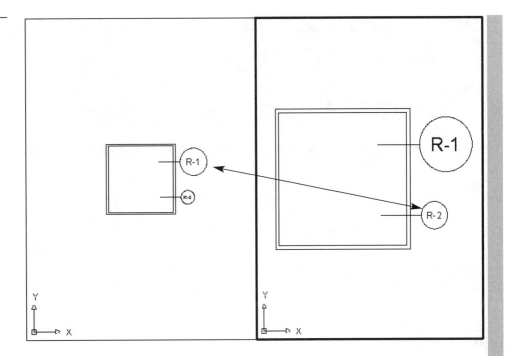

9. Erase all the Detail Marks.

10. Again set the left viewport to 1/4"=1'-0" with 1/2" as the Annotation Plot Size.

11. Again place <u>Detail Mark A-1</u>, and label it <u>R-3</u> upon placement.

12. Select the <u>Layer Key Overrides</u> icon from the Layer Management toolbar.

13. At the Layer Keys Overrides dialog box, select the <u>Minor Override</u>, type the number 2, and make sure <u>Enable All Overrides</u> is checked. **The number 2 is arbitrary; any figure will do** (Figure 20–9).

14. Activate the right viewport and set it to 1/2"=1'-0" with 1/2" as the Annotation Plot Size.

15. Again place <u>Detail Mark A-1</u>, and label it <u>R-4</u> upon placement.

Check the properties of both R-3 and R-4. You will now find that they are on different layers. Layer Key Overrides places the next annotation on a new override layer after the override is requested.

Figure 20–9

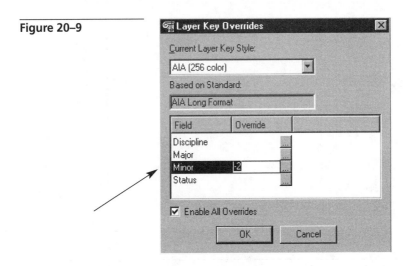

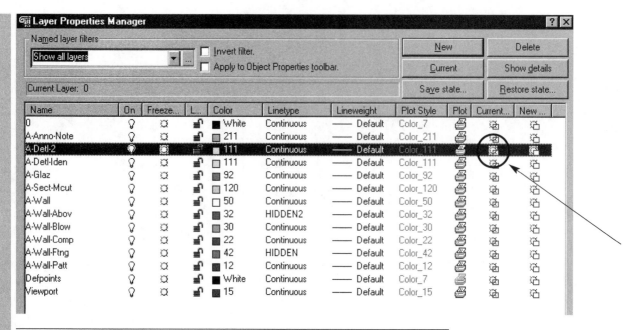

Figure 20–10

16. Activate the Left viewport, and then activate the <u>Layers</u> icon from the Object Properties toolbar.

17. Freeze the new override layer <u>A-Detl-2</u> in the current viewport (Figure 20–10).

18. Activate the right viewport and then freeze <u>layer A-Detl-Iden</u> in that viewport.

Now you have two different viewport scales for the same enclosure with the annotation plotting the same size (Figure 20–11).

Figure 20–11

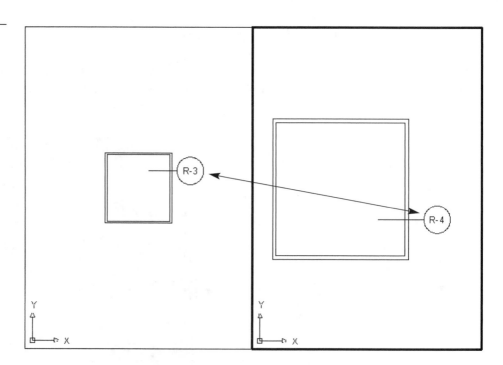

Section 21

AEC Dimension

When you finish this section, you should be able to do the following:

✔ Add, modify, and convert AEC Dimensions.
✔ Understand the associative dimension concept and how to add and remove Dimension Points.
✔ Set the dimension styles using the AEC Display Wizard.

The new AEC Dimensions are automatic dimensions based on Styles. Because there are so many variables in the dimension system, there are many dialog boxes. To make it easier, the developers have also added a "Wizard" to aid in variable setup.

Standard AutoCAD dimensions can be converted into AEC Dimensions, and AEC Dimensions can be mixed with the manual AEC and standard AutoCAD dimensioning systems.

You can add AEC Dimensions and modify dimension styles by selecting the appropriate icon from the AEC Dimension toolbar.

You can also add AEC Dimensions and modify Dimension Styles by selecting the Documentation | AEC Dimension menu from the Main toolbar. You can also get the AEC Dimensions menu by RMB in any viewport.

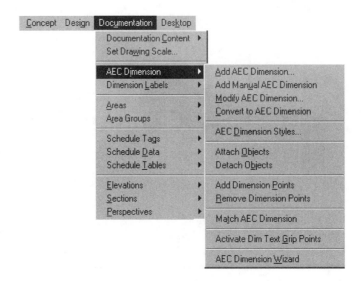

AEC Dimensions can dimension only AEC objects such as walls, windows, stairs, and structural members. If you add non-AEC objects to AEC objects, you have to add manual dimension points to the automatic AEC dimension or create manual AEC or standard AutoCAD dimensions.

The following table from the Autodesk Architectural Desktop 3 online help describes the difference between the three available dimensioning systems.

Automatic AEC Dimensions	Manual AEC Dimensions	AutoCAD Dimensions
Logical dimension points taken from object	Manual dimension points taken from drawing	Manual dimension points taken from drawing
Dimension AEC objects	Dimension picked points in drawing	Dimension picked points in drawing
Associative toward building elements	Associative or nonassociative toward points, depending on user settings	Associative toward points
Dimension groups	Dimension groups	Single dimensions
Support superscripting, variable-extension line length	Support superscripting, variable-extension line length	Supports no superscripting, variable-extension line length
Dimension texts cannot be edited	Dimension texts cannot be edited	Dimension texts can be edited
Defined by AEC dimension style and AutoCAD dimension style	Defined by AEC dimension style and AutoCAD dimension style	Defined by AutoCAD dimension style

Tip   Because the AEC Dimensions are based on AutoCAD's standard Dimensioning variables, it is imperative that you have a good understanding of that system and its operation. This includes an understanding of the relationship between dimensioning and Model - Paperspace. This book assumes that understanding.

AEC Automatic Dimensions

Hands On

1. Activate the <u>Viewports</u>, <u>Dimension</u>, <u>Walls</u>, and <u>AEC Dimension</u> tool-bars, and place them in a convenient place.
2. Select the <u>Dimension Style</u> icon from the <u>Dimension</u> toolbar.
3. At the Dimension Style Manager, select New and create a new dimension style called <u>TEST</u> Dimensions.

Before proceeding, change the Standard text style; you can use Stylus BT, which comes with Architectural Desktop.

4. Select <u>Format | Text Style</u> from the main toolbar.
5. At the <u>Text Style</u> dialog box, Select the <u>New</u> button and create a new style name called <u>NEW Text</u>.

 Tip   This is an AutoCAD, not Architectural Desktop, Style manager (Figure 21–1).

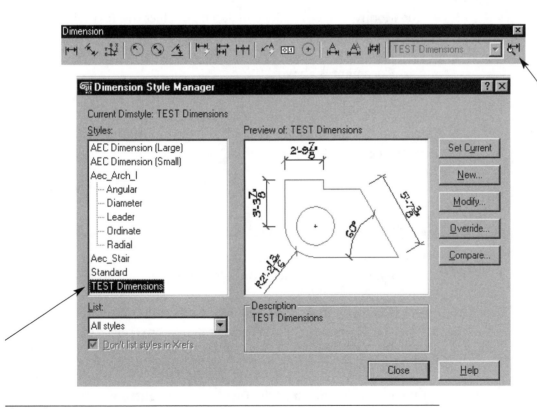

Figure 21–1

Figure 21–2

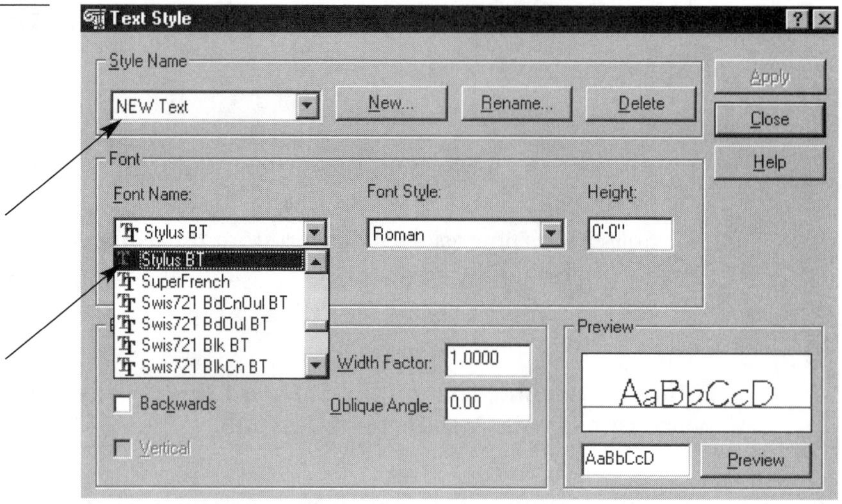

6. Set the NEW Text font to Stylus BT in the Font Name dropdown list and apply and close (Figure 21–2).
7. Again open the Dimension Style Manager.
8. Select Test Dimensions, and press the Modify button.
9. At the Modify Dimension Style dialog box, select the Text tab, and change the following:
   ■ Text style to NEW Text
   ■ Text Placement = Above
   ■ Text Alignment = Aligned with dimension line
10. Select the Fit tab, and set Use overall scale of: to **48**.
11. Select the Primary Units tab, and set the Unit format to Architectural.
12. Press the OK button and close the dialog boxes.

You have now set the AutoCAD dimension style for TEST Dimensions.

Creating AEC Dimension Styles

13. Select the AEC Dimension Styles icon from the AEC Dimension toolbar.
14. At the Style Manager dialog box, select the New Style icon, and rename it to TEST Style.
15. Select TEST Style, RMB, and select Edit from the Contextual menu.
16. At the AEC Dimension Style Properties dialog box, select AEC Dimension Style, select the Display Props tab, and press the Attach Override button.

You have now made the Edit Display Props button active (Figure 21–3).

Figure 21–3

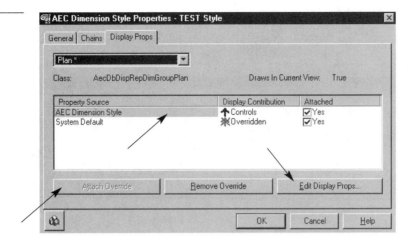

17. Press the <u>Edit display props</u> button to bring up the <u>Entity Properties dialog box</u>.
18. At the Entity Properties dialog box, select the <u>Contents</u> tab.
19. At the Contents tab, select <u>Wall</u> from <u>Apply to</u>, check the <u>Length of Wall</u> checkbox, check the Chain 1 checkbox, and select <u>Wall Length</u> from the dropdown list (Figure 21–4).

   This sets the Automatic AEC dimension string parameters for AEC walls.

20. Select the <u>Other</u> tab, and select <u>TEST Dimensions</u> at the Dimension Style dropdown list. Make sure the checkboxes are unchecked, and then press the <u>OK</u> button (Figure 21–5).

Figure 21–4

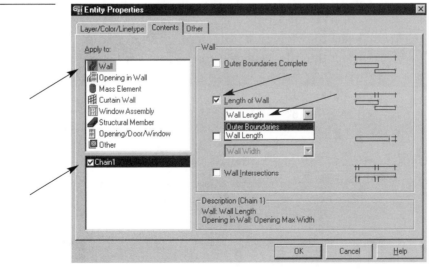

Figure 21–5

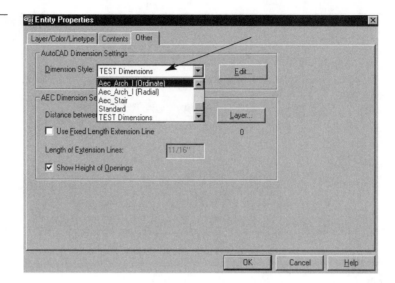

You have now created an AEC Dimension style called **TEST Style** using an AutoCAD dimension style called **TEST Dimensions**. **TEST Dimensions** uses **NEW Text** as its font.

Hands On

Using the New AEC Dimension Style You Have Created

1. Using the Aec arch [imperial-intl].dwt template, select the Work-FLR Viewport tab.
2. Activate the viewport, and change it to **Model** space.
3. Select the **Set Current Display Configuration** icon from the AEC toolbar, and select **Plot**.
4. Select the **Viewport Scale Control**, and set it to **1″=1′**.
5. Select the **Add Wall** icon from the **Walls** toolbar. Set the following settings:

   a. Style = Standard

   b. Width = 6″

   c. Justify = Left

Figure 21–6

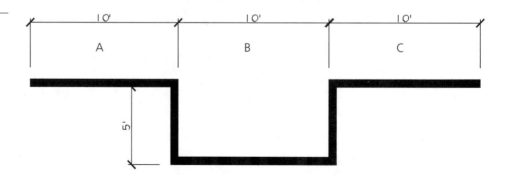

Figure 21–7

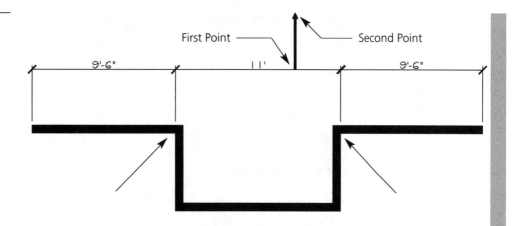

First Point —— | —— Second Point

9'-6"   1 1'   9'-6"

Tip The point that you pick will be where the dimension string is placed.

6. Create the walls shown in Figure 21–6. **Don't include the dimensions shown.**
7. Turn on the <u>ORTHO</u> button.
8. Select the <u>Add AEC Dimension</u> icon from the AEC Dimension toolbar.
9. At the <u>Add AEC Dimension</u> dialog box, select <u>TEXT Style</u> from the dropdown list.
10. Select walls **A** and **C,** and press the space bar or Enter key.
11. Pick the side above the walls when asked to pick a side in the command line.
12. When asked for the second point, pick a point <u>above</u> the first point (Figure 21–7).

   Notice that the AEC Dimensions dimensioned to the outside of the vertical walls.

13. Erase the AEC dimensions that you placed on the walls.
14. Repeat Steps 10 and 11.
15. When asked for the second point, pick a point <u>below</u> the first point (Figure 21–8).

Figure 21–8

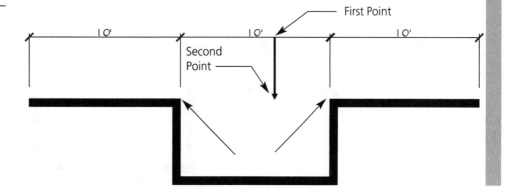

—— First Point

1 0'   1 0'   1 0'

Second
Point ——

Figure 21–9

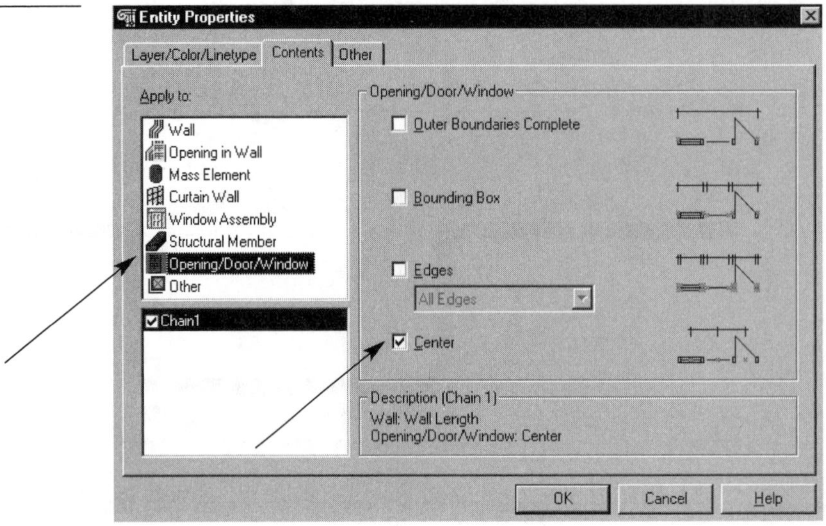

Entity Properties

Layer/Color/Linetype | Contents | Other

Apply to:

Wall
Opening in Wall
Mass Element
Curtain Wall
Window Assembly
Structural Member
Opening/Door/Window
Other

☑ Chain1

Opening/Door/Window

☐ Outer Boundaries Complete

☐ Bounding Box

☐ Edges
   All Edges

☑ Center

Description (Chain 1)
Wall: Wall Length
Opening/Door/Window: Center

OK   Cancel   Help

The direction that you select when asked for the second point determines which side of the wall is used for the logical point. Try this for the 5-ft walls.

Dimensioning Doors and Windows

16. Select the AEC Dimension Styles from the AEC Dimension toolbar again.

17. Again select Edit for TEST Style, and press the Edit Display Props button.

18. Select the Contents tab, and select Opening/Door/Window from the Apply to: list.

19. Check only the Center checkbox.

20. Make sure all the other AEC objects (except the Wall that you previously set) have their checkboxes unchecked (Figure 21–9).

21. Select wall B (Figure 21–6), RMB, and select Insert | Window from the Contextual menu.

22. Make sure to check the Automatic Offset/Center checkbox, and insert a Standard 3-ft-wide, 5-ft-high window in the center of the wall.

23. Select the Add AEC Dimension icon from the AEC Dimension toolbar, and select the TEST Style again.

24. Select wall A, the window, and wall C, and place a dimension point. Then place a second point below it. The result should look like Figure 21–10.

Figure 21–10

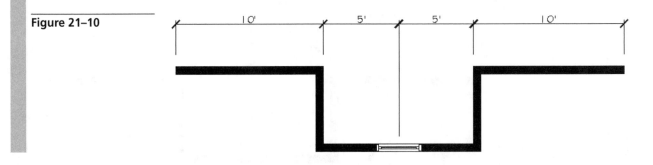

Figure 21-11

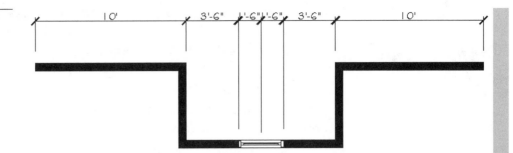

25. Select the dimension string, RMB, and select <u>Edit AEC Dimension Style</u> from the Contextual menu.

26. Go back to the <u>Contents</u> tab for <u>Opening/Door/Window</u>, and check the Bounding Box checkbox in addition to the previously checked Center checkbox. Press OK, and close the dialog boxes.

The Window is now dimensioned by its center and outer boundary (Figure 21-11).

27. Move the window 24 in. to the left. (Use the move command, or activate the window's grips.)

28. Select wall <u>B</u>, RMB, and again select <u>Insert | Window</u> from the Contextual menu.

29. At the <u>Add Windows</u> dialog box, set the <u>Automatic Offset/Center</u> to 18 in. and pick a spot near the right side of wall B.

You should now have two windows centered in wall B.

30. Select the <u>Attach Objects</u> icon from the <u>AEC Dimension</u> toolbar and select the dimension string; then press the space bar or Enter key.

31. When asked at the command line to Select building elements, select the new window, and press the space bar or Enter key.

You have now added a new AEC object to your dimension string (Figure 21-12).

Explore the other Display Props for Dimension Styles. Save this exercise.

Sometimes you will want to create an AEC dimension manually. Perhaps, you want to dimension somewhere else than the built-in logical points.

Figure 21-12

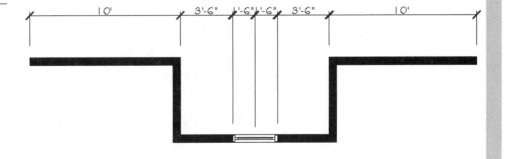

Adding a Manual AEC Dimension

Hands On

1. Lock your viewport (MVIEW | Lock).
2. Be sure the <u>MODEL</u> button is activated.
3. Zoom in close to the two windows.
4. Type <u>ddptype</u> at the command line, and press the space bar or Enter key.
5. At the <u>Point Style</u> dialog box, select the **X** (Figure 21–13).
6. Type <u>dimpointmode</u> at the command line, and press the space bar or Enter key.
7. Type **T** at the command line, and press the space bar or Enter key.

This sets the dimension points to transformable. Transformable dimension points move and are updated with the object, static points stay in place and do not move.

8. Set the Intersection Object Snap.
9. Select the <u>Add Manual AEC Dimension</u> icon from the <u>AEC Dimension</u> menu.
10. Pick the two corners of the two window jambs, and press the space bar or Enter key.
11. Pick a point to place the dimension string, and then pick a second point to complete the command (Figure 21–14).

Figure 21–13

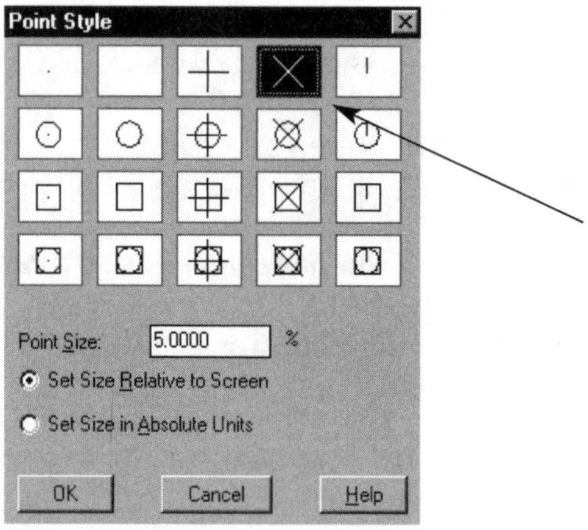

Figure 21–14

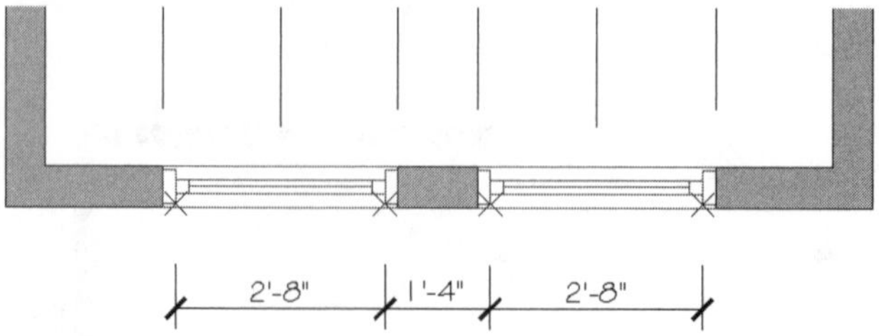

Figure 21–15

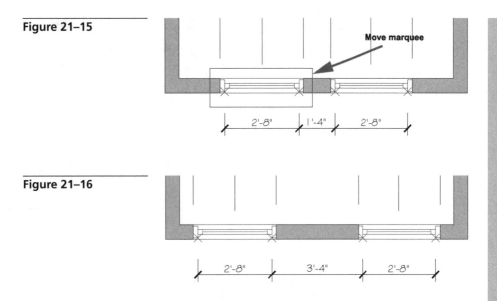

Figure 21–16

12. Select the <u>Move</u> icon from the <u>Modify</u> toolbar, and select the left window with a window marquee (Figure 21–15). Move it to the left 1'-0". Repeat with the right window (Figure 21–16).

   You must move the points with the window to maintain the associative dimensions. Repeat Steps 7–12, but select S (Static) when prompted for dimpointmode points. Note that the dimensions don't move.

Adjusting the Dimension Text

13. Select the dimension string shown in Figure 21–16, RMB, and select <u>Activate Text Grips</u> from the Contextual menu.
14. Select the dimension string again to activate its grips.
15. Activate the 3'-4" dimension, and move it to a new location (Figure 21–17).
16. **Save this exercise.**

Figure 21–17

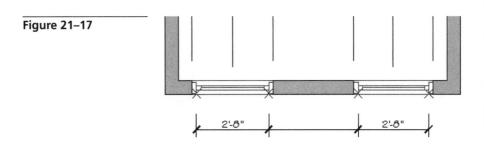

Figure 21–18

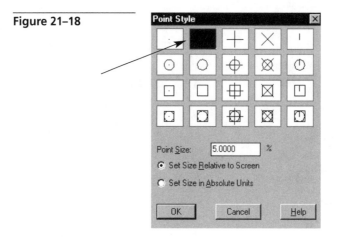

17. The point style you set in Step 5 will cause the points to show as an **X** when you plot. To stop this, type ddptype again, and change the point style to none (Figure 21–18).

If you need to remove an AEC object from an AEC Dimension Group (dimension string), Architectural Desktop 3 has a method.

Detaching Objects

Hands On

1. Zoom Extents (because the viewport is locked, the Paper Space view will Zoom Extents).
2. Select the <u>Detach Objects</u> icon from the <u>AEC Dimension</u> toolbar.
3. Select the top <u>AEC Dimension Group</u> (dimension string), and press the space bar or Enter key (Figure 21–19).
4. Select the left window object, and press the space bar or Enter key (Figure 21–20).

Figure 21–19

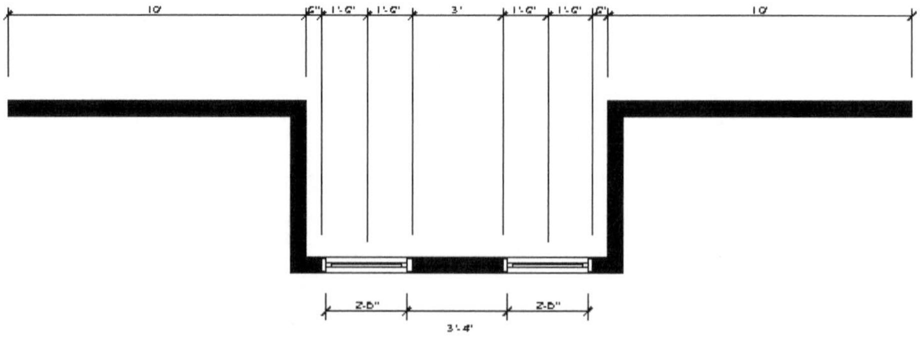

Figure 21–20

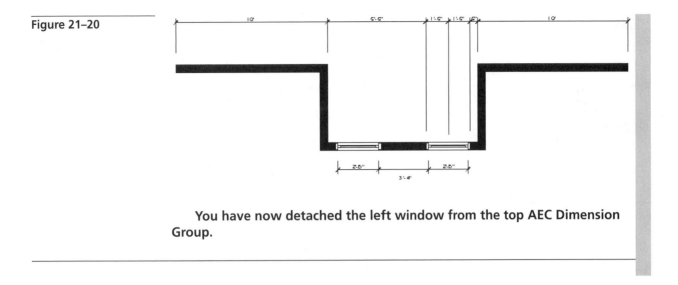

You have now detached the left window from the top AEC Dimension Group.

The AEC Dimension Wizard

Although you can set the AEC Dimension display manually as shown at the beginning of this section, Autodesk Architectural Desktop 3 has provided a Wizard to aid you in setting the display.

Selecting the AEC Dimension Wizard icon from the AEC Dimension toolbar activates the following dialog boxes in Figures 21–21, 21–22, 21–23, and 21–24.

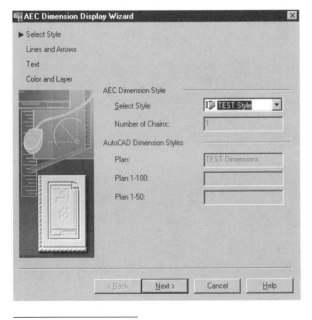

Figure 21–21

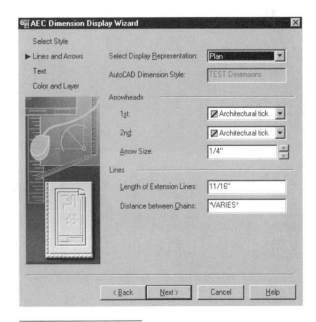

Figure 21–22

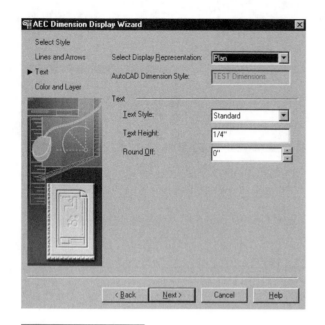

Figure 21–23

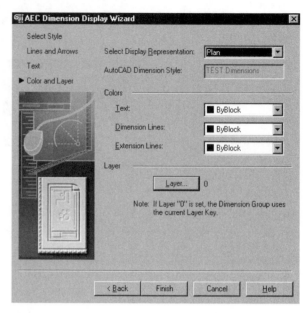

Figure 21–24

Section **22** | Schedule Tags, Schedule Data, and Schedule Tables

When you finish this section, you should be able to do the following:

✔ Place and control schedule tags.
✔ Understand Property Set Definitions.
✔ Attach and edit Schedule Tables and Schedule Data.

You can input Schedule Tags, Data, and Tables and modify them by selecting the appropriate icon from one of the Schedule toolbars.

You can also input Schedule Tags, Data, and Tables and modified them by selecting the appropriate selection from one of the Schedule menus. You can also get the Schedule menus by RMB in any viewport.

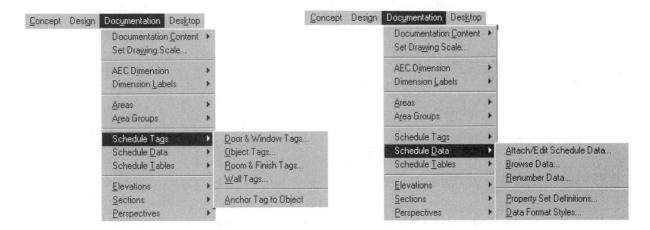

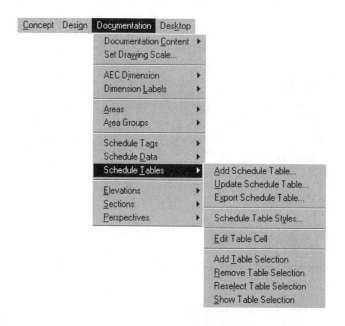

Schedule Tags

In order to compile data into a schedule, you must tag objects.

Autodesk Architectural Desktop 3 contains tags for the following objects:

- Doors
- Windows
- Room number
- Room finish
- Spaces
- Beams, braces, and columns
- Equipment
- Furniture
- Walls

Hands On

Use the Aec arch [imperial-intl].dwt template.

1. Activate the Walls, Viewports, and Schedule-Imperial toolbars, and place them in a convenient place.
2. Select the Work -FLR Layout tab.
3. Select Documentation | Set Drawing Scale from the main toolbar.
4. Select the Scale tab. Set the Drawing Scale to ¹/₂"= 1'-0" and the Annotation Plot Size to 1/8".
5. Activate the Top Viewport and using the Viewports toolbar, set the viewport scale to ¹/₂" = 1'-0".

Figure 22–1

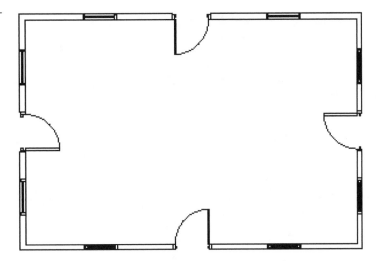

6. Using the <u>Add Wall</u> icon, create a 30'-0"x 20'-0" enclosure. Make the walls <u>Standard</u> 6 in. wide 8 ft high.

7. Select a wall, RMB, and select <u>Insert | Door</u> from the Contextual menu.

8. Place a 3'-0" <u>Standard</u> door in each wall.

9. Repeat Steps 7 and 8, placing 3-ft x 5-ft windows along side the doors (Figure 22–1).

10. Select the <u>Door and Window Tags</u> icon from the <u>Schedule-Imperial</u> toolbar.

11. When the <u>Design Center</u> window appears, select the Door Tag symbol, RMB, and select <u>Insert</u> from the Contextual menu.

12. Select one of the doors, and then click below the door.

13. The <u>Edit Schedule Data</u> dialog box will now appear, and you can add data if you wish (Figure 22–2).

Figure 22–2

Edit Schedule Data

| Alphabetical | Categorized |

⊟ **DoorObjects**
Firerating	
Glazing	--
KeySideRoomNumber	--
Number	001
Remarks	--
SetNumber	--

Add...   Remove...   OK   Cancel   Help

Figure 22–3

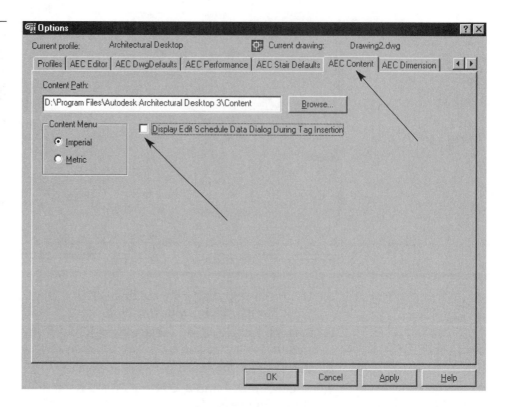

14. When you are finished, press the OK button to place the schedule tag.

If you do not need the Edit Schedule Data dialog box, do the following to turn it off:

a. RMB in the viewport, and select <u>Options</u> from the Contextual menu.

b. Select <u>AEC Content</u> from the Options dialog box.

c. Uncheck the <u>Display Edit Schedule Data Dialog During Tag Insertion</u> checkbox (Figure 22–3).

15. Zoom close to the doors.

Notice that they are automatically numbered incrementally. To change the settings of the tag, do the following:

a. Select <u>Documentation | Schedule Data | Property Set Definitions</u> from the Main toolbar to bring up the <u>Style Manager</u> dialog box.

b. At the Style Manager dialog box, select <u>Door Objects</u>, RMB, and select <u>Edit</u> from the Contextual menu.

<u>Property Set Definitions</u> are groups of properties for particular objects that you want to manage in schedules. They can be automatic, deriving their values from the properties of objects, or user-defined.

c. At the <u>Property Set Definition Properties</u> dialog box, select <u>Number</u>.

Figure 22–4

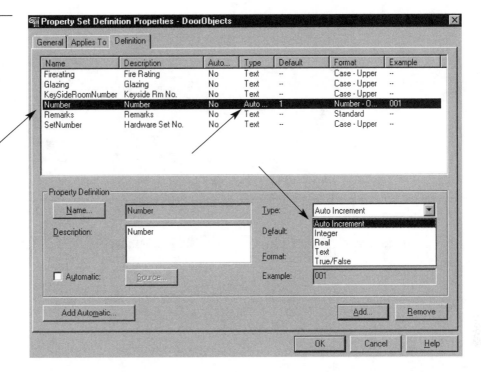

In the Property Definition, you can now set the <u>Type</u>. If you want to automatically increment the objects number system, select <u>Auto Increment</u>, and set the start number as the <u>Default</u>. The tags can also be created or modified to display the information defined in the property definition (Figure 22–4).

16. Place window tags for the windows. If the tags don't increment automatically, change their setting in the Property Definition Set for window objects. **Save this exercise.**

Schedules

Hands On

1. Using the previous exercise, select the <u>Add Schedule Table</u> icon from the <u>Schedule-Imperial</u> dialog box to bring up the <u>Add Schedule</u> dialog box.

2. At the <u>Add Schedule</u> dialog box, select <u>Door Schedule</u> from the <u>Schedule Table Style</u> dropdown list. Make sure all the checkboxes are checked (Figure 22–5).

3. Select all the doors (this can be done with a marquee).

4. Click in a spot on the page to start the upper-left corner of the schedule.

Figure 22–5

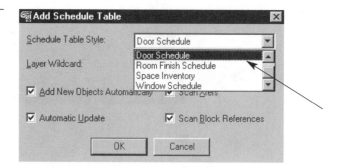

DOOR AND FRAME SCHEDULE

MARK	SIZE WD	SIZE HGT	THK	MATL	GLAZING	LOUVER WD	LOUVER HGT	MATL	EL	DETAIL HEAD	DETAIL JAMB	DETAIL SILL	FIRE RATING LABEL	SET NO	HARDWARE KEYSIDE RM NO	NOTES
001	3'-0"	6'-8"	2"	––	––	0"	0"	––	––	––	––	––	––	––	––	––
002	3'-0"	6'-8"	2"	––	––	0"	0"	––	––	––	––	––	––	––	––	––
003	3'-0"	6'-8"	2"	––	––	0"	0"	––	––	––	––	––	––	––	––	––
004	3'-0"	6'-8"	2"	––	––	0"	0"	––	––	––	––	––	––	––	––	––

WINDOW SCHEDULE

MARK	WIDTH	HEIGHT	TYPE	MATERIAL	NOTES
1	3'-0"	5'-0"	––	––	––
2	3'-0"	5'-0"	––	––	––
3	3'-0"	5'-0"	––	––	––
4	3'-0"	5'-0"	––	––	––
5	3'-0"	5'-0"	––	––	––
6	3'-0"	5'-0"	––	––	––
7	3'-0"	5'-0"	––	––	––
8	3'-0"	5'-0"	––	––	––

Figure 22–6

5. Press the space bar or Enter key when requested for the lower-right corner.

Pressing the Enter key (Architectural Desktop calls it Return in the command line) causes the schedule to automatically be scaled at the size set by the Set Drawing Scale command you set earlier.

6. Repeat Steps 1–5 for the Window Schedule (Figure 22–6).

Creating Custom Schedules

Hands On

The drawing

1. Activate the Viewports and Schedule-Imperial toolbars, and place them in a convenient place.
2. Select the Work-FLR Layout tab.
3. Select Documentation | Set Drawing Scale from the Main toolbar.
4. Select the Scale tab. Set the Drawing Scale to $1/2$"= 1'-0" and the Annotation Plot Size to 1/8".

5. Activate the Top viewport; using the Viewports toolbar, set the viewport scale to ½" = 1'-0".

6. Place three circles in the drawing with radii of 2 ft, 4 ft, and 6 ft, respectively.

You are going to create a schedule that records information about the circles in your drawing.

In order to make a schedule, you will need to create a Property Set Definition.

The Property Set Definition

7. Select Documentation | Schedule Data | Property Set Definitions from the Main toolbar.

8. At the Style Manager dialog box, select the New Style icon from the toolbar and name it Circle.

9. Select Circle, RMB, and select Edit from the Contextual menu.

10. At the Property Set Definition Properties dialog box, select the Applies To tab.

This dialog box contains all the objects from which schedules can be made. After this exercise, be sure to explore it.

11. Select the Entities radio button; then select the Clear All button at the lower left of the dialog box. After this is done, check the Circle checkbox (Figure 22–7).

12. In the same dialog box, select the Definition tab.

13. Press the Add button at the lower right side of the dialog box, and the New Property dialog box will appear.

Figure 22–7

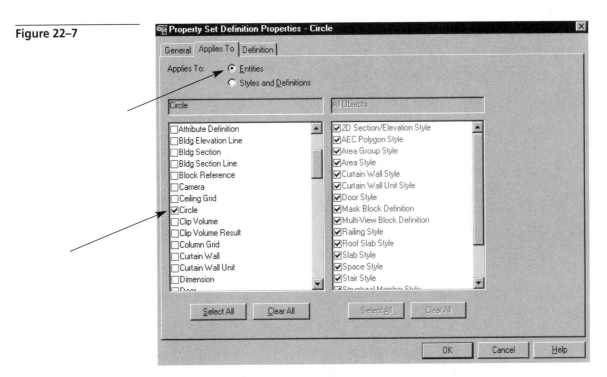

Figure 22-8

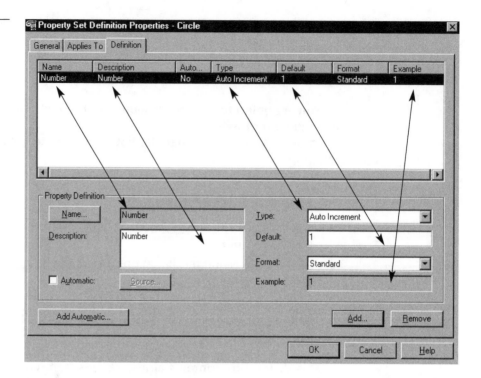

14. In the New Property dialog box, enter the word <u>Number</u> in the <u>Name</u> section, and press the <u>OK</u> button.

This brings up the Property Set Definition Properties dialog box. In Step 15 of the previous exercise you found that this dialog box is where you control the automatic increments. In this exercise you are creating a new Property Set Definition, and you want the schedule to automatically number each circle (Figure 22-8).

15. Set the Type to <u>Auto Increment</u> and Default to <u>1</u>. This will cause the property to be assigned automatically to an object and automatically increase in value as new objects are added.

16. Select <u>Add</u> again.

17. At the <u>New Property</u> dialog box, type and name <u>Radius</u>.

18. Check the <u>Automatic</u> checkbox, and select the <u>Source</u> button.

The Automatic Property Source dialog box appears. It shows all the properties of a circle (Figure 22-9).

19. At the <u>Automatic Property Source</u> dialog box, check the <u>Radius</u> checkbox, and press the <u>OK</u> button.

20. Repeat Steps 16 and 17, adding two more properties named <u>Circumference</u> and <u>Area</u>, respectively.

21. Again check the <u>Automatic</u> checkbox for each, and check the <u>Circumference</u> and <u>Area</u> checkboxes for their respective <u>Property Set Definition properties</u>.

22. Press the OK button until you exit all the dialog boxes.

You have now defined all the properties of circles that you wish to be recorded in a schedule (Figure 22-10).

Figure 22–9

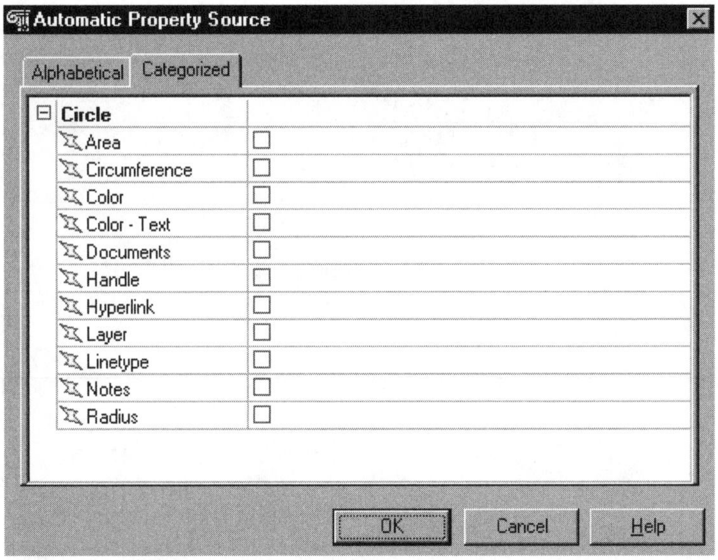

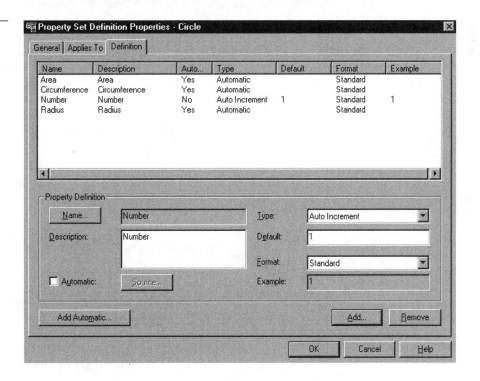

Figure 22–10

The Table Style

23. Select the Schedule Table Styles icon from the <u>Schedule-Imperial</u> tool-bar to bring up the <u>Style Manager</u> dialog box.

24. At the Style Manager dialog box, RMB in the right side of the dialog box and select <u>New</u> from the Contextual menu.

25. Enter the name <u>Circle Schedule</u>, and press the <u>Apply</u> button.

26. Select the <u>Circle Schedule</u> style, RMB, and select <u>Edit</u> from the Contex-tual menu to bring up the <u>Schedule Table Style Properties</u> dialog box.

27. At the Schedule Table Style Properties dialog box, select the <u>Applies To</u> tab.

Figure 22–11

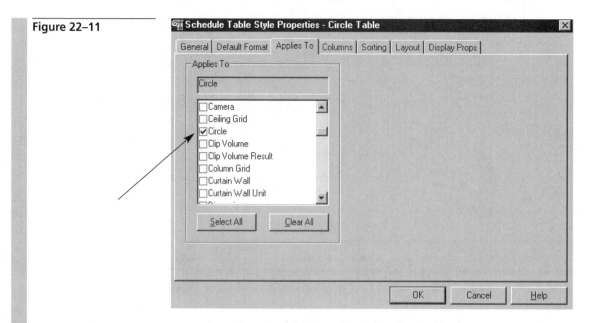

28.   Press the <u>Select All</u> button to clear the list, and then check the <u>Circle</u> checkbox.

This tells the program that the schedule applies to circles and their properties (Figure 22–11).

29.   Next, select the <u>Columns</u> tab and press the <u>Add Column</u> button at the lower left.

You should now see the Property Definition Set you created in Steps 7–22 (Figure 22–12).

30.   At the <u>Add Column</u> dialog box, select the <u>Number</u> property; then press the <u>OK</u> button to return to the <u>Schedule Table Style Properties</u> dialog box.

Figure 22–12

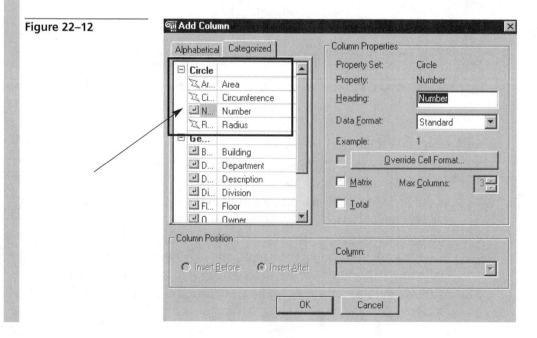

Figure 22–13

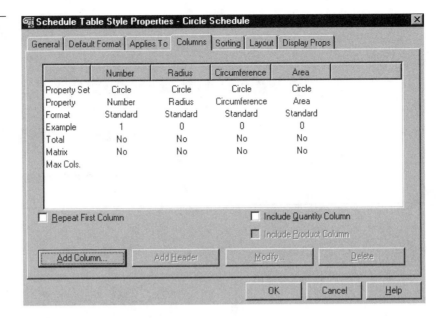

31. At the Schedule Table Style Properties dialog box, again press the <u>Add Column button</u>.

32. Repeat Steps 30 and 31, adding <u>Radius</u>, <u>Circumference</u>, and <u>Area</u> columns (Figure 22–13).

33. At the <u>Schedule Table Style Properties</u> dialog box, hold down the <u>CTRL key</u> and select the Radius and Circumference3 headers.

34. Press the <u>Add Header</u> button at the bottom of the Schedule Table Style Properties dialog box.

35. Enter a header name of <u>CIRCLE DATA</u> (Figure 22–14).

36. Change to the <u>Sorting</u> tab in the Schedule Table Style Properties dialog box.

37. In the Sorting tab, press the <u>Add button</u> at the top left.

Figure 22–14

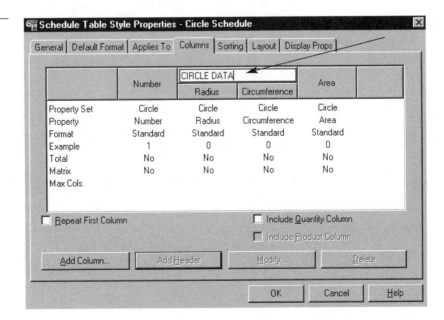

Figure 22–15

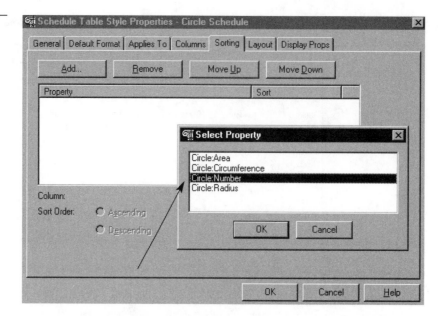

Figure 22–16

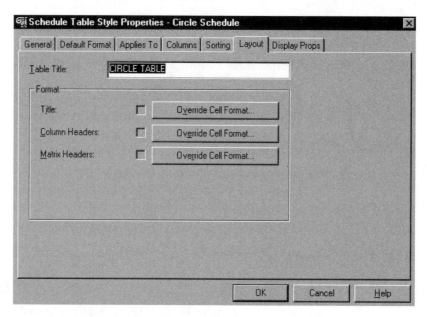

38. At the <u>Select Property</u> dialog box, select <u>Circle : Number</u> and press the <u>OK</u> button (Figure 22–15).

39. Select the <u>Layout</u> tab in the <u>Schedule Table Style Properties</u> dialog box.

40. Enter a Table Title of <u>CIRCLE TABLE</u>, and press the <u>OK</u> until you are out of all dialog boxes (Figure 22–16).

You have now created the Table Style and named the columns and title.

Using the Table

41. Return to your drawing of the three circles (Figure 22–17).

42. Select the <u>Add Schedule Table</u> icon from the <u>Schedule-Imperial</u> toolbar.

Figure 22–17

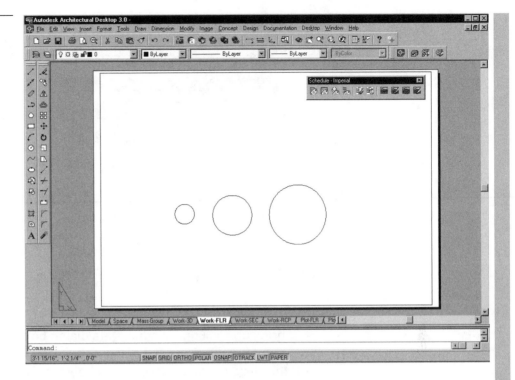

43. At the <u>Add Schedule Table</u> dialog box, select the <u>Circle Schedule</u> from the <u>Schedule Table Style</u> dropdown list, and press the <u>OK</u> button (Figure 22–18).

44. Select all the circles in your drawing, and press the space bar or Enter key.

45. Place the upper-left corner of the table, and press the space bar or Enter key.

46. Zoom in close to the schedule. Notice that the cells contain question marks (Figure 22–19). **This is because the data have not been attached.**

47. Select the <u>Attach/Edit Schedule Data</u> icon from the <u>Schedule-Imperial</u> toolbar.

 Tip

Remember, pressing the Enter key after placing the upper-left corner of a schedule table automatically places the table according to your annotation scale settings.

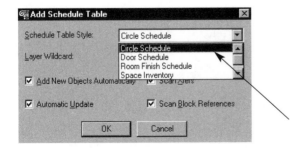

Figure 22–18

CIRCLE TABLE			
Number	CIRCLE DATA		Area
	Radius	Circumference	
?	?	?	?
?	?	?	?
?	?	?	?

Figure 22–19

Figure 22–20

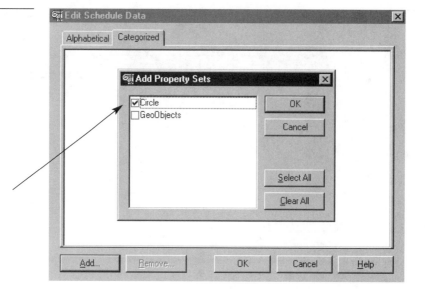

48. Select the circles in your drawing and press the space bar or Enter key to bring up the <u>Edit Schedule Data</u> dialog box.

49. At the Edit Schedule Data dialog box, press the <u>Add</u> button and check the <u>Circle</u> checkbox. Press the OK button, and close the dialog boxes (Figure 22–20).

     If you now check the table, it will contain information (Figure 22–21).

50. Select one of the circles, and using grips change its size.

     Notice that the schedule automatically updates to reflect the change in circle size.

51. Add some more circles.

     Notice that they automatically show up in the table, but their sizes are question marks.

52. Repeat Steps 47–49 to add the data to the table.

     Now changing any circle size or removing any circle will automatically change in the table.
     As mentioned at the beginning of this section, you can create tables to record many things in your drawing. You can even record XREF data from several drawings.

Figure 22–21

Number	CIRCLE TABLE		
	CIRCLE DATA		Area
	Radius	Circumference	
1	72	452.389	113.097
2	48	301.593	50.265
3	24	150.796	12.566

Section

23

Elevations

When you finish this section, you should be able to do the following:

✔ Create elevations of your projects.
✔ Update your elevations to reflect changes in your projects.
✔ Edit and merge elevation linework.

You can create elevations in a drawing by selecting the <u>Add Elevation Line</u> icon from the <u>Elevations</u> toolbar.

You can also create elevations in a drawing by selecting the <u>Documentation |
Elevations | Add Elevation Line</u> menu from the <u>Main</u> toolbar.

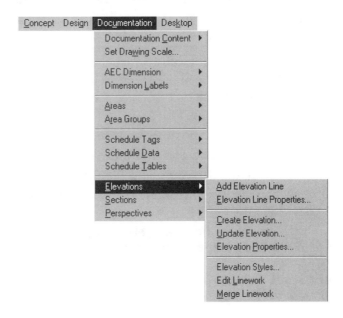

Figure 23–1

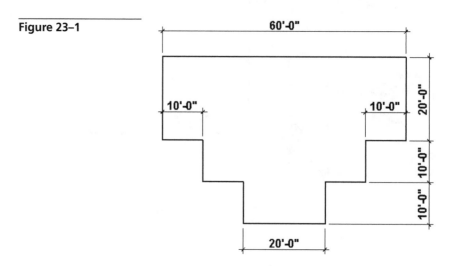

For this section, create a simple three-story building using the footprint shown in Figure 23–1.

Creating the Building

Hands On

1. Activate the Walls and Reference toolbars, and place them in a convenient spot.
2. Using the Aec arch [imperial-intl].dwt template, select the Work-FLR Layout tab.
3. Activate the Top View, and create the outline shown in Figure 23–1.
4. Select the Convert to Walls icon from the Walls toolbar, and select the outline.
5. Type **Y** at the command line to erase the geometry.
6. At the Wall Properties dialog box, select a standard wall, and set its dimensions to the following:
   - Wall Width = 8"
   - Base Height = 10'-0"
   - Justify = Baseline
7. Save the drawing as Floor 1.
8. Save the drawing two more times as Floor 2 and 3.
9. Start a new drawing and save it as Composite.
10. Open up all the drawings, and Tile them horizontally (Figure 23–2).
11. Activate the complete drawing and select the External Reference icon from the Reference toolbar.
12. Attach the three floors at Z elevation of 0 ft for floor 1, 10 ft for floor 2, and 20 ft for floor 3 (Figure 23–3).

You will get the AutoCAD message shown in Figure 23–4; just keep going and press the OK button.

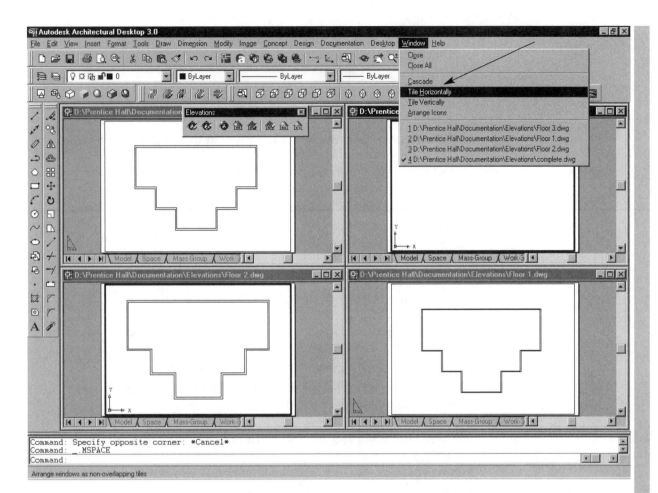

Figure 23–2

Figure 23–3

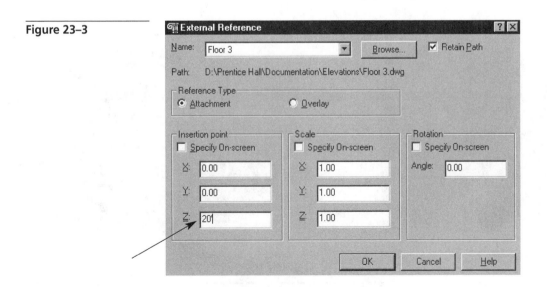

Figure 23–4

You should now have the building shown in the <u>composite</u> drawing.

13. Select the <u>Add Roof</u> icon from the <u>Roof-Roof Slabs</u> toolbar, and add a roof to the building.

14. Set the roof to the following:
    - Shape = SingleSlope
    - Plate height = 30'-0"
    - Rise = 6"

You have now created the building in Figure 23–5.

15. Select different walls in each floor, RMB, and insert windows and a door.

16. Save all your drawings except the <u>composite</u> drawing.

17. Activate the <u>composite</u> drawing and select the <u>External Reference</u> icon from the Reference toolbar.

18. In the Xref Manager dialog, select all the Floors, press the Reload button, and then press the OK button to close the dialog box.

Again, you will get the AutoCAD message shown in Figure 23–4; again disregard it and press the OK button.

You will now have a complete three-story building with windows, curtain wall, and revolving door (Figure 23–6). **Save this exercise.**

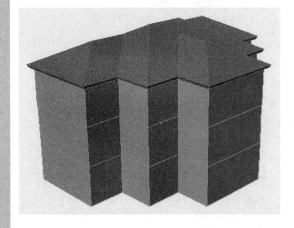

Figure 23–5

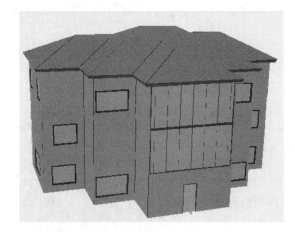

Figure 23–6

Making the Elevation

Hands On

1. Activate the <u>Elevations</u> toolbar, and place it in a convenient spot.
2. Using the previous exercise, select the <u>composite</u> drawing.
3. Select the <u>Work-FLR</u> tab, and activate the Top View.
4. Select the <u>MODEL</u> button. Then pan the building to the left until it takes up a little less than half the page and looks like Figure 23–7.
5. Select the <u>MODEL</u> button again, and toggle it to PAPER.
6. Select the Viewport border, RMB, and select <u>Display Locked | Yes</u> from the Contextual menu.
7. Press the <u>PAPER</u> button and toggle it back to <u>MODEL</u>.
8. Select the <u>Add Elevation Line</u> icon from the <u>Elevations</u> toolbar, and place an elevation line starting at the lower left of the building and ending at the lower right.

 Tip | Model button referes to the Model Space/Paper Space toggle, not the Model tab.

 Tip | Locking the viewport allows you to zoom in Model Space without changing the location of an object in relation to Paper Space.

Figure 23–7

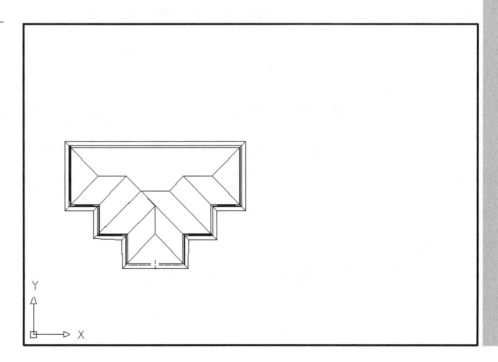

Figure 23–8

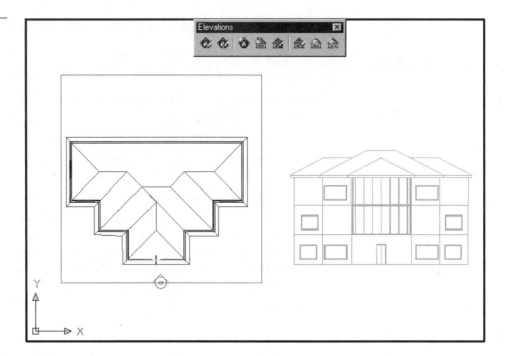

9. Select the elevation line, RMB, and select Elevation Line Properties from the Contextual menu. Make sure the Use Model Extents for Height checkbox is checked and then press the OK button.

10. Again select the elevation line; RMB and this time select Generate Elevation from the Contextual menu.

11. At the Generate Section/Elevation dialog box, select the 2D Section/Elevation Object with Hidden Line Removal radio button, and select the Pick Point button.

12. Pick a point to the right of the building floor plan show in Figure 23–7.

13. When the Generate Section/Elevation dialog box reappears, select the Select Objects button, and marquee the floor plan with a window or type All at the command line; press the space.

14. When the Generate Section/Elevation dialog box reappears again, press the OK button. **Save this exercise, and close all the drawings.**

The Elevation of the building will now appear (Figure 23–8).

Modifying the Elevation

Hands On

1. Open drawings Floor 1, Floor 2, Floor 3, and composite. Tile them horizontally.

2. Activate the Floor 1 drawing, and add a 3-ft × 5-ft-high window on either side of the entrance door.

Figure 23–9

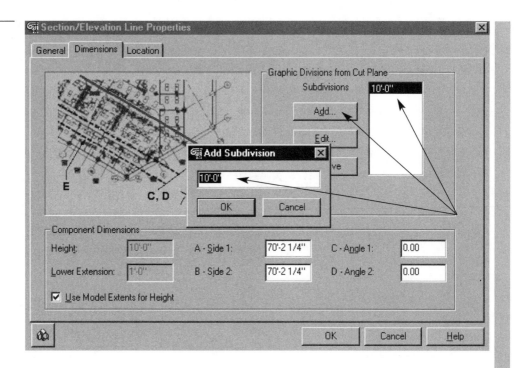

3.   Save the Floor 1 drawing.

4.   Activate the composite drawing.

5.   Select the <u>External Reference</u> icon from the <u>Reference</u> toolbar.

6.   At the <u>Xref Manager</u> dialog box, select Floor 1; then press the <u>Reload</u> button, and press the OK button. At the AutoCAD Message, press the <u>OK</u> button.

   You have now saved the Floor 1 drawing with the changes and Reloaded the composite drawing.

7.   In the <u>composite</u> drawing, select the elevation, RMB, and select <u>Update</u> from the Contextual menu.

   The Elevation now reflects the changes made in the floor plan.

8.   Select the elevation line, RMB, and select <u>Elevation Line Properties</u> from the Contextual menu.

9.   At the <u>Section/Elevation Line Properties</u> dialog box, press the <u>Add</u> button, and add a 10'-0" subdivision (Figure 23–9).

   <u>You have now created Subdivision 1.</u>

10.   Activate the <u>composite</u> drawing, select the elevation, RMB, and select <u>Edit 2D Section/Elevation Style</u> from the Contextual menu.

Tip

Once you have a subdivision, you can select the elevation and move the subdivision with grips (Figure 23–10).

Figure 23–10

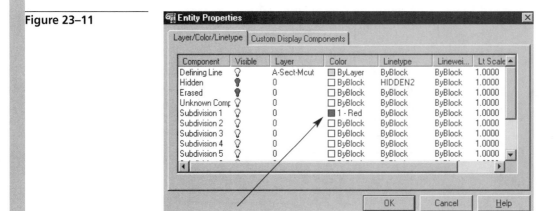

11. At the <u>2D Section/Elevation Styles</u> dialog box, select the Display Props tab, attach an override to the <u>2D Section/Elevation Style</u>, and then press the <u>Edit Display Props</u> button.

12. At the Entity Properties dialog box, select the <u>Layer/Color/Linetype</u> tab.

13. Change the <u>Subdivision 1</u> color to <u>red</u>, select OK, and close all the dialog boxes.

14. Select the elevation, RMB, and select <u>Update</u> from the Contextual menu.

You have now changed subdivision 1 to red color. Anything between the Defining line and Subdivision 1 will be red in the elevation. You can also set the line width to be different in a subdivision (Figures 23–11 and 23–12).

15. Select the <u>elevation line</u>, RMB, and add two more subdivisions.

Figure 23–11

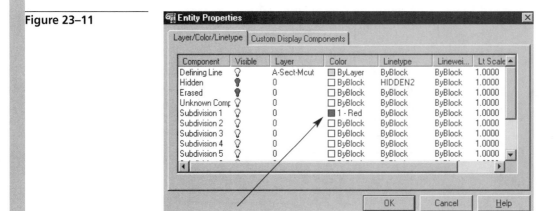

Figure 23-12

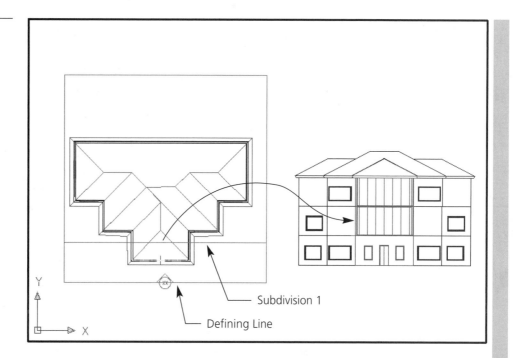

Subdivision 1

Defining Line

16. Select the elevation, RMB, and again select <u>Edit 2D Section/Elevation Style</u> from the Contextual menu.

17. Change the <u>Subdivision 2</u> color to <u>green</u> and <u>Subdivision 3</u> to <u>black</u>. Change the lineweight of Subdivision 3 to 2.00 mm; then select OK and close all the dialog boxes.

18. Select the elevation line to activate it, and using the grips (be sure your object snap is turned off), move the subdivisions to look like Figure 23–13.

Figure 23-13

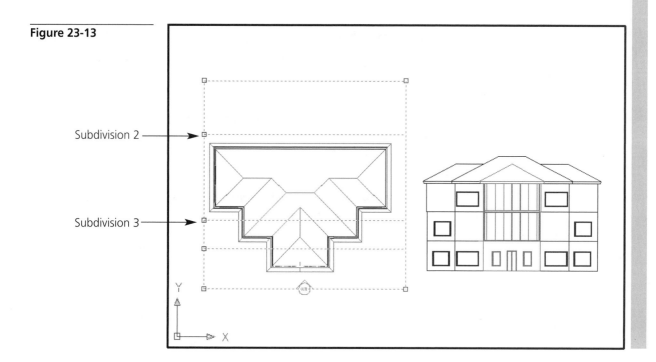

Subdivision 2

Subdivision 3

Figure 23–14

19. Select the elevation, RMB, and select <u>Update</u> from the Contextual menu. (Make sure the <u>LTW</u> button at the bottom of the screen is active.)

Viewing Figure 23–14, notice that the back outline of the building is black with a 2.00-mm outline. This is because everything between Subdivision 2 and 3 will have the attributes of Subdivision 3. Notice that there is a problem at the roof. Because the roof is pitched, it crosses both Subdivisions 2 and 3. You might also want the base to be all one color. To fix these problems, you will use the new <u>Edit Linework</u> command.

Edit Linework

Hands On

1. Select the <u>Edit Linework</u> icon from the <u>Elevations</u> toolbar, and select the lines shown in Figure 23–14.
2. Press the <u>F2</u> key on the keyboard.
3. In the AutoCAD Text Window that appears, choose number <u>3</u> for <u>Erased Vectors</u>, and enter it on the command line in the Text Window. Press the space bar or Enter key twice to end the command (Figures 23–15 and 23–16).

Now that the elevation has missing lines, use Merge Linework to merge AutoCAD entities with the elevation.

Figure 23–15

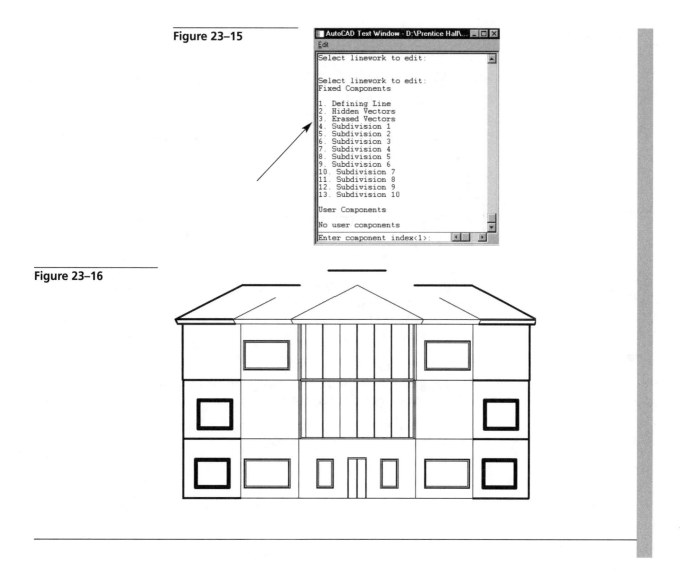

Figure 23–16

Merge Linework

Hands On

1. Using the previous exercise, add AutoCAD lines at the missing locations shown in Figure 23–16.
2. Select the Merge Linework icon from the Elevations toolbar, and select the lines placed in the previous step.
3. Select the elevation, and then select the lines at the roof outline.
4. Again, press the F2 key on the keyboard.

Figure 23–17

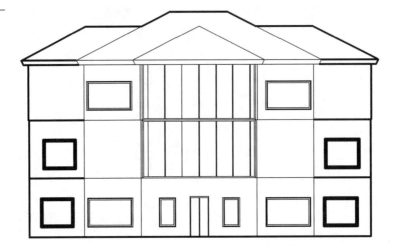

5. In the AutoCAD Text Window that appears, choose number <u>6</u> for <u>Subdivision 3</u>, and enter it on the command line in the Text Window. Press the space bar or Enter key twice to end the command. Repeat this process until you have the line colors and weight you desire (Figure 23–17).

    By using these methods, you have complete control of your elevations, their colors, and their line weights.

Section 24

Perspectives

When you finish this section, you should be able to do the following:

✔ Create and adjust perspectives of your projects.
✔ Create AVI flyby movies of your projects.

You can create perspectives in a drawing by selecting the <u>Add Camera</u> icon from the <u>Perspectives</u> toolbar.

You can also create perspectives in a drawing by selecting the <u>Documentation | Perspectives | Add Camera</u> menu from the <u>Main</u> toolbar.

Autodesk Architectural Desktop has the capability to create architectural flyby movies. A very popular movie format is the AVI. The Windows Media Player that is built into Windows 95-2000 and Windows NT can easily read this format. AVIs are easily transmitted over the Internet.

How to Create a Movie

Hands On

Create the Scene

1. Activate the Mass Elements and Perspective toolbars, and place them in a convenient spot.
2. Using the Aec arch [imperial-intl].dwt template, select the <u>Work-3D</u> Layout tab.
3. Select the <u>Box</u> icon from the <u>Mass Elements</u> toolbar, and create two Mass Elements 30 ft × 30 ft × 80 ft high and 30 ft × 30 ft × 30 ft high, respectively.
4. Create another Mass Element 20 ft × 20 ft × 20 ft high, and make a copy of it.
5. Finally, create a 20-ft × 20-ft × 12-ft-high Pyramid Mass Element, and make a copy of it.
6. Using the previous Mass Elements, create the buildings shown in Figure 24–1.
7. Array both buildings three times and arrange them as shown in Figure 24–2.

Setting Up the Camera

8. Zoom out in the Top View viewport.
9. Select the <u>Circle</u> icon from the <u>Draw</u> toolbar, and create a circle that circumvents all the buildings.
10. Select the circle, RMB, and select Properties from the Contextual menu.

Figure 24–1

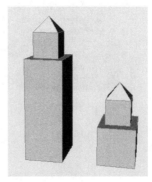

Figure 24–2

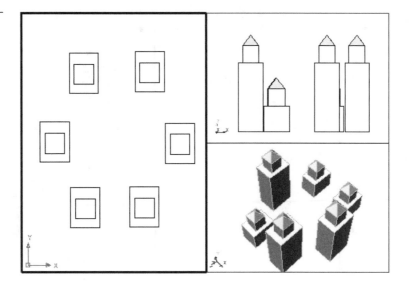

Figure 24–3

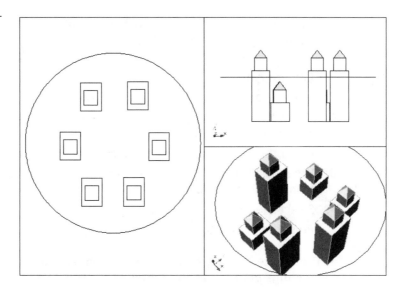

11. Set the Center Z to 70 ft. This will place the circle at an elevation of 70 ft (Figure 24–3).

The circle will become the path that the camera will follow.

12. Select <u>Add Camera</u> from the <u>Perspectives</u> toolbar, and place a camera in the Top View viewport.

13. When the command line asks for an <u>Insertion point</u>, just click anywhere in the viewport.

14. When the command line next asks for a <u>Target point</u>, just click anywhere in the viewport.

You have now placed a camera in the scene (Figure 24–4).

Figure 24–4

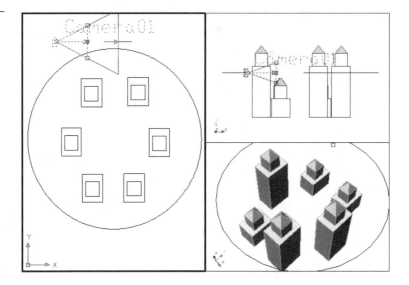

Making the Movie

15. Activate the Top View viewport, and select the <u>Create Video</u> icon from the <u>Perspectives</u> toolbar.

16. At the <u>Create Video</u> dialog box, select the <u>Pick Path</u> button under <u>Camera Path</u>.

17. Select the circle you placed in Step 9, and name it <u>TEST</u> path.

18. When the <u>Create Video</u> dialog box returns, select the <u>Pick Point</u> button under <u>Target Path</u>.

19. Using the <u>Center</u> object snap, select the circle again.

20. When the <u>Create Video</u> dialog box returns, select <u>Shade-256 Color</u> from the <u>Regen</u> dropdown list.

21. Select the <u>Dry Run</u> checkbox (Figure 24–5).

22. Press the <u>OK</u> button.

The Create Video dialog box will disappear, and the camera will circle the buildings pointing at the center of the buildings.

Figure 24–5

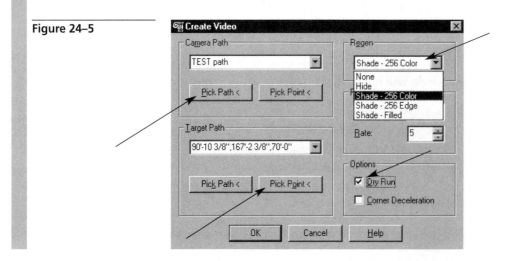

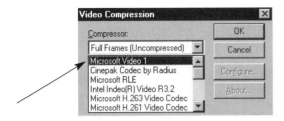

Figure 24–6

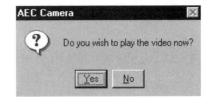

Figure 24–7

23. Again, select the Create Video icon from the Perspectives toolbar.

24. Uncheck the Dry Run checkbox, and press the OK button.

25. At the Camera Video File dialog box, enter a name in the File name box and press the Save button.

26. The Video Compression dialog box will now appear.

27. Select the Microsoft Video 1 compressor from the Compressor drop-down list and press the OK button (Figure 24–6).

The computer will now make the video. When it is finished, a dialog box will appear asking Do you wish to play the video now? (Figure 24–7).

Press the Yes button and the Windows media player will now play the movie (Figure 24–8).

28. If the movie needs adjustment, zoom out in the Top View viewport.

29. Select the circle path, select a grip, and drag the circle to a wider radius. (This can also be done through the Properties dialog box.) See Figure 24–9.

Figure 24–8

Figure 24–9

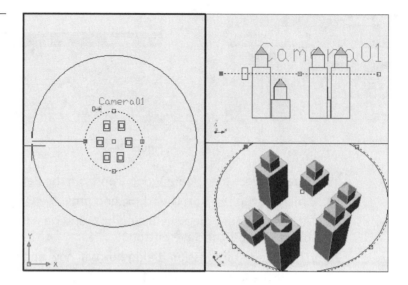

Repeat Steps 23–27, and create a new movie (Figure 24–10).

If the camera circles the buildings too quickly, you can slow it down by increasing the number frames made as it circles the buildings and by changing how many frames per second (rate) it will attempt to play (Figure 24–11).

Figure 24–10

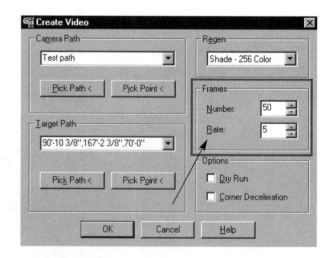

Figure 24–11

PART IV

Concept

Design

Documentation

Desktop

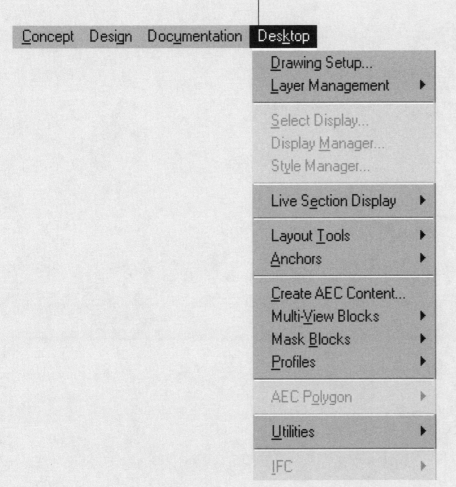

Concept   Design   Documentation   Desktop

| Drawing Setup... |
| Layer Management ▶ |
| |
| Select Display... |
| Display Manager... |
| Style Manager... |
| |
| Live Section Display ▶ |
| |
| Layout Tools ▶ |
| Anchors ▶ |
| |
| Create AEC Content... |
| Multi-View Blocks ▶ |
| Mask Blocks ▶ |
| Profiles ▶ |
| |
| AEC Polygon ▶ |
| |
| Utilities ▶ |
| |
| IFC ▶ |

Section 25

Layer Management

When you finish this section, you should be able to do the following:

✔ Understand the purpose of Layer Standards.
✔ Understand the purpose and operation of the Layer Manager.
✔ Understand the purpose and operation of Layer Key Overrides.

Autodesk Architectural Desktop 3 links all its objects to specific layers. When an object is input into a drawing, it automatically goes to a predetermined layer. In order to set up and manage the system called <u>Layer Keys</u>, you are provided with tools for Layer Management.

You can input <u>Layer Management Tools</u> into a drawing by selecting the desired tool icon from the <u>Layer Management</u> toolbar.

You can also input Layer Management tools into a drawing by selecting the desired tool from the Desktop | Layer Management menu from the Main toolbar. You can get the Layout Tools menu by RMB in any viewport.

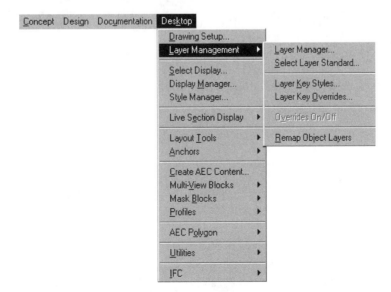

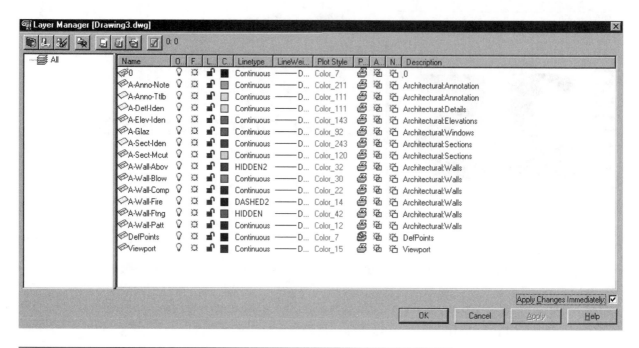

Figure 25–1

The Layer Manager

The Layer Manager is the main control panel for Architectural Desktop 3's Layering system. Although it is in some ways redundant to AutoCAD's layer system, it is a gateway to the layer key controls (Figure 25–1).

Layer Standards

Different offices and countries utilize different standards. To accommodate this, Architectural Desktop 3 includes eight standards. In the United States, the American Institute of Architects has created the AIA Long Format standard. The various standards can be reached from the Layering tab under the **Desktop | Drawing Setup** from the Main toolbar (Figure 25–2) or from the Layer Standards icon on the Layer Manager.

Figure 25–2

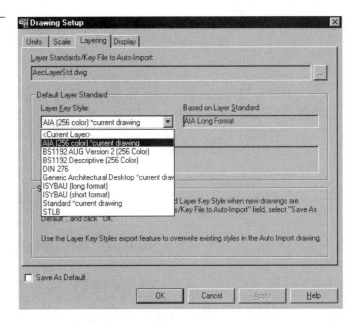

Hands On

1. Activate the <u>Layer Management</u> toolbar, and place it in a convenient place.

2. At the <u>Layer Manager</u> dialog box, select the <u>Layer Standards</u> icon (Figure 25–3).

Figure 25–3

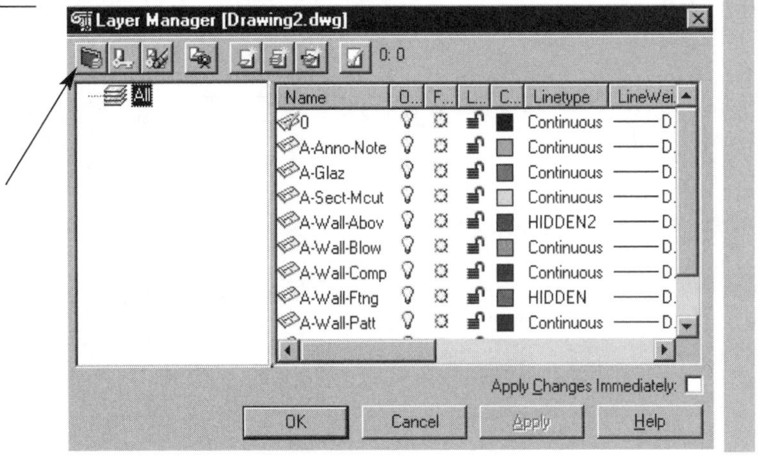

Figure 25–4

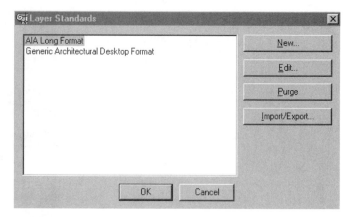

3. At the <u>Layer Standards</u> dialog box, select <u>Import / Export</u> button (Figure 25–4).

4. At the <u>Import / Export Layers Standards</u> dialog box, select the Open button (Figure 25–5).

5. Open the Autodesk Architectural Desktop 3 <u>Content</u> folder.

6. Open the <u>Layers</u> folder, and select the <u>AecLayerStd</u>.

The AecLayerStd drawing contains the eight standards included with the software.

7. Press the Import button, and Import the BS1192-Descriptive standard. Press the <u>OK</u> button.

8. Return to the <u>Layer Standards</u> dialog box, and press the <u>Edit</u> button.

9. At the <u>Layer Standards Properties</u> dialog box, select <u>AIA long Format</u> as the Layer Standard (Figure 25–6).

Figure 25–5

Import/Export Layer Standards	✕

Current Drawing:

AIA Long Format
Generic Architectural Desktop F

External File:

AIA Long Format
BS1192 - AUG Version 2
BS1192 - Descriptive
DIN 276 Format
Generic Architectural Desktop F
ISYBAU Long Format
ISYBAU Short Format
STLB Format

<<< Import
Export >>>

New...
Open...

External File Name: D:\Program Files\...\Content\Layers\EAecLayerStd.dwg
Recent Files: D:\Program Files\...\Content\Layers\EAecLayerStd.dwg

OK   Cancel   Apply

Figure 25–6

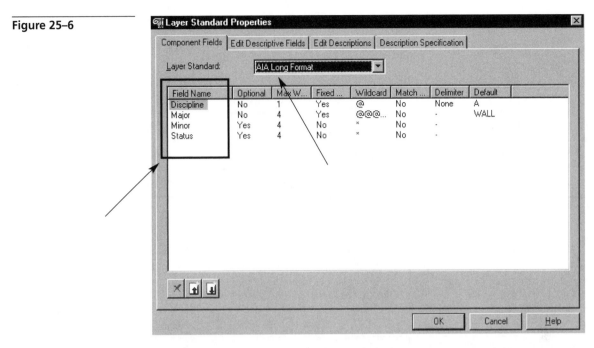

Figure 25–7

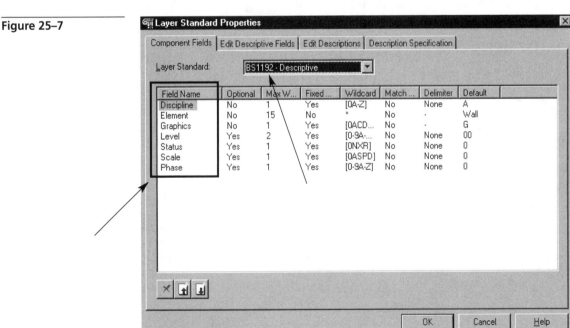

10.   Switch the Layer Standard to BS1192-Descriptive (Figure 25–7).

By switching between these two Layer Standards, you can see the different components of each standard.

The following default Layer Keys are built into the program. You cannot delete these layer keys.

ANNDTOBJ	Detail marks
ANNOBJ	Notes and leaders
ANNREV	Revisions
ANNSXOBJ	Section marks
ANNSYMOBJ	Annotation marks
APPL	Appliances
CAMERA	Cameras
CASE	Casework
CASENO	Casework tags
CEILGRID	Ceiling grids
CEILOBJ	Ceiling objects
COLUMN	Columns
COMMUN	Communication
CONTROL	Control systems
DIMLINE	Dimensions
DOOR	Doors
DOORNO	Door tags
DRAINAGE	Drainage
ELEC	Electric
ELECNO	Electrical tags
ELEVAT	Elevators
EQUIP	Equipment

EQUIPNO	Equipment tags
FINCEIL	Ceiling tags
FINFLOOR	Finish tags
FIRE	Fire system equipment
FURN	Furniture
FURNNO	Furniture tags
GRIDBUB	Plan grid bubbles
LAYGRID	Layout grids
LIGHTCLG	Ceiling lighting
LIGHTW	Wall lighting
MASSELEM	Mass elements
MASSGRPS	Mass groups
MASSSLCE	Mass slices
OPENING	Wall openings
PEOPLE	People
PFIXT	Plumbing fixtures
PLANTS	Plants—outdoor
PLANTSI	Plants—indoor
POLYGON	AEC Polygons
POWER	Electrical power
PRK-SYM	Parking symbols

ROOF	Roofs
ROOMNO	Room tags
SCHEDOBJ	Schedules
SEATNO	Seating tags
SECT	Sections
SITE	Site
SPACEBDRY	Space boundaries
SPACEOBJ	Space objects
STAIR	Stairs
STAIRH	Stair handrails
SWITCH	Electrical switches
TITTEXT	Border and title block
TOILACC	Architectural specialties
TOILNO	Toilet tags
UTIL	Site utilities
VEHICLES	Vehicles
WALL	Walls
WALLFIRE	Fire wall patterning
WALLNO	Wall tags
WIND	Windows
WINDNO	Window tags

You can create new Layer Keys on the fly if you need them by using a Layer Key Override. This will allow you to override the standard placement of an AEC object and place it on a new layer.

In order to be able to allow Overrides to the Layer keys, you must first check the Allow Overrides checkboxes (Figure 25–8).

To do this, double click on the Layer Standard you are using in the Style Manager dialog box.

To experience using Layer Key Overrides, try the following exercise.

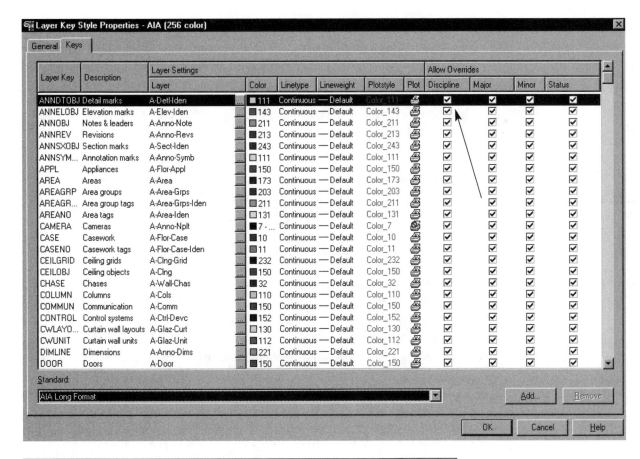

Figure 25–8

Hands On

In this exercise you will place walls on a special layer.

1. Activate the <u>Walls</u> and <u>Layer Management</u> toolbars, and place them in a convenient spot.
2. Using the Aec arch [imperial-intl].dwt template, select the <u>Work-FLR</u> Layout tab.
3. Activate the Top View viewport.
4. Select the <u>Add Wall</u> icon from the <u>Walls</u> toolbar, and add a 10'-0" square standard wall enclosure.
5. Select the wall, and notice that it is on the <u>A-Wall layer</u>.
6. Select the <u>Layer Key Overrides</u> icon from the Layer Management toolbar.

Tip

The layer of a selected object is shown automatically on the Object Properties toolbar. This toolbar comes automatically placed below the Main toolbar and Standard icon toolbars when you install Autodesk Architectural Desktop 3 (Figure 25–9).

Figure 25–9

 Tip This icon is a toggle. If the command line reads DISABLED, select the <u>Overrides ON/Off</u> icon again.

7. At the <u>Layer Keys Overrides</u> dialog box, select the <u>Minor Override</u>, type <u>Test</u>, and make sure <u>Enable All Overrides</u> is checked. **The word Test is arbitrary; any word will do.** The program automatically places a dash in front of the word (Figure 25–10).

8. Select the <u>Overrides On/Off</u> icon, and make sure that the command line reads Automatic Layer Overrides are now ENABLED.

9. Again, select the <u>Add Wall</u> icon from the <u>Walls</u> toolbar, and add another 10'-0" square standard wall enclosure.

10. Select the wall, and notice that this new wall is on the <u>A-Wall-test</u> layer (Figure 25–11).

11. Place a door in any wall of either enclosure.

12. Select the door, and see that it is on the **A-Door-test layer** (Figure 25–12).

Architectural Desktop will continue to create and place objects on new layers with the word test added until you disable Layer Key Overrides.

Try this exercise with your own overrides and settings until you are familiar with the system.

Figure 25–10

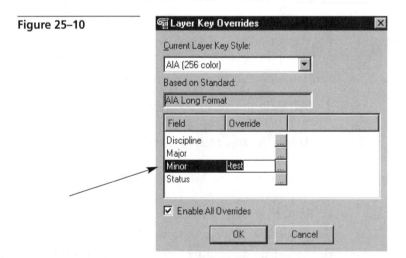

Figure 25–11   **Figure 25–12**

Section

26

Live Section Display

When you finish this section, you should be able to do the following:

✔ Understand the purpose and components of Live Sections.
✔ Place and modify section lines, section marks, and section objects.
✔ Create and modify Live Sections.

You can input <u>Live Sections</u> into a drawing by selecting the <u>Add Live Section Configuration</u> icon from the <u>Live Section Display</u> toolbar.

You can also input <u>Live Sections</u> into a drawing by selecting the <u>Desktop | Live Section Display | Add Live Section Configuration</u> menu from the <u>Main</u> toolbar. You can get the Live Section menu by RMB in any viewport.

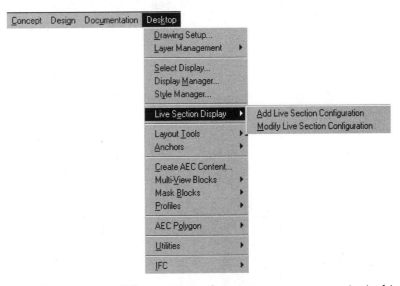

There are two different types of sections you can create in Architectural Desktop: <u>Standard Sections</u> and <u>Live Sections</u>. Live Sections cut only in Model views and are limited to the following AEC objects only:

- Cut walls
- Doors, windows, and window assemblies
- Mass elements and mass groups
- Stairs and railings
- Roofs and roof slabs
- Spaces and space boundaries
- Curtain wall layouts and units
- Structural Members

Unlike Standard Sections, Live Sections retain the original objects after sectioning, can set display properties for all objects in section, and can set hatching for section boundaries.

Live-Sectioned AEC objects consist of six components (Figure 26–1).

- **The Cutting boundary**—outside limit of the section (section line)
- **The Hatch**—graphic indication of area inside the Cutting boundary
- **Inside Cutting boundary**—remaining object cut by Cutting boundary <u>inside</u> Cutting boundary
- **Outside Cutting boundary**—remaining object cut by Cutting boundary <u>outside</u> boundary
- **Inside full body**—object completely <u>inside</u> section
- **Outside full body**—object completely <u>outside</u> section

Before a Live Section or any section can be created, a Section Mark or Section Line must be placed in your drawing to identify where the section is to take place.

Each new Live Section is displayed in a separate display configuration created specifically for that section. See p. 15, which discusses display configurations.

Figure 26–1

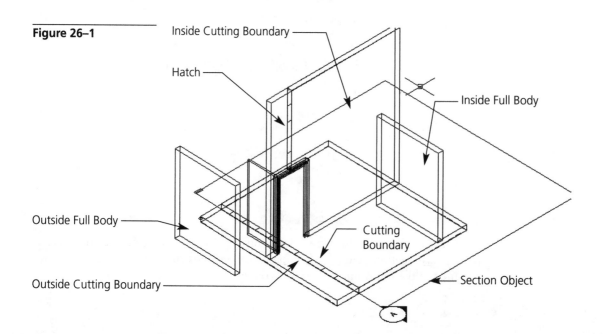

Using <u>Add Section Line</u> to Add a Section Line

Hands On

1. Activate the <u>Walls</u>, <u>Sections</u>, and <u>Documentation-Imperial</u> toolbars, and place them in a convenient place.
2. Select the Work-3D Layout tab.
3. Activate the Top Viewport; using the Add Wall icon, create a 10'-0" × 10'-0" enclosure. Make the walls <u>CMU-8 Rigid-1.5 Air-2 Brick-4 Furring</u>.
4. Select the left wall, RMB, and select <u>Insert Door</u> from the Contextual menu.
5. Place a 3'-0" standard door, centered in the left wall, swinging inward (Figure 26–2).
6. Select <u>Documentation</u> | <u>Set Drawing Scale</u> from the Main toolbar.
7. At the <u>Drawing Setup</u> dialog box, select the Scale tab, and set the <u>Drawing Scale</u> to 1/4" = 1'-0". Leave Annotation Plot Size at 1/8".
8. Select <u>Documentation</u> | <u>Sections</u> | <u>Add Section</u> Line from the Main toolbar.
9. Place the start point at the left of the door, place the second point to the right of the right wall, and press the <u>Enter</u> key.
10. Type <u>10'-0"</u> at the command line request for length, and press the Enter key.
11. Accept the height <10'-0">, and press the Enter key.

You have now created a Section Object (Figure 26–3).

Figure 26–2

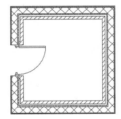

Figure 26–3

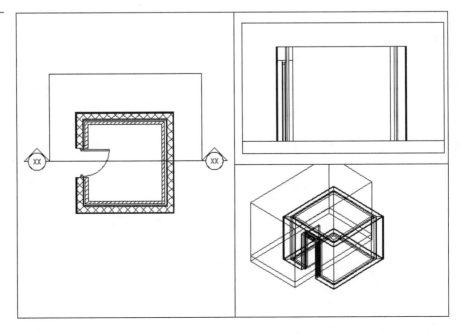

Figure 26–4

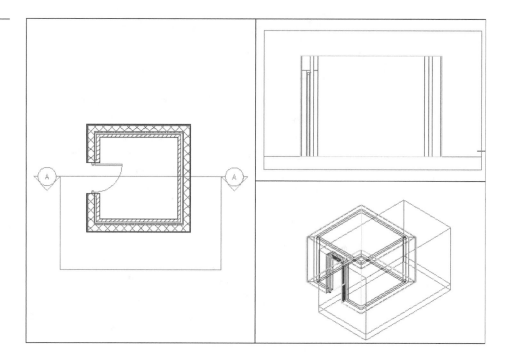

Reversing the Direction of the Section Object/Section

12. Select the Section Object, RMB, and select <u>Reverse</u> from the Contextual menu.

Changing the Direction Arrow Attributes

13. Select the left direction arrow, RMB, and select <u>Multi-View Block</u> Properties from the Contextual menu.

14. At the <u>Multi-View Block Reference</u> Properties dialog box, select the <u>Attributes</u> tab.

15. Change the Value from **XX** to **A**, and press the <u>OK</u> button.

16. Repeat Steps 13–15 for the right arrow (Figure 26–4).

Using <u>Documentation Content</u> to Add <u>Section Marks</u>

Hands On

1. Using the previous exercise, erase the Section Lines and Section Object.

2. Select <u>Documentation | Documentation Content | Section Marks</u> from the Main toolbar.

The Design Center will appear at the left side of your screen (Figure 26–5).

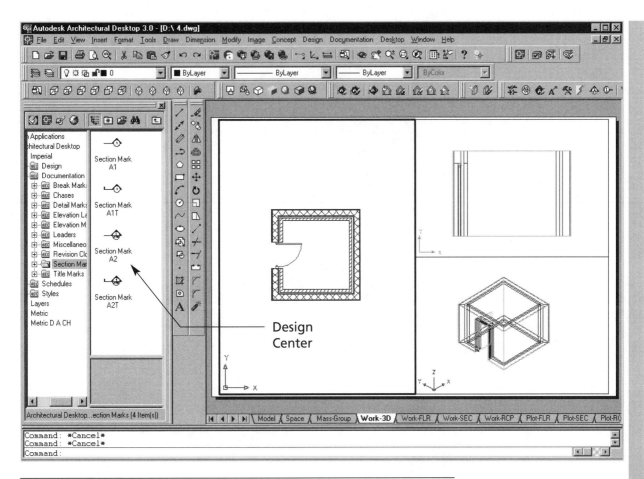

Figure 26–5

3. Select and drag <u>Section Mark A1T</u> to the left of the door in the Top View viewport.
4. Click to place the first point, drag to the right of the right wall, and click again. Press the <u>Enter</u> key.
5. At the Edit Attributes dialog box, change the <u>Section Mark Number</u> to **A**, and press <u>OK</u>.
6. Drag the arrow of the attribute in the Top View—upward and click.
7. Type <u>Y</u> at the command line question Add AEC Section Object? and press the <u>Enter</u> key. Then end the command.

You have again created a Section Object, but it does not have a 3D component.

8. Select the section object, RMB, and select <u>Selection Line Properties</u> from the Contextual menu.
9. At the Section/Elevation Line Properties dialog box, set A-Side 1 and B-Side 2 to 10'-0". Leave the <u>Use Model Extents for Height</u> checkbox checked and press the <u>OK</u> button (Figures 26–6 and 26–7). **Save this exercise.**

Figure 26–6

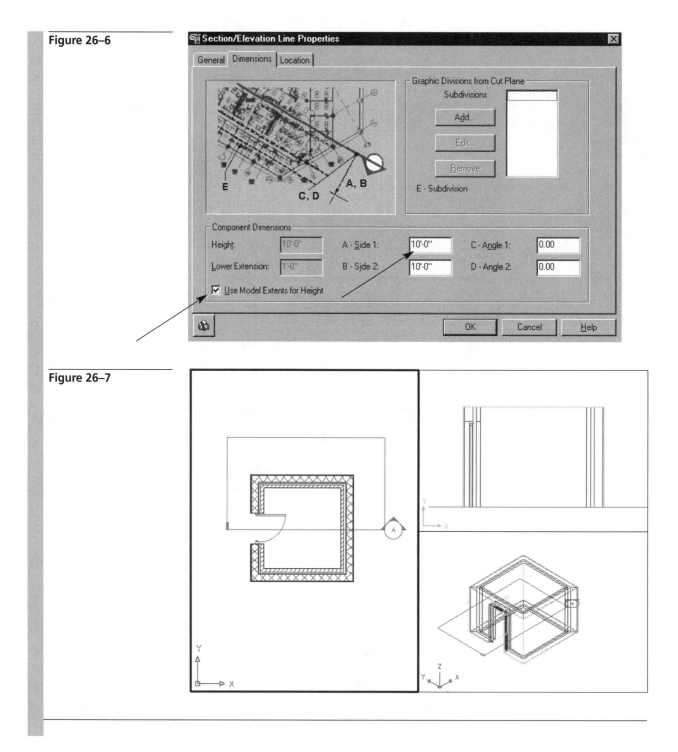

Figure 26–7

Making a Live Section Configuration

Hands On

1. Using the previous exercise, RMB, and select <u>Add Live Selection Configuration</u> from the Contextual menu.

2. At the <u>Add Live Selection Configuration</u> dialog box, <u>uncheck</u> the <u>Set Current</u> checkbox, and click the <u>Select Objects</u> button.

Figure 26–8

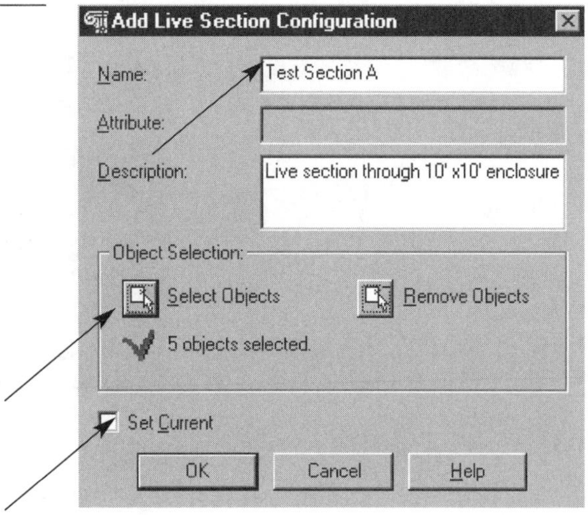

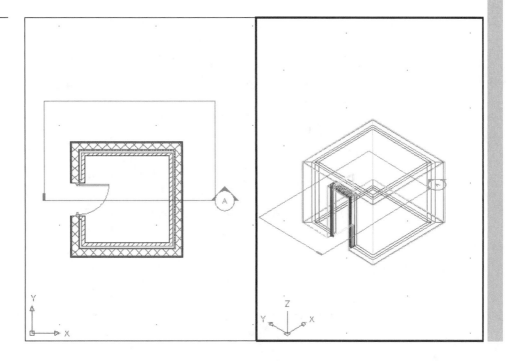

(Add Live Section Configuration dialog box)

3. Select everything in the Top View, and press the space bar or Enter key.

4. When the <u>Add Live Selection</u> dialog box reappears, type <u>Test Section A</u> in the Name field, and press the OK button (Figure 26–8).

Nothing will seem to happen, because you have created a display configuration but have not placed it in the present viewport. (<u>Set Current not checked</u>).

5. Change to the <u>Work-FLR</u> Layout tab, delete the existing viewports, and create two new vertical viewports.

6. Set the left viewport to <u>Top View</u> and the right viewport to <u>SW Isometric View</u> (Figure 26–9).

7. Make the <u>SW Isometric View</u> active.

8. Select the <u>Set Current Display Configuration</u> icon from the <u>AEC Setup</u> toolbar.

Figure 26–9

Figure 26–10

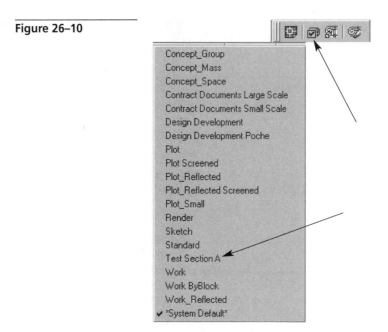

9. When the menu appears, pick <u>Test Section A</u> (Figure 26–10).

The result is the section shown in both Front View and SW Isometric View (Figure 26–11).
A Live Section allows you to modify components such as walls.

10. Select the wall of the section in the Front View, RMB, and select <u>Edit Wall Style</u> from the Contextual menu.

11. At the <u>Wall Styles Properties</u> dialog box, select the <u>Display Props</u> tab, attach an Override (override the default wall setting), and press the <u>Edit Display Props</u> button (Figure 26–12).

Figure 26–11

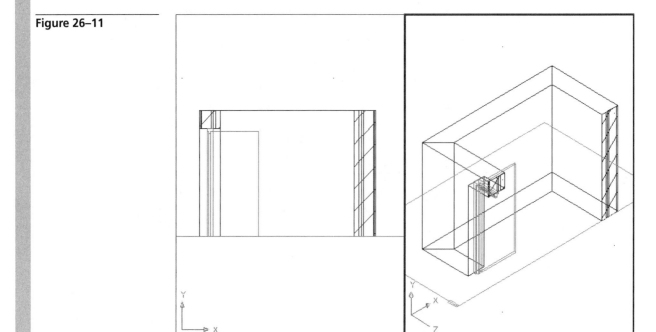

Figure 26–12

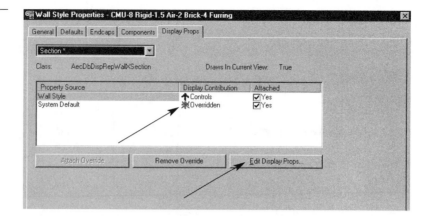

12. At the <u>Entity Properties</u> dialog box, select the <u>Hatching</u> tab.
13. Click on the <u>Hatch 4(CMU)</u> pattern and change it to the ANSI37 (crosshatch) pattern, 0° Angle. Press the OK button, and exit all the dialog boxes (Figure 26–13).

You have now changed the CMU wall hatch (Figure 26–14).

All the AEC components in the section, such as door size and hatching, can be changed in the section, and it will reflect in the 2D plan drawing. Change the door size in the section, and check it in plan.

Figure 26–13

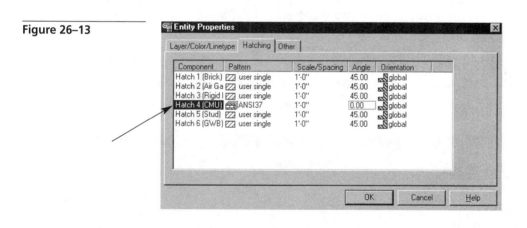

Figure 26–14

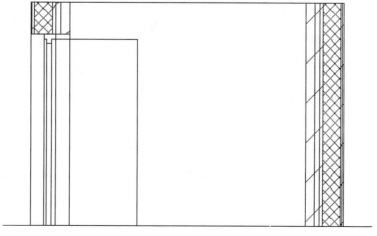

Figure 26–15

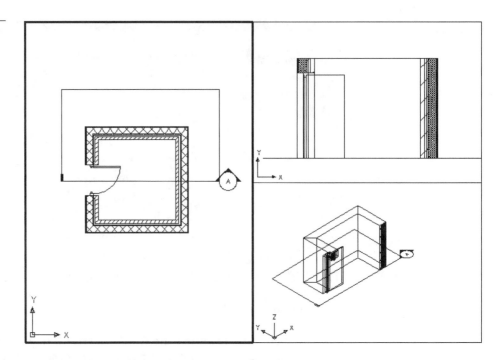

Hiding the Section Object

Return to the Work-3D Layout tab and notice that the Section Object is showing in all the views (Figure 26–15). **You will want only the section line and arrow to show.**

14.   Select the <u>Display Manager</u> icon from the <u>AEC Setup</u> toolbar.

15.   At the <u>Display manager</u> dialog box, open up the <u>Representations by Object</u> tree, and select the <u>Bldg Section Line</u> (Figure 26–16).

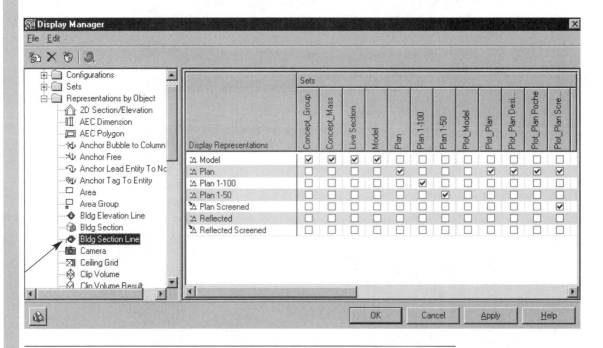

Figure 26–16

Figure 26–17

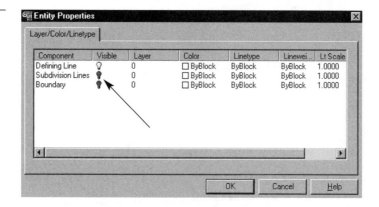

16. Still in the Display Manager, double-click on <u>Plan</u> under <u>Display Rep</u>-<u>resentations</u> to bring up the <u>Entity Properties</u> dialog box.

17. At the <u>Entity Properties</u> dialog box, turn off the visibility of the <u>Sub</u>-<u>division Lines</u> and <u>Boundary</u>; then press the <u>OK</u> button, and <u>Apply</u> the Display Manager (Figure 26–17).

The defining line is the Section Line and arrow that you want to show in plan view. The other components belong to the Section Object.

18. Repeat Steps 14–17 for the model Display Representation to finish the drawing (Figure 26–18).

Figure 26–18

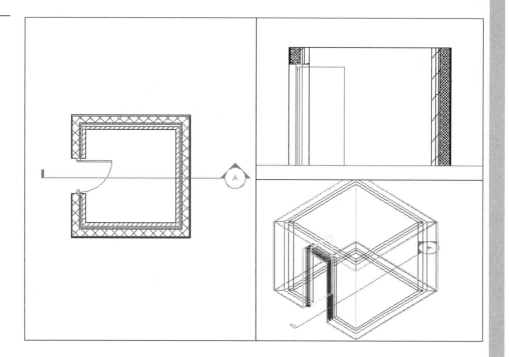

Section 27

Layout Tools and Anchors

When you finish this section, you should be able to do the following:

✔ Use the layout curve and layout grid.

✔ Understand the relationship between Layout tools and Anchors.

Layout tools and Anchors work together. First, you use the Layout tools to create the layout, and then you use Anchors to anchor objects to the layout. You can put **Layout tools** into a drawing by selecting the desired tool icon from the Layout Tools toolbar.

You can input <u>**Anchors**</u> or control them in a drawing by selecting the desired <u>Anchor</u> icon from the <u>Anchors</u> toolbar.

You can also input **Layout Tools** into a drawing by selecting the desired tool from the <u>Desktop | Layout Tools</u> menu from the <u>Main</u> toolbar. You can also input **Anchors** or control them in a drawing by selecting the desired tool from the <u>Desktop | Anchors</u> menu from the <u>Main</u> toolbar.

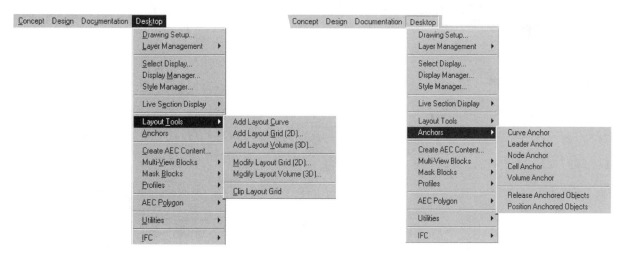

303

Layout Tools

There are three Layout tools: layout curve, layout grid, and layout volume (3D).

Layout Curve

In this exercise you are asked to place a series of bollards evenly spaced at 6'-0" outside your new pavilion. Using Layout Tools and Anchors, the job is a snap.

1. Activate the <u>Roofs-Roof Slabs,</u> <u>Walls,</u> <u>Layout Tools,</u> and <u>Anchors</u> toolbars.
2. Using the Aec arch [imperial-intl].dwt template, select the <u>Work-3D</u> Layout tab.
3. Activate the Top View viewport.
4. Using Standard AutoCAD commands, create the plan shown in Figure 27–1.
5. Offset the outlines 4'-0" as shown in Figure 27–2, and **modify them to be one joined polyline.**
6. Using the <u>Walls</u> toolbar, convert the floor plan to walls. Make the walls 8 in. wide and 8 ft. 0 in. high, with right justification.
7. Using the <u>Roof-Roof Slabs</u> toolbar, convert the Walls to a roof with a 6-in. rise.
8. Select <u>Concept | Mass Elements | Add Mass Element</u> from the Main toolbar.
9. At the Add Mass Element dialog box, set the following:
   - Shape = Doric
   - Height = 42"
   - Radius = 6"
10. Place the Doric shape in any convenient place on your drawing.

    The Doric shape Mass Element will become your bollards.

11. Select the <u>Add Layout Curve</u> icon from Layout Tools toolbar.

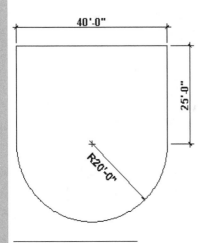

Figure 27–1

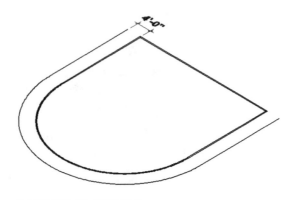

Figure 27–2

Figure 27–3

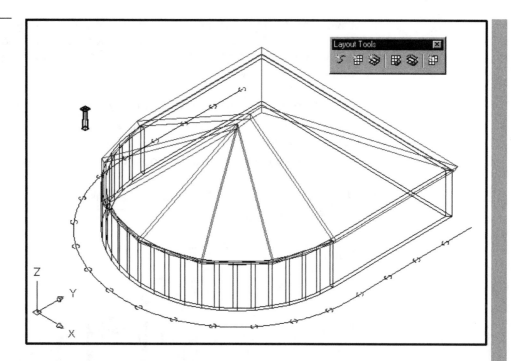

12. Select the offset polyline created in Step 5, and type **R** for repeat at the command line. Set Start and End Offset to **0**, and set the spacing to **6'-0"**.

   The offset polyline has now become a layout curve with nodes at 6'-0" o/c (Figure 27–3).

13. Select the <u>Node Anchor</u> icon from the Anchors toolbar.
14. Select **C** for Copy to each node at the command line, and press the space bar or Enter key.
15. Select the Doric column you placed in Step 10, and select one of the nodes on the layout curve. Exit from the command.
16. Freeze the layer on which the layout curve resides (Figure 27–4).

Figure 27–4

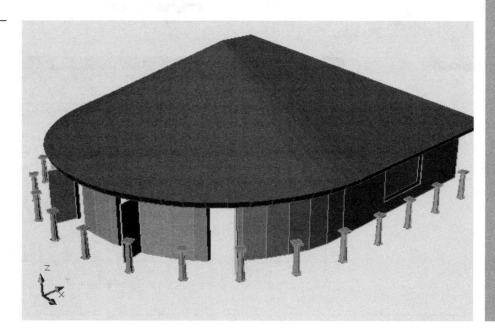

Layout grids are input and modified in the same manner as column grids. (See Section 18 for exercises showing how to add and modify Grids.) Layout Curve nodes can be adjusted by RMB on the node, and the anchored object will move with it.

17. Unfreeze the layer on which the layout curve resides.

18. RMB on any node, and select <u>Layout Curve</u> Properties from the Contextual menu (Figures 27–5 and 27–6).

19. At the <u>Layout Curve</u> dialog box, turn off the <u>Automatic Spacing</u> checkbox.

20. You can now adjust the node locations (and the bollards) parametrically (Figure 27–7).

Figure 27–5

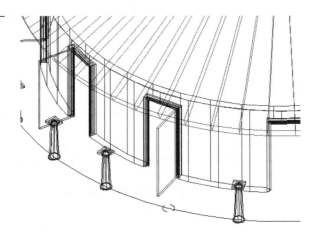

Figure 27–6

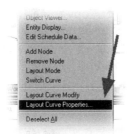

Figure 27–7

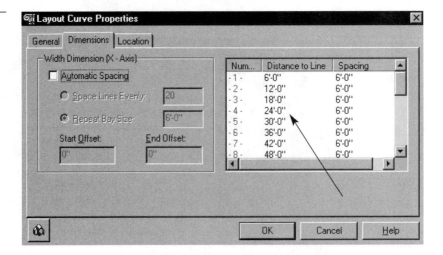

Hands On

Layout Grid (2D)

1. Activate the <u>UCS</u>, <u>UCS II</u>, <u>Roofs-Roof Slabs</u>, <u>Walls</u>, <u>Layout Tools</u>, and <u>Anchors</u> toolbars.
2. Using the Aec arch [imperial-intl].dwt template, select the Work-3D Layout tab.
3. Activate the Top View viewport.
4. Create a 40-ft-long × 30-ft-wide building with a 6-in.-rise roof (Figure 27–8).
5. Convert the Roof to <u>Roof Slabs</u>.
6. Select the <u>Object UCS</u> from the UCS toolbar, and select the front roof slab. (Make sure the ucsicon OR option is on). See Figure 27–9.
7. Select the <u>Add Layout Grid (2D)</u> icon from the Layout Tools toolbar.
8. Center a 15-ft × 10-ft grid on the front roof slab with three divisions in the X direction, and two divisions in the Y direction. **(The grid will**

Figure 27–8

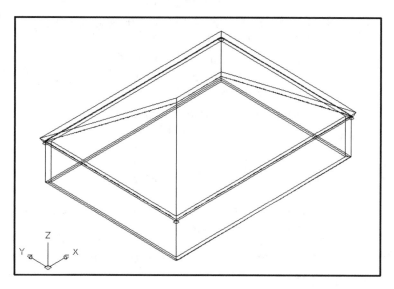

Figure 27–9

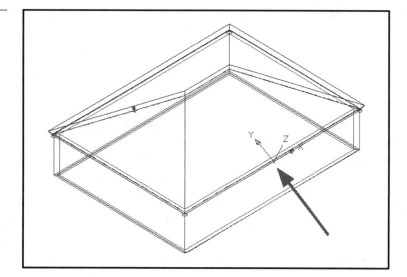

Figure 27–10

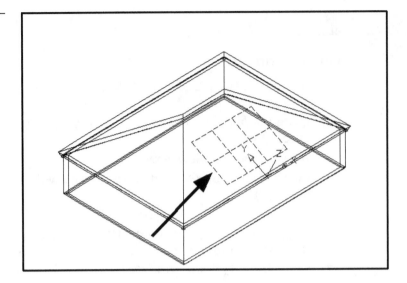

lie parallel to the roof because the UCS was set parallel to the roof in Step 6). See Figure 27–10.

9. Place a 5'-0" high × 1'-0" radius <u>Mass Element Cylinder</u> in a convenient place in your drawing.

10. Select the <u>Cell Anchor</u> icon from the Anchors toolbar.

11. Type **C** at the command line to copy to each cell, and press the space bar or Enter key.

12. Select the Mass Object; then select the layout grid on the roof slab (Figures 27–11 and 27–12).

Notice in Figures 27–11 and 27–12 that the Mass Elements in the cells of the layout grid match the size of the grid.

13. Change the grid size to 5'-0" in the X-Width and 5'-0" in the Y-Depth, and press the Apply button.

Notice that the Mass Elements in the cells automatically change size (Figures 27–13 and 27–14).

Figure 27–11

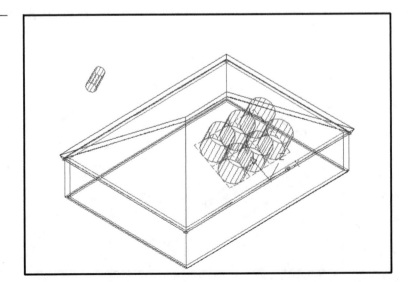

Figure 27–12

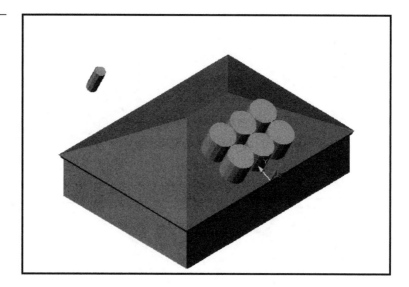

Figure 27–13

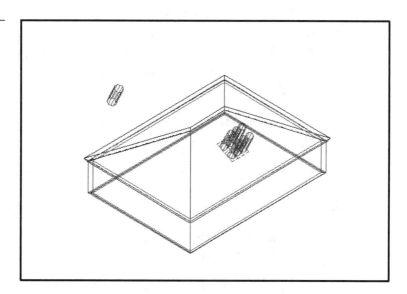

Figure 27–14

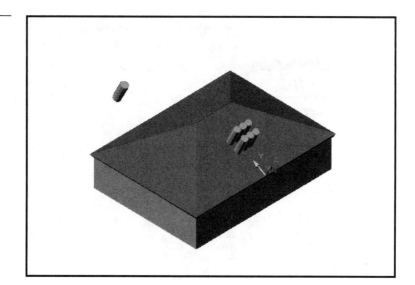

Figure 27–15

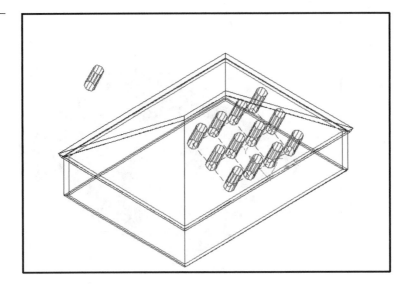

14. UNDO back to Step 9 (after the Layout Grid was placed).
15. Select the <u>Node Anchor</u> icon from the Anchors toolbar.
16. Type **C** for Copy to each node, and press the space bar or Enter key.
17. Select the Mass Element, and then select the layout grid (Figure 27–15).

Note that the Mass Elements are attached to the nodes of the layout grid. Moving or modifying the grid will then move the anchored objects.

18. Select all the Mass Elements, RMB, and select <u>Element Properties</u> from the Contextual menu.
19. At the Mass Element Properties dialog box, select the Anchor tab.

Notice that the Anchor tab has replaced the typical Location tab. This is because the layout grid location governs location of the element.

20. Change X Rotation to 333.43 (slope of the roof slab subtracted from 360°). See Figure 27–16.

Figure 27–16

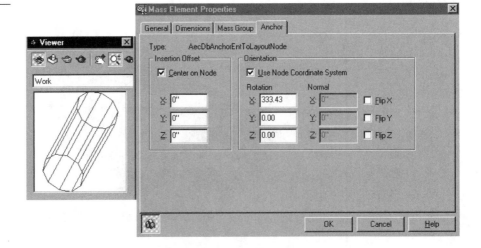

Figure 27–17

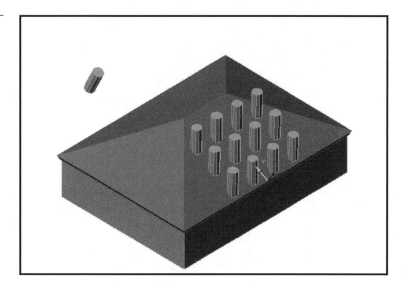

The Mass Elements rotate vertically to the roof slab (Figure 27–17).

The layout volume grid (3D) works and is modified in a similar manner to the 2D layout grid.

Experiment with all the different settings, and try anchoring and rotating different kinds of content to AEC objects and AutoCAD entities. Do not forget that you can use the layout grid to put a series of skylights or windows on a roof or wall.

Section 28

Create AEC Content

When you finish this section, you should be able to do the following:

✔ Add AEC content to the Design Center.

In Autodesk Architectural Desktop 3, the <u>Creating AEC Content</u> command places AEC content into the Design Center for quick and easy access. You can place <u>AEC Content</u> in the <u>Design Center</u> by selecting the <u>Create AEC Content</u> icon from the <u>AEC Blocks-Profiles</u> toolbar.

You can also place <u>AEC Content</u> in the <u>Design Center</u> by selecting the <u>Create AEC Content</u> from the <u>Desktop | Create AEC Content</u> menu from the <u>Main</u> toolbar. You can get the Create AEC Content menu by RMB in any viewport.

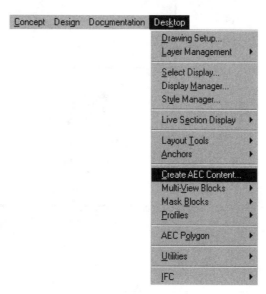

Tip To better understand this section, please read Sections 5, 28, and 29 before reading this section.

In Section 29 you create a Multi-View block of a piece of furniture and call it <u>Chair</u>. In this section you will place that block in the Design Center.

Hands On

1. Open up the last exercise in Section 29 (the Chair) (Figure 28–1).
2. Activate the <u>AEC Blocks-Profiles</u> toolbar, and place it in a convenient place.
3. Select the Model Layout, and change its color to white.
4. Select the Left View icon from the View toolbar (Figure 28–2).
5. Select the <u>Create AEC Content</u> icon from the <u>AEC Blocks-Profiles</u> toolbar.
6. At the <u>Create AEC Content Wizard</u> dialog box (Content Type) select the <u>Multi-View Block</u> radio button, and add the Chair to the Content File, and press the <u>Next</u> button (Figure 28–3).

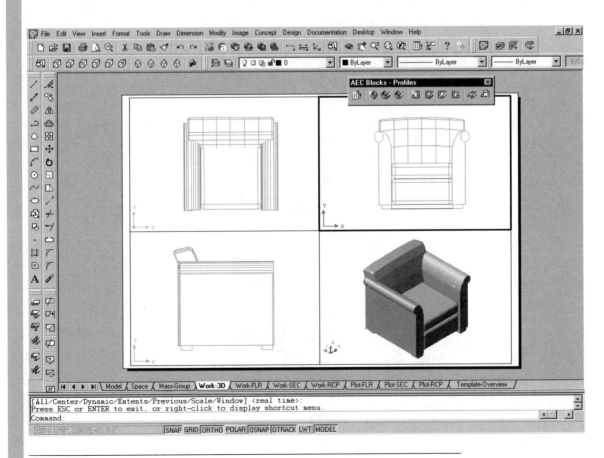

Figure 28–1

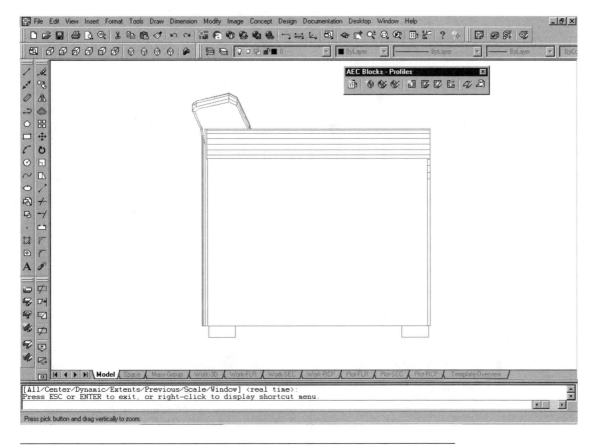

Figure 28–2

Figure 28–3

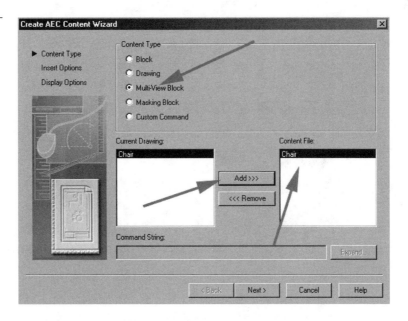

7. At the next <u>Create AEC Content Wizard</u> dialog box (Insert Options), press the <u>Select Layer Key</u> button.

8. At the <u>Select Layer Key</u> dialog box, select the <u>FURN</u> layer key, and press the OK button. Select the <u>Next</u> button.

Selecting the FURN layer key assures you that when you insert the content it will be placed on that layer. (See Section 25.)

9. At the next <u>Create AEC Content Wizard</u> dialog box (Display Options), press the <u>Browse</u> button to bring up the <u>Save Content File</u> dialog box.

10. At the Save Content File dialog box locate the <u>Autodesk Architectural Desktop 3\Content\ Imperial\Design\Furniture\Chair</u> folder, and name the file <u>TEST CHAIR</u> (Figure 28–4).

11. When you return to the <u>Create AEC Content Wizard</u> dialog box, type in a description of the MV block in the <u>Detailed Description</u> space, and press the <u>Finish</u> button (Figure 28–5).

Notice that the Model View drawing is shown as an icon.

Figure 28–4

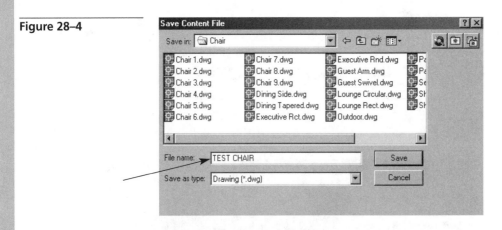

Figure 28–5

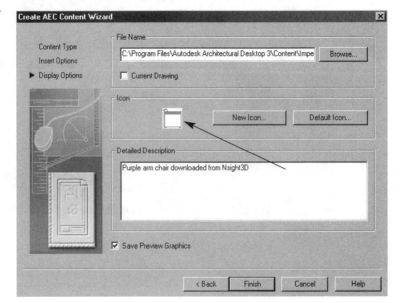

12. Start a new drawing using the Aec arch [imperial-intl].dwt template.

13. Select the Work-3D <u>Layout</u> tab.

14. Erase the existing viewports, and using <u>View |Viewports | 3 Viewports</u> from the <u>Main</u> toolbar, create 3 viewports. Make the left viewport <u>Top</u> view, the lower right viewport <u>SE Isometric</u> view, and the upper right viewport <u>Right</u> view.

15. Activate the Top Viewport.

16. Select <u>Design | Design Content</u> | Site from the <u>Main</u> toolbar.

17. Select and open the <u>Furniture</u> Folder.

18. Select and drag the <u>TEST CHAIR</u> icon into your drawing, and Zoom Extents all viewports (Figure 28–6).

The create AEC Content Wizard will place blocks, drawings, masking blocks, and custom command strings in the Design Center. The process is essentially the same for all these different forms of content.

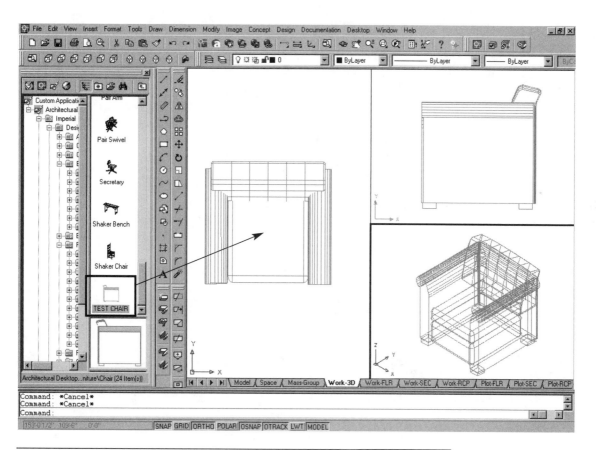

Figure 28–6

Section 29

Multi-View Blocks

When you finish this section, you should be able to do the following:

✔ Understand the purpose of Multi-View blocks.
✔ Create and use Multi-View blocks.

You can <u>define</u>, <u>add</u>, and <u>modify Multi-View Blocks</u> by selecting the desired icon from the AEC Blocks-Profiles toolbar.

You can <u>define</u>, <u>add</u>, and <u>modify Multi-View Blocks</u> by selecting the desired tool from the <u>Desktop | Multi-View Blocks</u> menu from the <u>Main</u> toolbar. You can also get the Multi-View Blocks menu by RMB in any viewport.

In combination with Autodesk Architectural Desktop's display system, the program uses a multiview block system. This system allows you to place content in one view and have the appropriate view appear in the other viewports. Although the program comes with a great deal of content, it includes controls that enable you to create your own custom content.

The following exercise illustrates the creation of a custom Multi-View Block.

The Chair

For this exercise you will need to go to the Web for content. You can go directly to the Web from inside Architectural Desktop 3 by activating the <u>Autodesk Point A</u> icon from the <u>Main</u> Icon toolbar. Go to <u>http://www.nsight3d.com/nsfree1.htm</u>. The owner of the site has given us permission to use one of his free objects for this exercise (Figure 29–1). Download the Nsight Onsite 3DS file, unzip it, and place it in a folder on your computer.

Figure 29–1

[Please read this legal stuff first.]
The files on this page are provided as-is. Nsight Studios expressly denies all warranties, either expressed or implied, including warranties of design, fitness for a particular purpose, and merchantability. Under no circumstances shall Nsight Studios be liable for any lost revenue or profits or for any damages resulting from the use or misuse of these files.

Sample Files:

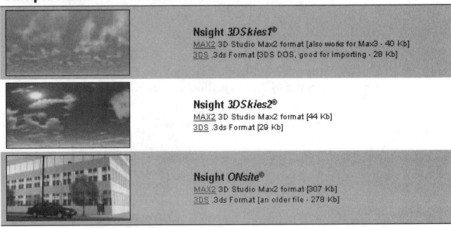

Nsight *3DSkies1*®
<u>MAX2</u> 3D Studio Max2 format [also works for Max3 - 40 Kb]
<u>3DS</u> .3ds Format [3DS DOS, good for importing - 28 Kb]

Nsight *3DSkies2*®
<u>MAX2</u> 3D Studio Max2 format [44 Kb]
<u>3DS</u> .3ds Format [29 Kb]

Nsight *ONsite*®
<u>MAX2</u> 3D Studio Max2 format [307 Kb]
<u>3DS</u> .3ds Format [an older file - 278 Kb]

See Also:

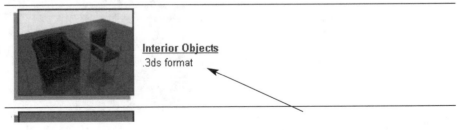

<u>Interior Objects</u>
.3ds format

Creating the Content

Hands On

1. Activate the <u>Utilities</u>, <u>Viewports</u>, and <u>AEC Blocks-Profiles</u> toolbars, and place them in a convenient place.

2. Select the Work-FLR Layout tab.

3. Activate the <u>SW Isometric</u> View.

4. Select <u>Insert | 3D Studio</u> from the main toolbar, and import the Onsit3ds file that was downloaded and unzipped from the Web.

5. At the <u>3D Studio File Import Options</u> dialog box select the **Chair-V01** mesh from the Available Objects and add it to the Selected Objects.

6. Select the <u>Don't Assign a Material</u> radio button, and press the OK button (Figure 29–2).

7. Zoom Extents in all the viewports.

   You have now imported a 3D mesh model of a chair (Figure 29–3).

8. Change to left view, and select the <u>Hidden Line Projection</u> icon from the Utilities toolbar.

9. Select the chair, and press the space bar or Enter key.

10. Select any Block insertion point, and type **Y** at the command line to insert in plan view.

Figure 29–2

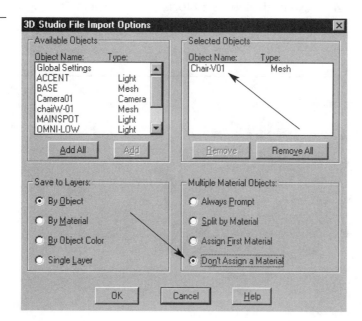

Figure 29–3

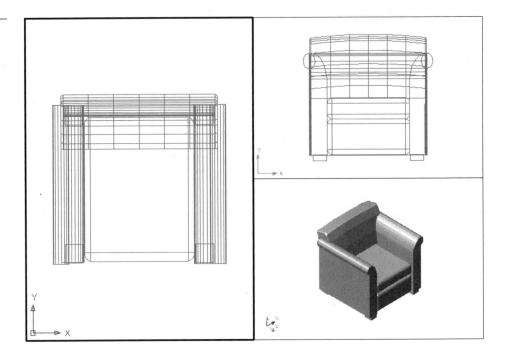

11. Return to an SW Isometric View to see the chair and its new 2D hidden-line projection.

   You have now created a 2D hidden-line projection of the right view of your model (Figure 29–4).

12. Repeat this process for the top and front views (Figure 29–5).

13. Select <u>Modify | 3D Operation | Rotate 3D</u> from the <u>Main</u> toolbar, rotate the front and side views, and place them as shown in Figure 29–6. Create insertion points that align all the views and the model.

14. Save each view as a block, naming them <u>Chair Front</u>, <u>Chair Side</u>, <u>Chair Top</u>, and <u>Chair Model</u>, respectively. Use the insertion points also shown in Figure 29–6.

Figure 29–4

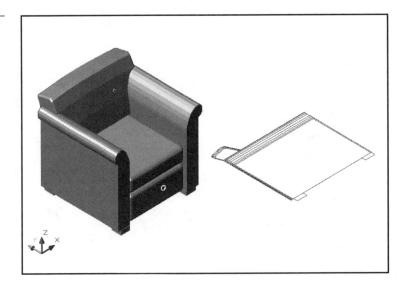

Figure 29–5

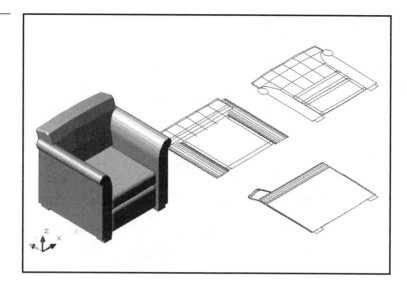

Figure 29–6

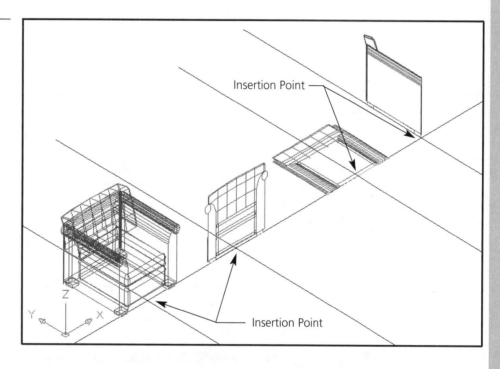

Insertion Point

Insertion Point

Creating the Multi-View Block

Hands On

1. Select the <u>Multi-View Block Definitions</u> icon from the AEC Blocks-Pro-files toolbar.

2. At the <u>Style Manager</u> dialog box, select the <u>New Style</u> icon and create a new style; name it <u>Chair</u>.

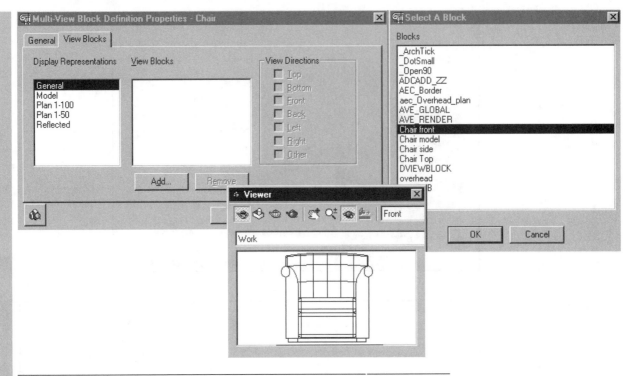

Figure 29–7

3. Select the definition, RMB, and select <u>Edit</u> from the Contextual menu.

4. At the <u>Multi-View Block Definition Properties</u> dialog box, select the <u>View Blocks</u> tab. Select <u>General</u>; then press the Add button and select the <u>Chair Front</u> block (Figure 29–7).

5. After adding the <u>Front</u> block, check the <u>Front</u> and <u>Back</u> checkboxes under View Directions. Repeat this process for the Side, and Top blocks, selecting the checkboxes as shown (Figures 29–8, 29–9, and 29–10).

6. Select Model from the Display Representations; then add the Model block, and check the <u>Other</u> checkbox (Figure 29–11).

    You have now created a Multi-View Block.

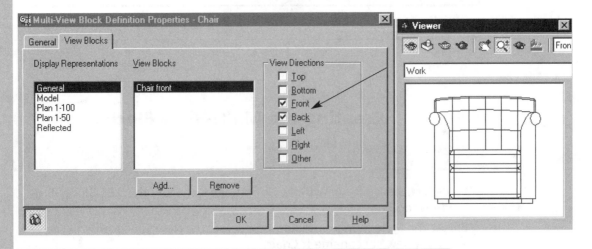

Figure 29–8

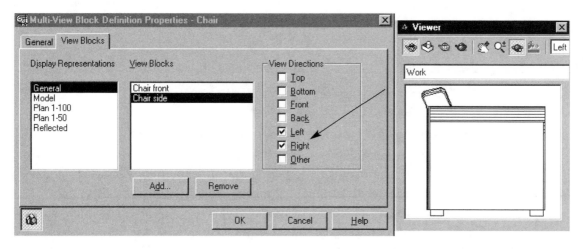

Figure 29–9

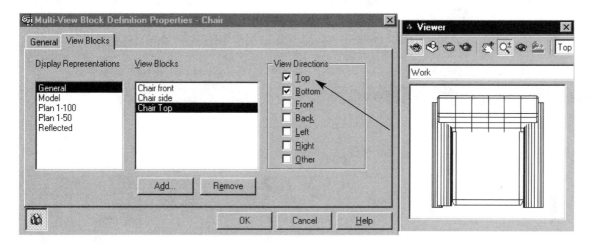

Figure 29–10

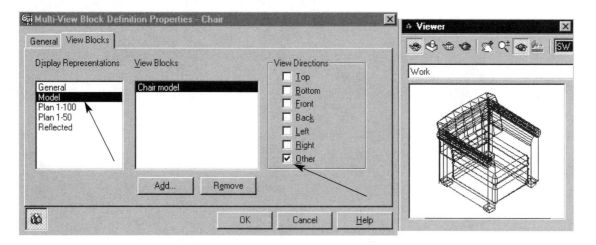

Figure 29–11

Testing the Multi-View Block

Hands On

1. Create a new drawing.
2. Activate the Work-3D tab.
3. Press the <u>PAPER</u> button in order to be in Paper Space.
4. Erase the Paper Space viewports.
5. Select the <u>Display Viewports Dialog</u> icon from the Viewports toolbar.
6. At the Viewports dialog box, select <u>Four: Equal</u>.
7. Select <u>Fit</u> at the command line.
8. Change to Model Space and set the viewports to Top, Right, SW Isometric, and Front views.
9. Activate the Top View viewport.
10. Select the <u>Add Multi-View Block</u> icon from the <u>AEC Blocks-Profiles</u> toolbar.
11. At the <u>Add Multi-View Blocks</u> dialog box, choose <u>Chair</u> from the dropdown list (Figure 29–12).
12. The correct view of the car appears in all the different viewports. Zoom Extents in each viewport (Figure 29–13). **Save this exercise.**

Figure 29–12

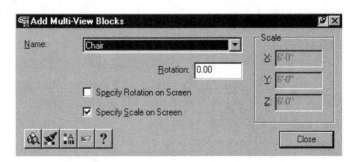

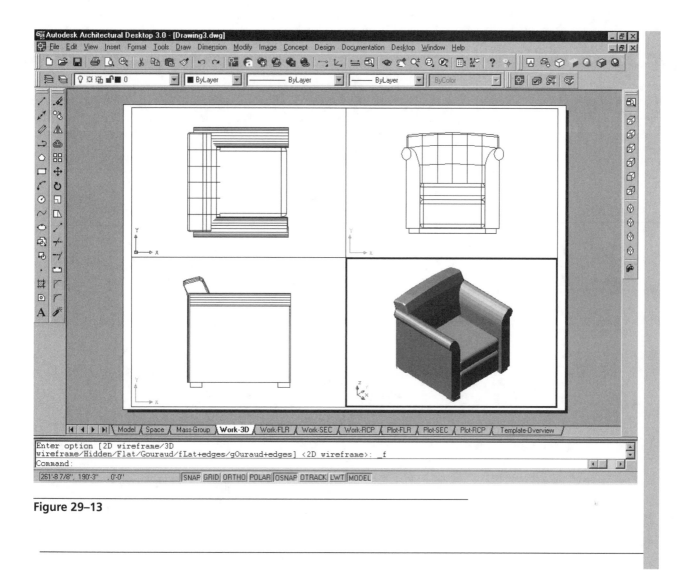

Figure 29–13

There are many ways to make 3D content. You can use AutoCAD's 3D modeling capability, 3D Studio Viz, or go to the Web and search for free content. With Multi-View Blocks, the sky is the limit.

Section

30

Mask Blocks

When you finish this section, you should be able to do the following:

✔ Understand the purpose of Mask Blocks.
✔ Create, modify, and use Mask Blocks.

Mask Blocks are two-dimensional blocks that mask the graphic display of AEC objects in plan view.

You can <u>add</u> and <u>modify Mask Blocks</u> by selecting the desired icon from the <u>AEC Blocks-Profiles</u> toolbar.

You can <u>add</u> and <u>modify Mask Blocks</u> by selecting the desired tool from the <u>Desktop | Mask Blocks</u> menu from the Main toolbar. You can also get the Mask Blocks menu by RMB in any viewport.

Mask Blocks are often combined with AutoCAD objects such as lay-in fluorescent fixtures to mask the AEC ceiling grid. With a thorough understanding of Masking Blocks, you will probably find a myriad of uses for these objects.

Creating a Custom Fluorescent Fixture Called New Fixture

Hands On

1. Activate the <u>AEC Blocks-Profiles</u> and <u>Grids</u> toolbars.
2. Using the Aec arch [imperial-intl].dwt template, select the <u>Work-FLR</u> Layout tab.
3. Activate the Top View viewport.
4. Using the standard AutoCAD drawing commands, draw the ceiling fixture shown in Figure 30–1.
5. Select <u>Modify | Polyline</u> from the <u>Main</u> toolbar, and select the outline.
6. Join the outline into a closed polyline.
7. Select the <u>Mask block Definitions</u> icon from the <u>AEC Blocks-Profiles</u> toolbar.
8. At the Style Manager dialog box, select the <u>New Style</u> icon, and name the new style <u>New Fixture</u>.
9. Select the <u>Set From</u> icon from the Style Manager dialog box's toolbar, and select the outline when asked to Select a Close Polyline at the command line.

Tip If you don't know how to convert and join a line into a polyline, consult the AutoCAD 2000i help for <u>Pedit</u>.

Figure 30–1

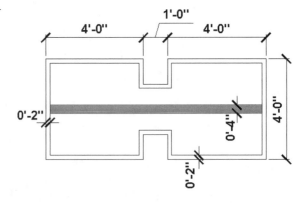

10. Accept **N** when asked to <u>Add Another Ring?</u> at the command line.

11. Make the insertion point for the Mask the center point of the outline.

12. When asked to <u>Select Additional Graphics</u> at the command line, select everything except the outline.

13. At the Style Manager dialog box, press the <u>Apply</u> button; then press the OK button.

The outline will become the Mask block, and the interior objects of the drawing will become the fixture graphics.

Testing the <u>New Fixture</u>

14. Erase everything.

15. Change to the <u>Work-RCP</u> Layout tab, and activate the top viewport.

16. Select the <u>Add Ceiling Grid</u> icon from the Grids toolbar, and add a 20-ft × 20-ft ceiling grid with 2-ft × 2-ft bay sizes (Figure 30–2).

17. Select <u>Add Mask Block</u> from the AEC Blocks-Profiles toolbar.

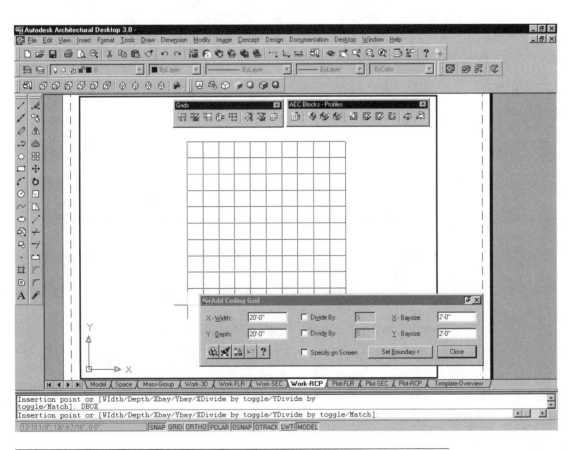

Figure 30–2

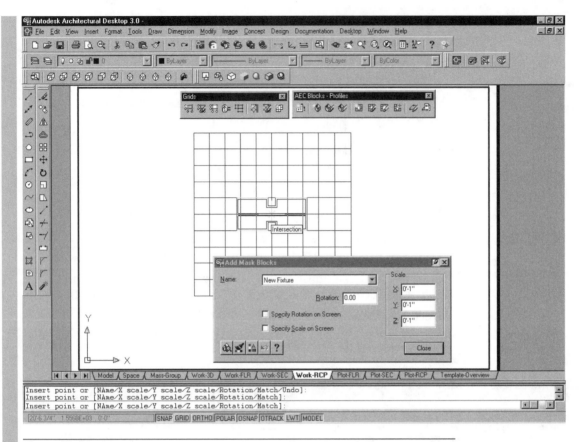

Figure 30–3

18. When the Add Mask Blocks dialog box appears, select New Fixture from the Name dropdown list. Place the block at the center of the grid, and close the dialog box (Figure 30–3).

19. Select the Attach Mask to Objects icon from the AEC Blocks-Profiles toolbar.

20. Select the Mask Block. Then press the space bar or Enter key.

21. Select the ceiling grid (AEC entity), and accept the current view (AecDbDispRepCeilingGridRcp). See Figure 30–4.

Notice that in Figure 30–4, before you attached the mask block, the ceiling grid shows through the block.
In Figure 30–5 the attached Mask Block hides the grid.

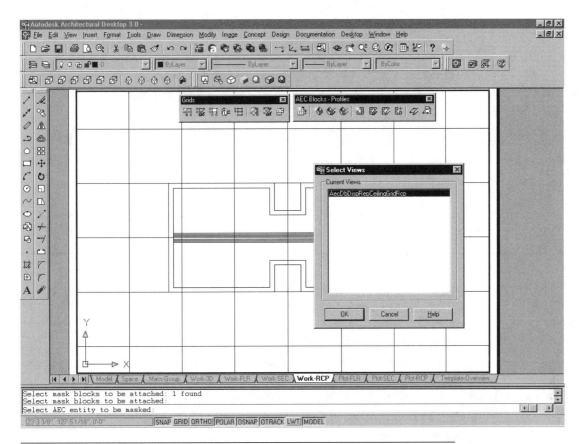

Figure 30–4

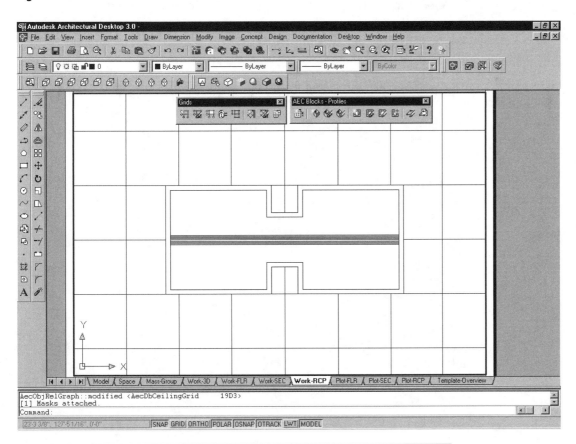

Figure 30–5

Using Create AEC Content to Place the New Fixture in the Design Center

Hands On

1. Erase the grid in the Work-RCP Layout tab, but leave the installed New Fixture.

   The icon that will be used in the design center will be taken from the current view.

2. Select the <u>Create AEC Content</u> icon from the AEC Blocks-Profiles toolbar.

3. At the <u>Create AEC Content Wizard</u> dialog box (Content Type), select the <u>Masking Block</u> radio button, add the New Fixture to the Content File, and press the Next button (Figure 30–6).

4. At the next <u>Create AEC Content Wizard</u> dialog box (Insert Options), press the <u>Select Layer Key button</u>.

5. At the <u>Select Layer Key</u> dialog box, select the <u>LIGHTCLG</u> layer key, and press the OK button (Figure 30–7).

   Selecting the LIGHTCLG layer key assures you that when you insert the content, it will be placed on that layer. (See Section 25.)

6. Select the <u>Next</u> button in the Create AEC Content Wizard.

7. At the next <u>Create AEC Content Wizard</u> dialog box (Display Options), press the <u>Browse</u> button.

Figure 30–6

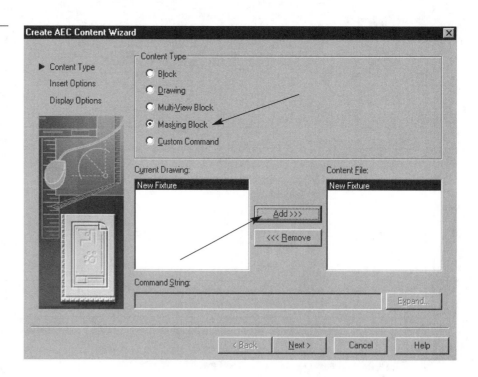

Figure 30–7

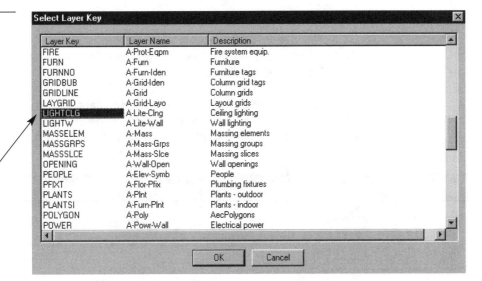

8. At the Save content File locate the <u>Autodesk Architectural Desktop 3\Content\ Imperial\Design\Electric\Fluorescent</u> folder, and name the file <u>New Fixture</u>.

9. When you return to the <u>Create AEC Content Wizard</u> dialog box, type in a description of the Masking block in the <u>Detailed Description</u> space, and press the <u>Finish</u> button (Figure 30–8).

Notice that the current viewport drawing is shown as an icon.

Figure 30–8

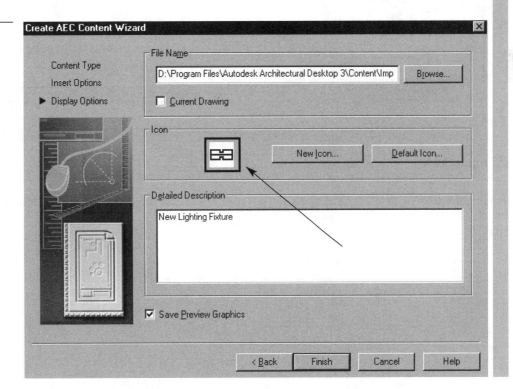

10. Select <u>Design | Design Content | Electric Fixtures</u> from the Main toolbar.

11. Select and open the <u>Fluorescent</u> Folder.

12. Select and drag the <u>New Fixture</u> icon into a new drawing, and Zoom Extents (Figure 30–9).

The create AEC Content Wizard will place Blocks, Drawings, Masking Blocks, and custom command strings in the design center. The process is essentially the same for all these different forms of content.

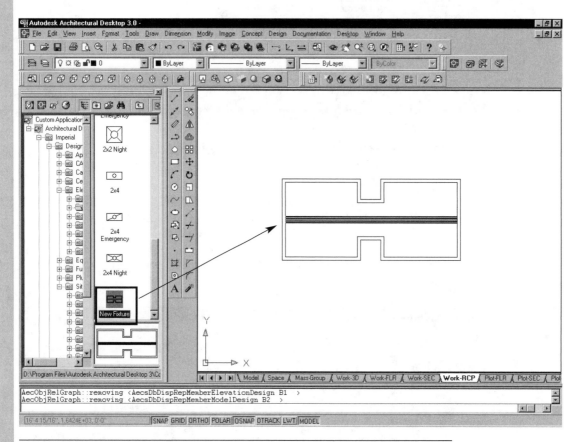

Figure 30–9

Section 31

AEC Polygon

You can add, modify, or convert AEC Polygons by selecting the desired Anchor icon from the Anchors toolbar.

You can add, modify, or convert AEC Polygons from the Desktop | AEC Polygon menu from the Main toolbar. You can also get the AEC Polygon menu by RMB in any viewport.

Section 32 | Utilities

When you finish this section, you should be able to do the following:

✔ Use the AEC utilities.

There are five utilities: Notes, Object Viewer, Quick Slice, Reference AEC Objects, Hidden Line Projection, and Explode AEC Objects.

Selecting the desired <u>Utility</u> icon from the <u>Utilities toolbar</u> will give the specific utility.

You can get the utilities from the <u>Desktop | Utilities</u> menu from the <u>Main</u> toolbar. You can also get the utilities menu by RMB in any viewport.

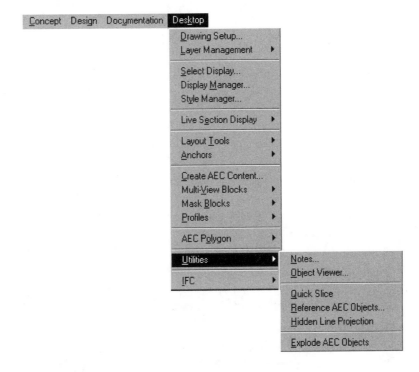

Notes

You can add notations as well as Document files (.doc), Drawing files (dwg), Rich Text files (rft), and AutoCAD drawings to any object for recall. If you want to keep the specifications on that stairwell, just add a Word, WordPerfect, or rtf document to the stairway or door using the Notes utility. You can even add notes to a circle or line or use notes to attach a drawing detail to an object (Figure 32–1).

Figure 32–1

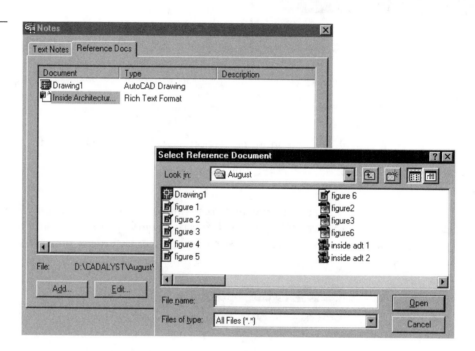

Object Viewer

Object Viewer is very similar to AutoCAD's 3D Orbit command, but it doesn't have 3D Orbit's clipping plane controls. The Viewer creates a separate window for the view and has slightly better shading capability.

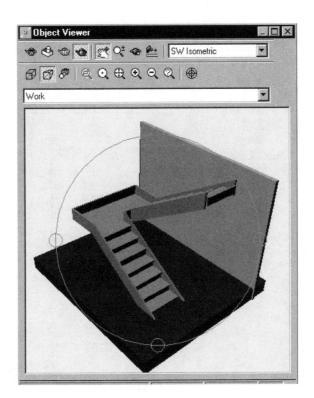

Figure 32–2

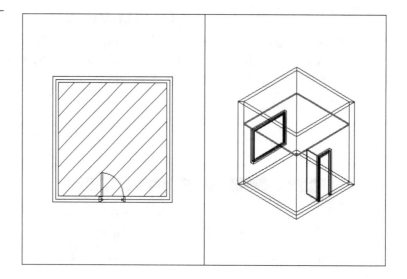

Figure 32–3

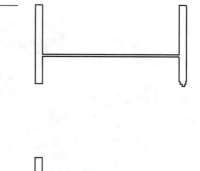

Quick Slice

If you need a quick section through objects, Quick Slice suits the bill. Just select the objects you want to section, and drag the cursor across the object (Figure 32–2). You can then Explode the resulting polylines to use as a basis for details (Figure 32–3).

Reference AEC Objects

Referencing is a term usually used in 3D programs when a copy changes as its parent is changed. If you reference several columns to a parent column, for instance, changing the parent column's height will change the height of all the referenced columns.

In the following example, a simple AEC Object enclosure A has been referenced, mirrored, and flipped to B (Figure 32–4).

Selecting a grip and changing parent A changes B (Figure 32–5).

Figure 32–4

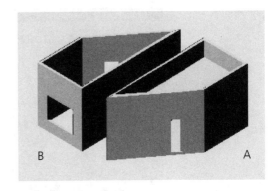

Figure 32–5

Figure 32–6

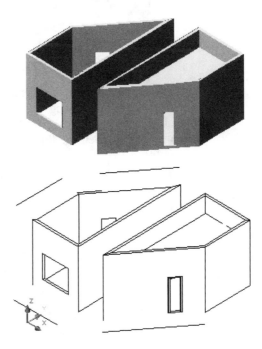

Hidden Line Projection

Use the Hidden Line Projection to quickly create 2D representations of your drawings. Although it is often used for elevations, it can make hidden line sections and flattened 3D views.

Hidden-line projections make flattened views of the viewport in which they are taken. Figure 32–6 shows the 3DAEC objects and the flattened 2D view that has been exploded and has the lines moved.

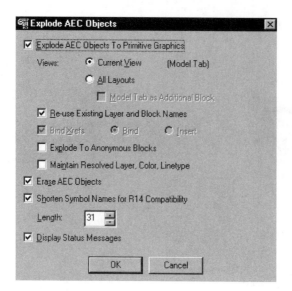

Explode AEC Objects

Use Explode AEC Objects to explode AEC objects back to standard AutoCAD entities. Although the drawing file gets bigger, users of AutoCAD or programs that read dwg files will be able to easily read your drawings. Because the AEC objects have been converted, their intelligence will be lost.

Index